Meaning in English

An Introduction

This lively, compact textbook introduces readers to semantics – the study of how we construct meaning in communication. Easy to follow, and with a clear structure, it explains formal terminology in a simple and understandable way, without using formal notation or logic, and draws on dozens of examples from up-to-date empirical research findings. Offering a tight integration of classic semantic issues with cognitive science, Javier Valenzuela provides a complete and coherent overview of the main topics in this area, including a review of the empirical methods used in semantic theorizing and discussions of both non-traditional and new topics such as how meaning is acquired by children and how meaning is constructed cross-linguistically. Featuring illustrations, exercises, activities, suggestions for further reading, highlighted key terms and a comprehensive glossary, this book is accessible to beginners and undergraduates, including those from non linguistic backgrounds with no prior knowledge of linguistic analysis. It will be an essential resource for courses in English language, English studies, linguistics and the cognitive sciences.

JAVIER VALENZUELA is a Tenured Professor in Linguistics at the University of Murcia. He is the author of *Lingüística y cognición: el lenguaje desde la lingüística cognitiva* (with Iraide Ibarretxe-Antuñano, forthcoming, 2017) and editor of *Lingüística Cognitiva* (with Iraide Ibarretxe-Antuñano, 2012) and he has published in journals including *Cognitive Science, Journal of Pragmatics, Frontiers in Human Neuroscience* and *Language Sciences*. He also served as President of the Spanish Cognitive Linguistics Association from 2012 to 2016.

Cambridge Introductions to the English Language

Cambridge Introductions to the English Language is a series of accessible undergraduate textbooks on the key topics encountered in the study of the English language. Tailored to suit the needs of individual taught course modules, each book is written by an author with extensive experience of teaching the topic to undergraduates. The books assume no prior subject knowledge, and present the basic facts in a clear and straightforward manner, making them ideal for beginners. They are designed to be maximally reader-friendly, with chapter summaries, glossaries and suggestions for further reading. Extensive exercises and discussion questions are included, encouraging students to consolidate and develop their learning, and providing essential homework material. A website accompanies each book, featuring solutions to the exercises and useful additional resources. Set to become the leading introductions to the field, books in this series provide the essential knowledge and skills for those embarking on English Language studies.

Books in the series

The Sound Structure of English Chris McCully

Old English Jeremy J. Smith

English Around the World Edgar W. Schneider

English Words and Sentences Eva Duran Eppler and Gabriel Ozón

Meaning in English

An Introduction

Javier Valenzuela

CAMBRIDGE
UNIVERSITY PRESS

University Printing House, Cambridge CB2 8BS, United Kingdom

One Liberty Plaza, 20th Floor, New York, NY 10006, USA

477 Williamstown Road, Port Melbourne, VIC 3207, Australia

4843/24, 2nd Floor, Ansari Road, Daryaganj, Delhi – 110002, India

79 Anson Road, #06–04/06, Singapore 079906

Cambridge University Press is part of the University of Cambridge.

It furthers the University's mission by disseminating knowledge in the pursuit of education, learning and research at the highest international levels of excellence.

www.cambridge.org
Information on this title: www.cambridge.org/9781107096370
10.1017/9781316156278

First published 2017

Printed in the United States of America by Sheridan Books, Inc. in 2017

A catalogue record for this publication is available from the British Library.

ISBN 978-1-107-09637-0 Hardback
ISBN 978-1-107-48016-2 Paperback

Contents

Figures

Tables

Preface

When I was commissioned by Cambridge University Press to write an introduction to semantics, I was elated; I knew I was in for a great ride. This is the case even if I was perfectly aware of an unavoidable fact: it's impossible to write an introduction to semantics that will satisfy everybody. Many great scholars will feel you are ignoring them (or more probably, just plain wrong about your choices). While it's evident that different traditions have very smart people in their camps who cannot be completely wrong, there's really no way around it: in a book like this, you have to choose sides. And then face the music.

So, as expected, some level of disagreement can be found in almost any topic in semantics we choose: whether the tools of logic are useful or not; whether meaning is something embodied or symbolic, whether metaphor is useful or useless, whether semantics and pragmatics are to be distinguished or not, whether language influences thought significantly or not, and a very long etcetera. That's why I said that writing a book on semantics (especially an introduction, where there's not much space to give all possibilities their due), is probably a surefire way of creating enemies. Well, that's life.

I am in complete agreement with the saying that 'education is not the filling of a vessel, but the lighting of a fire'. This is the approach I've tried to take here: even more important than the facts themselves is the feeling of excitement and enthusiasm that emanates from all the work that is being carried out in the field right now. As I see it, the story of semantics is not a mere recollection of facts from the past, but something that is being written in these very moments. I firmly believe these are topics that are central to our understanding of language, our minds and ourselves, and in this sense, they should be interesting for just about anyone (especially for anyone interested in how language and our minds work).

A great deal of effort in this book has gone into two goals: first, aiming for an explanation of topics accessible to anyone, while trying to avoid over-simplification at the same time. This is really tricky, because most issues in semantics are notoriously complicated and each single point can be modified, qualified and nuanced *ad nauseam*. The second goal has been trying to provide an 'organic' feel to the whole book. As much as possible, I have tried to convey a coherent and homogenous view of how meaning is constructed and expressed, and how it structures our cognition. This is why there are a number of (intended) recurrences throughout the book: frames are mentioned in Chapters 4, 5, 8 and 9; intention-reading in Chapters 6 and 9; the distinction between symbolic and embodied approaches show up in Chapters 1, 2 and 3, 7 and 8; metaphor is mentioned in chapters 2, 5, 6 and 7, and so on. The objective is to let the reader perceive semantics as a single system, more than as a collection of unrelated phenomena.

On a more practical note, the book can be read by anyone on their own, or be taught by an experienced teacher. There are suggested answers to the exercises on the book's website; for instructors, there are also some suggested activities that have worked wonderfully for me during the years. Oh, and I'm also thinking about starting a t-shirt company with some of the great illustrations that my friend Sergio has created for the book.

But the conclusion, again, is that I had a great time writing it, and I hope that all my readers will enjoy it as much as I did.

Acknowledgments

This book is the result of many years of teaching semantics, which means that I have a lot of people to thank: many friends and colleagues have helped shape my view of language throughout the years. First among them should be Joe Hilferty; but also Iraide Ibarretxe, Ana Rojo, Cristina Soriano, Julio Santiago, Paco Calvo and Cristóbal Pagán, who have informed me and often challenged my views (and continue to do so). Liz Murphy, Jose Antonio Mompeán (and Joe and Iraide again) have helped me sound a bit less foreign. Many people in Cambridge University Press have been really helpful and offered great collaboration; Helen Barton should be mentioned in the first place, but also three anonymous reviewers who provided many suggestions which I have been grateful to accept; many thanks also go to Valerie Appleby and Jennifer Miles Davis. On a more formal note, I gracefully acknowledge the help of the Spanish Ministry of Economy and Competitiveness under Grants FFI2013-45553-C3-1-P & FFI2015-70876-P and the Fundación Séneca under grant 19482/PHCS/14.

And last but not least, thanks to my students, for their explicit feedback, for their blank stares informing me when the material was too hard or too boring, and for the twinkle in their eyes telling me I was on the right track.

CHAPTER 1

What is Semantics?

In this chapter ...

In this chapter, we introduce the subject of semantics, stressing its essential role in linguistics and other cognitive disciplines. We will look at some common definitions, and will come up with a list of questions about meaning that we would be interested in answering. We also review briefly the place of semantic studies in linguistic theorizing in the last century; in order to get a feel of the difficulties involved in semantic analysis, we will examine the meaning of a single word. The second part of the chapter will be devoted to reviewing the ways in which meaning can be expressed, both non-linguistically (introducing the discipline of semiotics) and linguistically, examining the different types of meaning expressed by the different linguistic levels (phonology, morphology, lexicon and syntax). The chapter ends with some notes on the general organization of the book.

1.1 Some Preliminaries

Meaning controls memory and perception. Meaning is the goal of communication. Meaning underlies social activities and culture. To a great degree, what distinguishes human cultures are the meanings they give to natural phenomena, artifacts, and human relations (Glenberg and Robertson, 2000).

The importance of semantics for the study of language cannot be overstated. Understanding how we construct meanings from the words and expressions we hear can be said to be the core of linguistic studies, since it amounts to understanding how language performs its main task, which is to convey meaning. Semantics is thus essential for all aspects of language study: how language is acquired (be it a first language or a second one) and how it is structured; how language changes over time and how it varies in different social contexts; how languages should be taught and how we (or machines) translate it; how language-related conditions such as aphasias work, etc. You could say that semantics lies at the very heart of the study of language. The practical applications of knowing in an accurate and detailed way how people associate their thoughts to linguistic objects, and how hearers use those objects to recover the intended meaning in a communicative exchange, are obviously enormous. Semantic search in the web has been called 'the holy grail of computer-assisted research' (McCloskey, 2013); natural-language computer query systems such as Apple's Siri or IBM's Watson would be delighted to have a complete story of how meaning really works.

But semantics goes even further than that: it is also relevant for learning about the way in which we structure our thoughts. Indeed, many authors think that there are deep connections between our language and our conceptual structure and that semantics is a window that allows us to peek into the functioning of a substantial part of our cognitive system. Language has been shown to be one of the driving forces in our evolution, influencing our hearing range and the specific shape of our larynx and our vocal organs. In all probability, our semantic system and our brain structure also co-evolved, transforming us into the species we are today. The capacity to produce and understand language seems to be uniquely human, distinguishing our species from other animals in our world. It is thus easy to understand why the problem of meaning has stirred the interest of scholars of many different traditions, including philosophers, linguists, anthropologists, sociologists, psychologists and neuroscientists, among other scholars.

The present book will provide an overview of the main areas of interest of semantics, specifying the main mechanisms involved in meaning production and comprehension, and the methodologies used to learn about these mechanisms, pointing along the way to the connections with a variety of neighbouring disciplines, such as linguistics, psychology, philosophy and neuroscience.

1.2 What is Semantics? Some Definitions

Many introductions to semantics begin by asking the following question: *what is semantics?* What does semantics actually study? This seems like

Table 1.1 *Some Definitions of Semantics*

Semantics is the study of meaning	Lyons (1977)
Semantics is the study of meaning in language	Hurford and Heasley (1983)
Semantics is the study of meaning communicated through language	Saeed (1997)
Semantics is the part of linguistics that is concerned with meaning	Löbner (2002)
Linguistic semantics is the study of literal, decontextualized, grammatical meaning	Frawley (1992)
Linguistic semantics is the study of how languages organize and express meanings	Kreidler (1998)

a sensible way to start a course on semantics, so we can begin by looking at some of the answers that different authors provide.

Table 1.1 provides a selection of definitions. As can be immediately noticed, there is no complete agreement. For some authors, semantics concerns the study of meaning as communicated through language, while for some others, semantics studies *all* aspects of meaning and they have to add the label 'linguistic' to arrive at a more precise definition. However, probably most authors would agree with Kreidler's definition (to choose just one of them): *linguistic semantics is the study of how languages organize and express meanings.*

This leaves us with a second question, though: what do we understand by 'meaning'? What are those 'meanings' that are organized and expressed by languages? In very general terms, speaking consists of communicating information: somebody (the speaker) has something in his/her mind (an idea, a feeling, an intention, or whatever), and decides to communicate it linguistically. Vocal noises are then emitted that are heard by a second person (the hearer), who seems to 'translate' these noises back into ideas, with the result being that this hearer somehow knows what the first person had in mind. That 'something' that was at first in the speaker's mind and now is also in the hearer's mind is what we call meaning. What can it be? The problem is that it can be virtually anything: objects (concrete, abstract or imaginary), events and states (past, present, future or hypothetical) or all sorts of properties of objects, feelings, emotions, intentions, locations, etc. We can talk about anything we can think of (or perhaps almost). And even if we were to arrive at a rough idea of what meaning is, we would nevertheless have another list of questions waiting in line. These are some of them, in no particular order:

- How can the meaning of a given word or expression be defined or measured?
- How can the meaning of a word or expression be represented?

- What is the relationship between language and thought? Do we think *in* language or a similar format? What is the relationship between word meanings and conceptual structure?
- Can language express all meanings or are there meanings that cannot be expressed linguistically? If you cannot express something in your language, can you think about it?
- Are there different types of meaning?
- Should semantics study *all* aspects of the meaning of a word, or only those that are important or necessary for linguistic processing? (i.e., should we distinguish semantics and pragmatics, and if so, where do we draw the line?)
- How do children learn the meaning of words? Do they first develop the necessary cognitive structures and then learn the corresponding linguistic labels or do some cognitive relations depend on language? That is, does cognitive development drive language, is it the other way round, or do they evolve in tandem?
- How exact is the 'copy' of the meaning that goes 'from' the speaker 'into' the hearer? That is, how faithful or unambiguous is linguistic communication?
- What are the laws governing the changes of meaning that words undergo over time?
- How are the meanings of words combined in phrases and sentences?
- Do different languages structure and express meaning in significantly different ways?
- How are the meanings of the different words related to each other?

And perhaps the most crucial question for linguists:

- Which parts of the linguistic code correspond to which parts of meaning?

These are some of the questions that semantics has to try to answer; throughout the history of semantics, different theories have chosen to focus on some of them and have ignored the rest, and have also provided radically different answers to some of these questions.

Figure 1.1 Meaning Communication

1.3 A Very Short History of Semantics

The history of semantics is not straightforward. In a way, semantic studies can be traced back to the first studies of language. From the very first moments in which man started to explore the phenomenon of linguistic communication, semantics had a central place in that endeavour. Aristotle's first reflections on language or Panini's grammar (both around the fourth century BC) included questions about meaning in language. Such questions have continued to be present in most linguistic discussions up until this century.

The attempt to find the correspondence between parts of the linguistic code and parts of meaning can be considered the goal of any linguistic theory in general. Still, there have been many disagreements on how to approach this question, and there are even disagreements on the overall importance of the study of meaning in a linguistic theory. In the century or so of existence of linguistics as an autonomous discipline (since Saussure), semantics has been awarded different degrees of importance or centrality in linguistic analyses. For example, semantics was banned from linguistics by American structuralism (e.g., Bloomfield); it was not something 'observable', and therefore it could not form part of any scientific study of language. The prohibition of using mental constructs in theorizing was lifted by the next linguistic theory, probably the most popular of the twentieth century: Chomskyan generativism.

However, generativists also decided that semantics was not a central part of linguistic analysis; in their view, the central concern of language is syntax: linguistic knowledge is basically knowledge about how words are combined and grouped. This is the information that is 'pre-wired' in children's brains, in the form of Universal Grammar. The connection between words and phrases and their meanings is something that is achieved in a second phase by 'general purpose devices', that is, psychological mechanisms that are not specifically linguistic in nature, and thus fall outside the scope of linguistic study. According to generativists, you can study language, and you can explain a significant part of its behaviour, if not all, just by looking at syntax, at the rules for the different combinations of words. You don't have to worry about the meanings of words and expressions in order to capture the true essence of linguistic behaviour.

As a summary, then, during most of the twentieth century, the study of semantics as an integral and essential part of language was shunned from linguistic studies (especially in American circles), first by Bloomfieldean structuralism and then by Chomskyan generativism. By the end of the century, however, some scholars started to rebel against this state of affairs in the belief that this theoretical stance was incorrect and artificial. The linguist Ronald Langacker, for example, speaks about the 'centrality of meaning to virtually all linguistic concerns'. In his view:

> Meaning is what language is all about; the analyst who ignores it to concentrate solely on matters of form severely impoverishes the natural and necessary subject matter of the discipline and ultimately distorts the character of the phenomena described (Langacker, 1987: 12).

A similar view is expressed by the artificial intelligence scholar Robert Wilensky, who also warns about the difficulties of incorporating semantics into our theories:

> The notion of meaning is central to theories of language. However, there appears to be considerable disagreement regarding what a theory of meaning should do, and how it pertains to other linguistic issues (Wilensky, 1989: 249).

1.4 Some Problems for Semantic Studies

While the study of other linguistic levels can undoubtedly prove difficult, the study of meaning presents difficulties that can seem insurmountable. Phonetics, for example, studies phenomena that are quite concrete and tangible: the linguistic sounds produced by humans. These sounds can be recorded with several methods (sometimes, very sophisticated ones); the organs involved in their production can be examined; the acoustic composition of the sound wave can be analysed, as can the combinations of sounds allowed in each language or the way context affects their production or interpretation. In the same way, morphology and syntax also have an object of study which is concrete: morphology studies the different parts of words and their order of combination, and syntax studies the order in which words are placed when formulating a message and the different structures that can be formed when different words are grouped together (i.e., phrases). In both cases, the object of study can be observed directly: recording conversations, looking at texts that have been produced in different ways (written or oral form), etc.

But the object of study of semantics is much more slippery, more elusive: the goal is to analyse the 'meaning' that linguistic elements express. This is a much harder problem, since meaning cannot be observed directly, no matter how sophisticated our brain imaging systems become. The problem of the nature of meaning is a question that has been with us since the beginning of time, and it is not clear whether we have arrived at a completely satisfactory answer (though as we hope to show in this book, significant headway has been made).

In spite of the difficulties, we cannot choose to ignore semantics; over the years, only two plausible functions of language have been considered: a communicative function and a representational function. In both of them, semantics has to be placed at the very heart of the process. If language evolved as a means of communication and this is its real and original function and *raison d'être*, then we find meaning at the beginning and at the end of the communication process, and it must be considered, therefore, to be a central part of the nature of language itself. On the other hand, some scholars have proposed that the primary function of language is not communication but mental representation (i.e., language is a way of representing the world in our minds). This would confer on humans the advantages of performing certain manipulations of those representations, allowing us to conceive hypothetical scenarios and quite complex reasoning patterns, which would be impossible without language. If this view of language is the correct one, we again find meaning in a central place: if the function of language is to represent reality in our minds, that representation is what we would call meaning.

To get a grasp of the difficulties involved, let us try to think for a moment about the meaning of one specific word: *coffee*. Can we provide a precise answer to the question 'What is the meaning of coffee?' Is it the mental information that we have about the concept and that is evoked by the sounds [kofI]? How much do we know about *coffee*? Below you can find a list of facts that we know about coffee.

Some facts we know about coffee

We know that coffee is a drink, made of some plant beans (that have to be roasted); that it is black, has a particular smell and a strong taste; that normally we put sugar in it; that it has a particular effect (stimulating); that it is usually drunk hot; that we can consume it in other forms (ice-cream, cakes). We know how to prepare coffee in different ways, the devices we use to prepare coffee (the Italian-type household coffee-pot, the professional cafeteria espresso machine, the filter version, etc.), the recipients where you put the coffee when it's made (a cup, a jug, etc.), when you have coffee or how many times a day (at breakfast and after lunch are the most typical, and then, mid-morning coffee, probably, sometimes after dinner, but only when you go out), the varieties of forms in drinks (latte, espresso, macchiato, mocha, cappuccino and then all the variants in Starbucks). You know how expensive it is (depending on whether you buy it in a shop, in a coffeehouse, in a hotel, in an airport, etc.), where they sell it, which companies sell it (Nescafé, Illy,

Lavazza – you might even have heard about Juan Valdés, the Colombian coffee symbol), the varieties in shops and supermarkets (regular or decaffeinated, in whole beans, so you can grind it yourself, or already ground, in powder, ready to be brewed in a specific device, or instant or soluble coffee). More recently, you can also buy coffee with added flavours, such as cinnamon or hazelnut. You know it's produced in countries like Brazil or Colombia, the type of shops where they sell coffee so you can prepare it yourself (supermarkets) or buy the beverage ready to be drunk (cafés). You know the difference between a cafeteria (where they serve food, like in a University cafeteria) and a coffeehouse or coffee shop (where they serve primarily coffee or hot beverages). You know the social occasions in which coffee is the typical drink (think of the expression 'go for a coffee', which implies that you will talk, possibly about informal or personal matters; if somebody you've recently met asks you 'would you like to get coffee sometime?', that person wants to know you better). You know that students drink coffee during exam preparation to stay awake, that too much coffee is bad for your health, that smokers feel compelled to smoke when they drink coffee, that you must store it in a cool and dry place, that in planes the option is normally either tea or coffee. You probably know that when you have coffee on a plane, you're supposed to put your cup on the flight attendant's tray, that the substance which coffee has that makes you nervous is called caffeine, that other related beverages with caffeine are colas, that there are national varieties of coffees such as Turkish-Greek, Italian-Espresso or English-American, that stains from coffee are difficult to clean, that there is a 'coffee' hour, or a 'coffee break' during which you stop your work and have a coffee (or even something else: you can have 'tea' during a coffee-break), etc.

This list could probably go on almost indefinitely. We could have more 'personal' information, things that belong to the private sphere (in my case, coffee has a special connection with my childhood memories, because of the coffee pudding that my mother used to make for me), or perhaps the associations it could have for someone with the songs 'Night Café' by the British group Orchestral Manoeuvres in the Dark or 'One More Cup of Coffee' by Bob Dylan. To this we could even add highly contextual information, like the fact that coffee, being a liquid, can be used to put out a fire (at least, a very small one), and a very long etcetera.

Now we can get a feel of the real problems of doing semantic analysis. Which part of this knowledge is to be accounted for by a theory of linguistic semantics? Is all the information we have about a word and its concept relevant for language use or only a subset of it? Can we draw a line between the dictionary and the encyclopaedia? And how can we decide which part is going to be relevant across all contexts of use? The questions are numerous, and many of them will prove exceedingly difficult. But all journeys, no matter how long, always start with the first step.

Figure 1.2 Is this Part of What you Know about Coffee?

1.5 How can Meaning be Communicated?

In our definition, we have been careful to add that 'semantics is the study of meaning *in language*'. And the reason for this is that language is not the only way in which we can communicate meaning. We can do it, for example, just by showing people our hands, as can be seen in Figure 1.3:

Figure 1.3 Hand Shapes with Different Meanings

Almost everybody in our Western culture knows the meaning of these 'signs' (approximately, disapproval, victory (or peace), approval, attention request and greeting). There are lots of non-linguistic symbols that are used to communicate meaning: almost all traffic signs, for example. If you want to communicate that something is dangerous, you can attach this drawing to it (Figure 1.4):

Figure 1.4 Sign for Danger

The study of meaning in general is carried out by **semiotics**. Semiotics studies how 'signs' mean, that is, how we can make one thing stand for another (a 'signifier' stands for a 'signified'). For example, in Western culture, black clothes are used to indicate mourning, and on our beaches a red flag means that it's dangerous to swim. It is clear that many of these signs are culturally based: for example, in some Eastern cultures, the colour to indicate mourning is white. However, not all of them are cultural; normally, semioticians find it useful to make a three-way distinction, first established by C. S. Pierce:

- **Icon:** a relation of similarity between the sign and what it represents; for example, a portrait of a person.
- **Index:** a cause–effect relationship; contiguity in space or time; for example, smoke and fire or yawning and boredom.
- **Symbol:** an arbitrary, conventional relationship between sign and meaning: for example, red flag and danger.

Clearly, linguistic meaning will be (mainly) circumscribed to the third type, since the connection between a collection of sounds and a particular meaning is arbitrary and subject to different cultural conventions by different languages. This does not mean that *all* aspects of language are symbolic: it is easy to find iconic aspects in language, from phonology (as we shall see in the next section) to syntax (e.g., word order aspects); the amount of literature devoted to examining cases of iconicity in language is indeed substantial. Be that as it may, semantics must probably be seen as a part of semiotics, and this is how most scholars regard language.

As a final thought, we should warn that it is not always easy to distinguish these three types of signs. Often, we find cases in which a sign is at the same time, icon, index and symbol, since these are often built upon one another: symbols on indices and indices on icons.

1.6 How is Meaning Communicated through Language?

'Everything in language conspires to convey meaning' (Wierzbicka, 1988: 1).

It is clear then that one of the main questions that semantics must ask is how meaning is communicated linguistically. What resources does language have to convey or express meaning? We can try to review the different linguistic levels one by one and see what types of meaning can be expressed.

1.6.1 Phonology

Can we express meaning by uttering isolated sounds? Do linguistic sounds have meaning by themselves? At first sight, the answer is no. The phoneme /l/ or the phoneme /o/ have no meaning by themselves. However, this immediate answer can be reconsidered and modified slightly if we take a look at what has been called **sound symbolism**, also known as **phonosemantics**. Sound symbolism states that there is a certain association between the sound of an utterance and its meaning. Other definitions could be 'a non-arbitrary connection between sound and meaning' or 'words that sound like what they mean'. There are a number of linguistic areas and phenomena that are sound symbolic:

- **Diminutives.** There seems to be an association of the sound /i/ with small things. Many languages form the diminutive with this sound (see Table 1.2).

Table 1.2 *Some Diminutive Affixes Containing the Sound /i/*

-(t)je	(Dutch)	-ling, -ie, -y	(English)
-ino	(Italian)	-cik	(Turkish)
-ito/a	(Spanish)	ki-	(Swahili)
-chik	(Russian)	-in	(Irish)

The reason for this, it seems, lies in the way in which this sound is produced. To utter the phoneme /i/, we have to raise the tongue and leave a very small space in our mouth; the contrast between this sound and /o/ is evident. That is why /i/ sounds have a certain tendency to be associated with small things, and /o/ sounds with big things (Table 1.3).

Table 1.3 *'Small' and 'Big' Words with /i/ and /o/ Sounds*

a bit	a lot
teeny	humongous
squeak	roar
tweeters	woofers
wee	colossal
tiny	enormous
mini	jumbo

- **Maluma vs. Takete.** Gestalt psychologists (e.g., Köhler, 1947) thought of a very interesting experiment. They gave people two different forms; one of them was spiky and angular, and the other round and soft. They told subjects that one of them was called 'takete' and the other 'maluma', as seen in Figure 1.5.

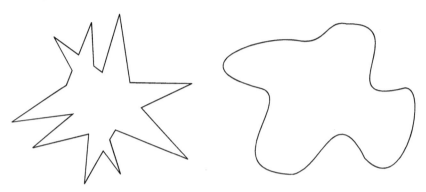

Figure 1.5 Which one is 'Maluma' and which 'Takete'?

Interestingly, a vast majority of people tended to associate the name maluma with the round, soft figure and the name takete with the spiky one. This experiment was initially carried out in Germany during the 1940s, but it has been replicated with many other different languages (e.g., English, Spanish, Swahili and Tamil, among others), essentially with the same results. This is also known as the *bouba–kiki* effect, since those words have also been used in the same experiments. Children as young as two and a half, still unable to read, are also sensitive to this distinction (Maurer *et al.*, 2006); a study by Oztürk *et al.* (2013) found similar behaviours even in four-month-old babies! Thus, phonetic symbolism seems to be a rather universal phenomenon.

According to the neuroscientist V. S. Ramachandran, these could be considered examples of synaesthesia, in which we mix information from different modalities. Examples of synaesthesia are found in many common phrases of English, like *loud colour*, that mixes sound and vision, or *soft voice*, which mixes sound and touch. In this case, the shape of the mouth imitates the shape of the thing being described (to a certain extent) and the brain areas controlling the mouth muscles are adjacent to the visual centres (Ramachandran and Hubbard, 2001).

- **Meow, plunge and glint.** Another example of a certain relationship between sound and meaning is to be found in phenomena such as **onomatopoeia** (roughly, the linguistic mimicking of non-linguistic sounds, such as *bow-wow* for the barking of a dog), **phonesthesia** (when the sound of the word reminds us of the action or object they describe as in *plunge, whisper, crack* or *frizzle*) and **phonesthemes**, which corresponds to an association of certain sound combinations with a given meaning, in a rather random way. For example, the consonant cluster *st-* is associated with verbs indicating movement, e.g., *stomp, stampede, step, stride, stroll*; another example is the combination *gl-*, associated with verbs related to light or vision, e.g., *glimmer, glisten, gleam, glitter, glow* and *glint*.

These associations of sounds with meanings (which have a really old story, from Plato and Aristotle, or Jespersen at the beginning of the twentieth century), have more recently attracted the interest of marketing companies; apparently, the commercial brand name 'Viagra' was chosen for its phonosemantic properties, as was the antidepressant Prozac (which had originally been given the less-appealing name of 'fluoxetine').

Having said all this, however, it seems that it's not very clear that we can predict a certain meaning from a given sound. In all these cases, all we can find is a certain association of sounds with some shades of meaning, but never a well-defined, crisp, specific meaning.

So far in this section, we have been talking about the (possible) meanings of phonemes, also known as 'segments' of speech. However, there is another part of phonology, known as prosody, which is described as 'suprasegmental', since it applies to more than one segment of sound (i.e., more than one phoneme), be it syllables, words, sentences or longer chunks of speech. Prosody includes phenomena such as rhythm, stress or intonation; the latter is the most versatile of the three, and it could to a certain extent be called 'the Cinderella of language', since it does a lot of work but is largely ignored by everybody (though this seems to be slowly changing in recent times). By varying the pitch of the words we utter, we can express quite different variations in meaning. That is so even in languages such as English which are 'non-tonal'. Tonal languages use pitch in a more defined way: depending on the intonation of the word, its lexical meaning can change; the most cited example is the Mandarin Chinese word *ma*, which depending on which of the four existing 'tones' you apply, can mean *mother, hemp, horse* or *scold*.

Even if English is not a tonal language, intonation can indeed be used to convey meaning. Sometimes the difference among several interpretations of an utterance can lie in intonation only, which often proves essential for recovering the communicative intention of the speaker (that is, identifying the type of speech act). For example, phenomena such as irony or sarcasm depend crucially on this. It is well known that intonation is processed in a different part of the brain and forms a somehow separate system; this could explain why we can distinguish whether someone is insulting us or paying us a compliment in an unknown language. Intonation is in fact a universal feature of language: all languages in the world use some type of intonational patterns.

Some of the 'meanings' that can be expressed with intonation are related to our emotional attitude when we say something: whether we are sad, happy, enthusiastic, bored, proud, surprised, angry, friendly, aggressive, reluctant, relieved or frightened. Intonation is also connected with grammatical form and communicative intention. For example, the sentence *this is the answer* can be a statement, or, when uttered with a rising intonation at the end, be turned into a question and thus express doubt. The sentence *Can you play the piano?* can be an invitation to play (e.g., *we know you're a famous concert pianist so please, can you play the piano for us?*), an expression of surprise (e.g., *Oh, can you play the piano? I didn't know you could*) or a simple request for information. Intonation is also used to convey the distinction between new information and old or shared information (a distinction that receives many names, such as topic-comment, theme-rheme, given-new, or presupposition-focus) and helps us segment sentences into phrases and understand the relationships between discourse chunks.

As a final example, think about the problems of topic-selection in structures such as negated sentences. There is no way of knowing syntactically which is the element being negated in *I didn't phone Peter on Sunday*; stressing each of its components will put it on focus, as can be seen in the following sentences in (1):

1. a. *I* didn't phone Peter on Sunday (your brother did)
   b. I didn't *phone* Peter on Sunday (I sent him an email)
   c. I didn't phone *Peter* on Sunday (I phoned Paul)
   d. I didn't phone Peter on *Sunday* (I phoned him on Saturday)
   e. I didn't phone Peter on Sunday (I did nothing).

1.6.2 Morphology

Morphology studies word structure. Words are the 'carriers' of meaning *par excellence*: we use words to convey meaning. However, if we look at the internal structure of words, we see that the different parts of words indicate different types of meaning. Morphemes may be free (standing alone, without any other morpheme) or bound (those which have to be attached to a word stem). The study of morphology is normally focused on bound morphemes, which can be inflectional or derivational. Each type of morpheme is used to convey a different type of meaning.

The way to distinguish between **inflectional** morphemes and **derivational** morphemes is the following: inflectional morphemes do not change the grammatical category of the stem. If you take the noun *dog* and add the plural marker 's', the result (*dogs*) is still a noun. **Derivational** morphemes, on the other hand, do change the grammatical category of the stem; if we combine the verb *work* with the morpheme '*er*' what we get is *worker*, which is no longer a verb, but a noun. Derivational morphemes sometimes do not change the category of the word, but alter its meaning in a significant way. For example, *treasure* is a noun, and after the addition of *–er*, we get *treasurer*, which is still a noun. However, a *treasure* and a *treasurer* are completely different types of things; the first one is an object and the second, a person. In contrast, inflectional meanings do not change the meaning of the word in dramatic ways, but just introduce some modification on basically the same type of element. In English, we find that the meanings that are associated with inflectional morphemes are rather limited in number, while the meanings associated with derivational morphemes are of a wider type. Let's examine each of them in turn.

- **Inflectional meanings in English.** The meanings of inflectional morphemes in English form a small set. They can be grouped depending on whether we are talking about morphemes attached to nouns or morphemes attached to verbs. For example, in English nominal morphemes we typically find the following meanings:
  - *Plurality:* if we want to indicate that there is more than one element of the thing we are referring to, we attach a specific morpheme: *-s*. So, *cats* indicates that there is more than one *cat* in our scene. Of course, there are other ways to indicate plurality in English; we have 'apophonic' plurals (*man–men, foot–feet*), invariant forms (*sheep–sheep*), etc.
  - *Possession:* we can indicate who the possessor of an element is by attaching another morpheme: *-s* (e.g., *John's hat.*)
  - *Gender:* in some English nouns, especially those referring to animals or human professions, we can distinguish male from female by attaching a special morpheme to indicate that the sex is female: *lioness, waitress*, etc. This only works for some words, though; quite often, this gender distinction is indicated by a totally different word (e.g., *king–queen, bull–cow, boy–girl*), or cannot be indicated at all (e.g., *doctor, engineer, eagle*).
  - *Size:* sometimes we can indicate the size of an object with a morpheme: this is the case of the diminutive. Thus, a *booklet* is a small book, a *gosling* is a small goose and a *piglet* is a small pig. Nevertheless, although the most concrete meaning of diminutives is size, their most frequent meaning is affection (e.g., *doggie, sweetie*), perhaps due to the connection between small things and endearment (e.g., babies).

Then we have the meanings typically expressed by verbal inflectional morphemes:

- **Tense:** if we add *-ed* to the stem of the verb, we indicate that the action was performed before the time of speaking (in the case of regular verbs, of course): e.g., *she worked a lot*. Other languages establish more distinctions, like a tense for events that relate to today (called 'hodiernal' tenses), 'hesternal' tenses for yesterday, 'crastinal' for tomorrow or 'post-crastinal' for the day after tomorrow; there are also 'historical tenses' (for things that happened in a distant past).
- **Person and number:** if we add *-s* to the stem, we indicate that the action was performed by a third person (not the speaker or the hearer) in the singular number, and the tense is present: e.g., *she works hard*.
- **Aspect:** if we add *-ing* we indicate that the action is still going on; see the difference between *she has worked here* vs. *she is working here*.

The full gamut of variations in meaning of the verb's tense and aspect are actually achieved by combination with other words (known as 'auxiliaries'): e.g., *was working, has worked, will work, will be working*, etc. With these combinations, we can indicate quite precisely the time at which the action is performed, or its duration, etc. (see Figure 1.6). In English, grammatical aspect allows us to indicate whether the action is to be construed as already finished or still in progress (perfective vs. imperfective) or whether the action is typically repeated (habitual); we can even have 'relative' tense, like 'past with respect to some future time' (e.g., *Tomorrow you will see I was right about this movie*) and other variations.

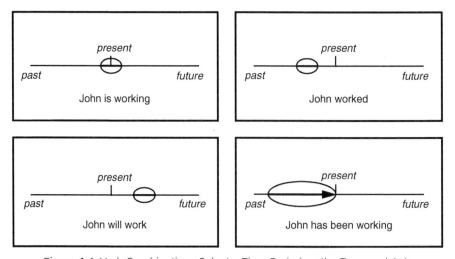

Figure 1.6 Verb Combinations Select a Time Period on the Temporal Axis

- **Derivational meanings in English.** The number of derivational morphemes in English is much higher than that of inflectional morphemes. Additionally, the range of meanings associated with derivational morphemes is much broader. Table 1.4 shows a few examples:

Table 1.4 *Some Derivational Morphemes and their Meanings*

Morpheme	Meaning	Example
-er	the one that does X	worker, drinker
-less	without X	penniless, spotless
-al	relative to X	derivational, colloquial
-ation	the result of X-ing	realization, levitation
-ness	state or condition of X	brightness, happiness
-ian	pertaining to X	Russian, utopian
-ly	to act in a X way	slowly, discretely
-able	able to be X-ed	readable, drinkable
-ful	full of X	wonderful, joyful
-ology	the science of X	biology, musicology

Although the list is not infinite, there are clearly many more meanings that can be expressed with a derivational morpheme than with an inflectional one. The question of to what extent derivational morphology is limited in its expression of meaning is quite interesting and also complicated. For example, there is no morpheme in English that attached to a given name will express its taste (a sort of morpheme for *bitter*). But the limitations are not that clear: in Polish, there seems to be a morpheme (*-ówka*) which means 'type of vodka made from X'; in Spanish, there is a morpheme that when attached to any object means 'blow given with X' (*-azo*).

Another problem with the meaning of derivational morphemes is that quite often the semantic contribution of the morpheme is not so transparent. For example, we have listed the meaning of *-ful* as 'full of X'. This works for words such as *wonderful*, which means approximately 'full of wonder'; the same is applied to words like *shameful, careful* or *delightful*. However, the word *spoonful* refers to 'the quantity that a spoon holds', and not 'full of spoons'; the same can be found in words like *fistful, handful* or *pocketful*. Neither of these meanings apply in the case of the word *grateful*, which is neither 'full of grates' nor 'the amount that a grate holds', because, actually, the noun *grate* does not exist on its own. Finally, the morpheme *-ful* can also attach to a verb stem (not a noun, as in the previous examples) and then its meaning has to be construed in a different way, as in *forgetful* or *helpful*. Most of these cases can be dealt with as cases of polysemy (that we will cover in Chapter 5).

1.6.3 Lexicon

Finally, we reach free morphemes, that is, what most people understand by the notion of 'word'. This is probably the hardest part of all, since we can express virtually anything with a word. For example, all the grammatical meanings of morphemes that have been mentioned before can also be expressed lexically: number, for example, can be expressed with a numeral (*one, two, three, four*, etc.) or a quantifier (*some, many*). It looks as though we can refer to anything with a lexical word: to things (animate, inanimate, concrete or abstract, real or invented), to events, to feelings and maximally abstract concepts, such as cause, force, etc.

It is helpful to distinguish between two types of words: on the one hand, we have '**open-class words**', such as nouns, adjectives, verbs and adverbs (also known as 'content' or 'lexical' words), and on the other '**closed-class words**' (e.g., conjunctions, prepositions, pronouns and determiners; also known as 'function' or 'grammatical' words). They are quite distinct in many ways: in number (open words are more numerous), frequency (closed-class words are more frequent), length (closed-class words are shorter), or in their 'age of acquisition' (open words are acquired earlier). These two types of words are also different neurologically: open- and closed-class words elicit different brain-waves. Moreover, some aphasic patients lose only closed-class words, speaking in what is called 'telegraphic speech'; there is a huge amount of research on this intriguing topic. Finally, if you look at neologisms, almost all of them are open-class words: Oxford's new word for 2014 was *vape*, means 'to inhale and exhale the vapour produced by an electronic cigarette or similar device'. Other recent neologisms we can think of (many of them coming from technology, such as *app, spam, to google, a (forum) troll, drone, noob, emoji, geek, selfie, sms, hashtag, tweet* or *retweet*) are typically nouns, sometimes verbs and, more rarely, adjectives. Sometimes, new words are created by combining existing morphemes (which belong to the closed-class category) with parts of existing words: this is the case of words such as *prequel* or *webinar*. In contrast, new additions to the closed-class category (e.g., new conjunctions, new articles or new prepositions) are much harder to find.

These differences are not always completely clear-cut (things rarely are in language); for example, for many authors, prepositions are in-between these two classes (since we can have complex prepositional groups that function as prepositions and that contain open-class words, such as nouns, cf. *in front of, to the back of, in addition to, in place of*, etc.). However, in general, the distinction between open- and closed-class items holds. Let us consider each of them in turn and look at the types of meanings they usually express.

- **Open-class words.** As mentioned above, there are no clear limitations to the meanings that can be expressed with open-class words. There are only broad connections to the type of meaning they express. This is what we find in the two main ones, nouns and verbs:

- *Nouns*: they basically express things, though not always; for example, *redness* is a quality, more than an object and *destruction* is an event.
- *Verbs*: they are normally used to express actions or states.

These two types of words are the most basic of all; they are probably universal, since there are languages that have no adjectives, articles or adverbs, but it is not clear that there are any languages without something similar to nouns and verbs, (but see Gil, 2013). To these two categories, a third one can be added:

- *Adjectives*: they are basically used to express qualities of things.

For many authors, these are the three most 'basic' types of words; they refer to entities, events and properties, roughly. We have seen that this has to be modified slightly, but still holds in general. The next category that is normally listed in the 'open' class of words is the *adverb*.

- *Adverbs*: they are used mostly to modify actions and states, as well as properties.

- **Closed-class words**. While open-class words can express any type of meaning, 'closed' or 'grammatical' word classes are quite different. They seem to behave rather like grammatical morphemes (or even inflectional morphemes); the range of meanings they can express is rather limited (compared to open-class words, anyway). These are some closed or grammatical words and their usual meanings:
  - *Prepositions*: they are used to indicate relations of place, time and other abstract notions such as manner, causality, etc. For example, in the sentence *the cat is on the mat*, the preposition *on* indicates the location of vertical superiority of *the cat* with respect to *the mat*.
  - *Determiners*: they are used to indicate reference. They help to clarify whether something has been mentioned before or not, or whether we are referring to all the instances of the entity or a particular one, etc. As we shall see later, determiners are one of the crucial instruments in determining the reference of a given word. For example, if we say *I saw the car*, we are assuming that our interlocutor knows which specific car we are talking about.
  - *Conjunctions*: they are used to connect bigger chunks of meaning; we use them to indicate causality, coordination, etc. so that we help the hearer integrate what we are saying with our previous speech, building coherent discourse. For example, we know that whatever comes after the word *and* is going to be added to the information presented until that moment (instead of being contrasted, as would be the case with the word *but*).

1.6.4 Syntax

Can meaning be expressed by ordering words in a specific way? Clearly, the answer is yes. In English, indicating 'who did what to whom' is done in this way: the sentences *The dog bit the man* and *the man bit the dog* contain the same words in a different order, and their meanings are obviously different. The same goes for the different ways in which we group words, another of the issues syntax is concerned with. For example, *[the mother of the boy] and [the girl]* refers to two persons; *the mother of [the boy and the girl]* refers to only one.

Apart from organizing elements in the sentence, the meanings of different words can be combined by joining them syntactically, like putting together an adjective and a noun, or a noun and another noun. However, the ways in which these combinations work are not very clear; language is clearly compositional, but its **compositionality** is far from straightforward. Knowing exactly which parts of meaning are contributed by each word, or how the meaning of the combination is arrived at can be very tricky, even in two-word combinations; as we shall see throughout the book, context can play an all-important role. To phrase it as a question, if *olive oil* is oil made from olives, where does *baby oil* come from? Another very graphic example comes from the combination of the words *blue, red* and *eye*: the part of the eye that is blue in *blue eye* (the iris) is different from the part of the eye that is red in *red eye* (the normally 'white' part of the eye, called the 'sclera'). Where does this information come from? Obviously, it cannot come from the meanings of these individual words. We will look in more depth at further problems of meaning combination and their dependence on context in later chapters.

The connections between syntax and semantics are quite solid, nonetheless. Many studies from the acquisition of English have shown that children use syntactic information to infer the meaning of unknown words. Syntactic categories are normally linked to more or less broad types of meaning: for example, mass nouns are linked to substances and count nouns to concrete objects. Children exploit these connections to narrow down the hypothesis space when guessing the meaning of new words. The name of this phenomenon is **syntactic bootstrapping**, and the first person to mention it was the psychologist Roger Brown in 1957. In his experiments, children saw a picture of somebody performing an unknown action involving a novel substance and a novel object. When asked about the meaning of a nonce word, children tended to think that *a sib* referred to the object, *some sib* to the substance and *sibbing* to the action, thus relating count noun syntax, mass noun syntax and verb syntax to different aspects of the scene. Later studies have confirmed these results and have expanded their scope. For example, Hirsh-Pasek *et al.* (1996) showed a couple of simultaneous videos to two-year olds: one showed Big Bird and Cookie

Monster turning at the same time, and the other showed Big Bird pushing Cookie Monster and making him turn. When children heard the transitive sentence *Big Bird is dacking Cookie Monster*, they tended to look at the video in which Big Bird was pushing Cookie Monster and making him turn; when they heard the intransitive sentence *Big Bird and Cookie Monster are dacking*, they tended to look at the video in which both characters were turning at the same time. This suggests that children are sensitive to the different types of meaning associated with transitive and intransitive verb frames. We will review the notion of syntactic bootstrapping again in Chapter 6, when talking about the acquisition of meaning.

The linguist Adele Goldberg (1995, 2006) has studied how grammatical constructions *per se*, without any lexical content, can convey a meaning of their own. In her theory, called Construction Grammar, grammatical constructions are complex linguistic signs (in a Saussurean sense): they link a certain form, for example, a grammatical configuration, with a certain content, its associated meaning, which is conveyed *by the construction itself*. For example, the combination [Subject + Verb + Object1 + Object2] is associated with the meaning 'to transfer something to someone'. When we insert a verb into that construction, the meaning of the verb is adapted to the meaning conveyed by the grammatical construction, so that the overall meaning is something like '*Subj made Object1 receive Object2 by V-ing*'. This is what we see in examples like these ones:

2. a. *She sent him a packet*
    b. *She baked him a cake*
    c. *She painted him a portrait*
    d. *She told him a story*

The meaning of sentences, thus, stems from the fusion of the meaning of the individual verb plus the meaning of the construction in which the verb is inserted (see Table 1.5 for some additional examples of constructions). Scholars working in this field have been able to evidence this type of

Table 1.5 *Some Examples of Constructions and their Associated Meanings*

Construction	Form	Meaning	Example
Transitive	Subject Verb Object	X acts on Y	John broke the window
Ditransitive	Subject Verb Object1 Object2	X causes Y to receive Z	She sent him a letter
Resultative	Subject Verb Object Complement	X causes Y to become Z	He painted the door blue
Caused motion	Subject Verb Object Oblique	X causes Y to move Z	He kicked the ball into the room

meaning expression in dozens of grammatical constructions. We will talk about Construction Grammar again in coming chapters (e.g., in Chapter 8, when discussing sentential semantics).

1.7 Organization of this Book

As we have already seen, some meanings can be expressed by different linguistic mechanisms (e.g., we can express the concept of 'number' with a morpheme – the plural morpheme –s, or with a lexical word – e.g., *many, two*, etc.), and at the same time, some linguistic elements will correspond to more than one meaning (think of the different meanings of the word *cold* in *cold weather*, a *cold person, to have a cold*, or in *cold-blood*). The rest of this book will try to look at this issue in some detail. Though we have only begun our survey, we can already foresee that the relationship between 'elements of meaning' and 'elements of language' is going to be a highly complex one; we can say that the mapping will be many-to-many, including not just 'one-to-many' or 'many-to-one', but even 'several-to-one' or 'several-to-several', as we see in Figure 1.7.

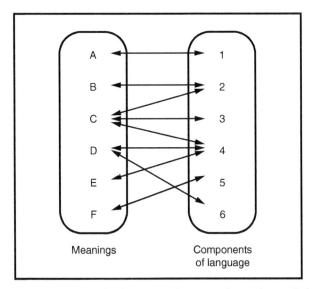

Figure 1.7 Many-to-Many Mapping between Elements of Meaning and Elements of Language

Since it is not possible to attack every point at the same time, we will divide our study into three levels, following a classic distinction (e.g., Givón, 1984). We will first look at the meaning of words (or **lexical semantics**). Then, we will examine the meaning of sentences, used to describe scenes; this is the realm of **sentential semantics**. Then, we will look at how meaning is established in a wider, more contextual way, which can be termed

discourse semantics. Though this distinction is somewhat artificial, it is not completely arbitrary. These three areas of meaning are processed by different psychological systems; words (lexical semantics) are often considered stable bits of information, stored in long-term memory, and are culturally based. Sentences, on the other hand, are created on-line; they are processed by short-term memory, and their limits and characteristics must be different from lexical semantics. Finally, discourse semantics is also short-term, though more contextual (cf Givón, 1984, 1998). Of course, this is also a methodological division. In some cases these levels will overlap, and we will have to speak of several levels at the same time. Sometimes, we will have to deal with issues that are normally covered in pragmatics courses along the way, though the most 'classic' pragmatic issues will be covered with more detail in our final chapter.

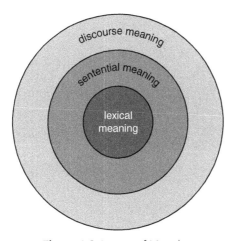

Figure 1.8 Layers of Meaning

Before starting with our examination of meaning by words, sentences and texts (Figure 1.8), the next two chapters in the book will cover general aspects of meaning; first, we will take a quick look at the different methodologies we have at our disposal to extract semantic information from language (Chapter 2), and then we will examine the thorny issue of the relationship between meaning and thought (Chapter 3).

1.8 Chapter Summary

This chapter has introduced the notion of semantics, trying to convey both the importance of its study and the difficulties of the task. We have seen the centrality of semantics for all types of linguistic analyses whatever you think the function of language might be; at the same time, we have shown the problems facing anyone trying to decide what should be included in a theory of meaning, by examining our knowledge of a single word. We have reviewed the differing views of the place of semantics in theories of language found in the last century. Then, we have examined how meaning is expressed, both non-linguistically (introducing the semiotic notions of icon, index and symbol) and linguistically. For this last purpose, we have been looking at the types of meanings that can be expressed in the different linguistic levels, from phonology (with its rather loose associations between some sounds and some meanings called 'sound symbolism' and a brief revision of the often ignored role of intonation in conveying meaning), morphology (distinguishing between the more restricted set of meanings of inflectional morphemes, closer to grammatical-type meanings, and the more open-ended set of meanings expressed with derivational morphemes), the lexicon (where we have distinguished between open-class words, which convey full lexical meanings, as in nouns, adjectives, verbs and adverbs, and closed-class words, with quite specific meanings closer to grammatical ones, and expressed by elements like prepositions, conjunctions or determiners), and syntax (reviewing how word order can indicate meanings, e.g., at event-level, indicating 'who-did-what-to-whom', how children use syntax to constrain their semantic hypotheses when learning new words, and also the possibility that syntactic constructions *per se* can carry meanings). The chapter closed with a brief look at the general organization of information in the book, which will follow a linear order that will take us from the meaning of words to sentential meaning and finally to discourse meaning.

Exercises

Exercise 1.1   Try to indicate all meaningful parts of the following texts:

In a hole in the ground there lived a hobbit. Not a nasty, dirty, wet hole, filled with the end of worms and an oozy smell, nor yet a dry, bare, sandy hole with nothing in it to sit down on or to eat: it was a hobbit-hole, and that means comfort.

'Twas brillig, and the slithy toves
Did gyre and gimble in the wabe
All mimsy were the borogoves
and the mome raths outgrabe

Beware the Jabberwock, my son!
The Jaws that bite, the claws that catch
Beware the Jubjub bird and shun
the frumious Bandersnatch

Exercise 1.2   Identify the following pictures as icons, indices or symbols:

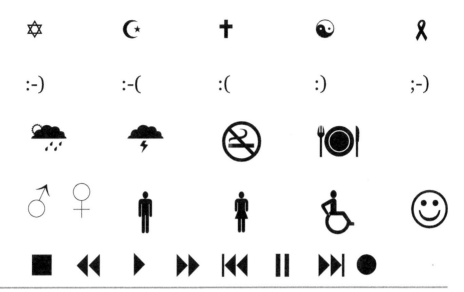

Exercise 1.3   All the information that we listed in our 'coffee' example is clearly culturally based. Quite probably, even within the same culture, nobody has exactly the same information about coffee as anyone else. You could say that there are no two *exact* meanings of the concept 'coffee' out there. How is it possible then that we can communicate? Do we really understand each other when we talk?

Exercise 1.4   The linguistic expression '*I saw a fish this big*' on its own is probably not enough to convey a complete meaning. What would be necessary as a complement? Is the expression then symbolic, iconic, indexical? Can you think of more examples like this?

There is a substantial amount of literature examining iconicity features in language. We have examined the case of sound symbolism, but iconic effects may be also found in other levels, such as the morphosyntactic. For example, think about the sentence *Veni, vidi, vici* ('I came, I saw, I conquered'). Can its syntactic order be considered iconic with respect to the temporal sequence of events it describes? Is this similar to the example in Carston (1988): '*it's better to meet the love of your life and get married than to get married and meet the love of your life*'?

What about complex syntactic structures such as conditionals or temporal adverb clauses, which join two different clauses in a given order? (e.g., *If you ask me, I will sing for you* or *You have to wash your hands before eating*).

What about the lexical reduplication effect in *he talks and talks and talks*, or in *far, far away*? Or the lengthening of a phoneme as in *a very loooong movie* or *a veeeeery nice one*? Can you think of other examples of iconicity like this?

Exercise 1.6   Complete the following:

'White hair' is an index of . . . .
'Thunder' is an index of . . . .
'Applause' is an index of . . .
'A baby cry' is an index of . . .
'Laughter' is an index of . . .

Can you think of more examples of indexical associations?

Exercise 1.7   What is the meaning of the following gestures?

- A nod of the head
- A repeated lateral head shake
- A shrug of your shoulders
- Crossing your fingers
- The 'cut-throat' sign (in which you run your index finger across your throat)
- The 'shush' sign (putting your finger across your lips)

Are these meanings iconic, indexical or symbolic? Can you think of more meaningful gestures?

Exercise 1.8   Go to the following webpage (http://www.cambridge.org/MeaninginEnglish) and listen to these sounds. With which meaning do you associate them? Is the association iconic, indexical or symbolic?

1.	2.	3.	4.
5.	6.	7.	8.
9.	10.	11.	12.

Exercise 1.9   Context can also alter the meaning of non-linguistic symbols. What is the meaning of a red light in a machine, in a radio studio, in a road or on a car dashboard? What about the expression *red-light district*?

Exercise 1.10   Try to identify the meaning of the following morphemes:

MORPHEME	EXAMPLE
-ish	*reddish, longish, tallish*
-ment	*enablement, excitement, development*
-ic	*metallic, aristocratic, dramatic, majestic*
-ize	*modernize, sterilize, familiarize*
-ing	*shooting, sleeping, reading*
-ate	*activate, elongate, facilitate*
-ity	*reality, stupidity, nobility, brutality*
-ous	*poisonous, gracious, prodigious, mysterious*

Exercise 1.11   Think of cases in which different intonations of a sentence alter its meaning. For example, how many ways of altering the meaning of the sentence *you are going to marry him* using intonation can you think of?

Key Terms Introduced in this Chapter
semantics
semiotics
icon
index
symbol
sound symbolism/phonosemantics
onomatopoeia
phonesthesia
phonesthemes
inflectional vs. derivational meanings
open-class vs. closed-class words
syntactic bootstrapping
constructional meaning

Further reading
Riemer (2010), Saeed (2015) and Cruse (2000) introduce in a clear way many aspects of semantics; they can be very useful as reference books. More specifically, grammatical semantics is thoroughly covered Frawley (1992). A popular introduction to semiotics is Sebeok (1994), while the classic reference for how constructional meaning is expressed is Goldberg (1995). Finally, Vigliocco and Vinson (2007) offer an overview of the problems of semantic representation from a psycholinguistic perspective.

CHAPTER 2

Analysing Meaning: Some Methods

In this chapter . . .

In this chapter, we take a look at some of the methods that have been used in semantic theorizing, from the more traditional to the ones being currently applied. After a short introduction situating the topic, we exemplify one of the more traditional methodologies: Semantic Feature Analysis, a classic example of the use of introspection in semantics. We review some of its advantages, and then point out some of its problems. Next, we cover statistical methods, focusing in particular on distributed-semantics methods, such as Hyper-space Analogue to Language or Latent Semantic Analysis. The next section deals with psycholinguistic methods, with tasks such as lexical decision, memory measures, reading times or eye-tracking, which notes the movement of our eyes to derive information about the mental models we construct as we are understanding language. We then go on to neurological methods, such as Event Related Potentials (ERPs) or Functional Magnetic-Resonance Imaging (fMRIs), and the latest addition of TMS, or Transcraneal Magnetic Stimulation. Finally, we discuss the possibilities of computational modelling. The chapter closes with a short reflection on the limits and place of empirical data in theorizing.

2.1 **Why Worry about Methods?**

One of the issues that are seldom discussed in courses on semantics is the methodology used by the different scholars to arrive at their analyses. Probably, the reason behind this fact is that, until now, most of the methods have been *introspective*, that is, based on the intuitions of the analyst (what is sometimes known as 'arm-chair linguistics', as in Figure 2.1). Introspection seems to be the most obvious method to study something

Figure 2.1 A Linguist using the Traditional 'Arm-chair Linguistics' Methodology

that goes on within our own minds (which is thus very personal) and is not externally visible in any obvious way. Clearly, it is not apparent how we can study meaning directly: even looking directly at our brain with a scanner would not show us 'meanings' there, but only brain activity, neural connections and so forth. Unfortunately, introspective methods are faced with many problems: the subjectivity of the analyst and also the lack of mechanisms for verifiability, to name just two of the main ones. Thus, their claim to usefulness as a method of increasing our knowledge about any topic has to be treated with the utmost caution.

Regarding semantics, there are currently a number of additional strategies, based on new methodologies, which can be used to extract meaning from linguistic expressions or, to put it another way, to try to pin down meaning, to delimit it more precisely, so that the different semantic phenomena (e.g., polysemy, synonymy, co-reference, etc.) can be appropriately described and explained. Most of these novel methodologies being applied come from the discipline known as **cognitive science**: the multidisciplinary study of conceptual systems, which tries to combine insights from linguistics, anthropology, cognitive psychology, neuroscience, artificial intelligence and philosophy in order to arrive at a richer understanding of cognition. This entails that the methodologies used in each of these disciplines can be applied to the same topics and, in this way, they can offer new views on old topics. Cognitive science has much to offer semantics; in this chapter we will review some of these methodologies which, when applied to semantic studies, will no doubt provide a firmer base for its theoretical foundation and improve, generally speaking, the rigour of the discipline.

This new emphasis on empirical approaches does not mean that everything that has been gathered using the classical introspective methods should be abandoned, or that this type of methodology should be radically banned from semantics. Nothing could be further from the truth. Even in the most experimental of methodologies there is a need for introspection: as the philospher Kant said, 'theory without experiment is empty but experiment without theory is blind'. Therefore, we will find many examples of initial explanations based on the intuitions of the analyst that are then subjected to more objective methods in order to confirm or reject the different hypotheses, or to choose between different alternatives.

A key notion used in cognitive science is that of **convergent evidence**: scholars try to find evidence from many different sources (e.g., reaction times when processing a word, the time you spend reading a text, the items you remember after reading a text, the speed with which you detect a grammatical error, your eye movements while processing language or brain activity in a specific area), to see if a whole range of different experiments points in the same direction and thus provides more support for a given explanation.

Let us then review some of these methods, starting with the more traditional (the decompositional approach of semantic feature analysis) and moving on to more recent and empirically based ones, using statistical, psycholinguistic, neurological or computational information.

2.2 Traditional Introspective Methods: Semantic Feature Analysis

A majority of the approaches to the analysis of meaning tend to assume that the meanings of most words are complex, and can be described as formed by different 'meaning components'. This strategy seems to fit our intuitions, since we somehow feel that (probably most) words do not have single meanings. For example, it is quite easy to identify pairs or groups of words whose meanings overlap to a certain extent. Those overlaps would be the 'part of meaning' that all these words share. In the case of *man* and *woman* it is easy to see that part of their meaning is shared: they are both [HUMAN]. At the same time, we can also identify how two words are different; in our example, what makes *man* and *woman* different is gender: the first one is [MALE] and the second [FEMALE]. This quite intuitive procedure suggests therefore an agenda of how to proceed: we can analyse the meaning of a word or expression by identifying those components that are shared with other groups of words, and then by identifying the parts of meaning that distinguish one word from the next one. These different components of meaning have traditionally been called **semantic features** (that, as we have seen, are often written in capital letters and between brackets).

Binary semantic feature analysis started as part of the theory of 'semantic fields', which is related to the structuralist approach (e.g., Trier, 1931; see also Lehrer, 1974 or Kittay, 1987), now almost a century old. Structuralists had started describing phonology using a method that employed binary features (e.g., 'mode of articulation' or 'place of articulation'), a method that is still applied today. This system allowed the comparison of the different sounds of a given language among themselves: for example, /p/ and /b/ are very similar in sound, but are distinguished by one feature: [±voice]. So, /p/ is [+bilabial][+stop][−voiced] while /b/ is [+bilabial][+stop][+voiced]. This method also allowed the comparison of sounds from different languages, and, generally speaking, turned out to be a very efficient and successful method. Thus, attempts to adapt the feature approach to other levels of linguistics, including semantics, were only natural.

According to semantic field theory, semantic representations arise from the relationships existing among the different words (Trier, 1931). A semantic field, then, is a group of words that are closely related in meaning; the meaning of each word in this field is defined by the relationships it holds to other words in its semantic field. The ways in which the different words are contrasted within a semantic field depend on the semantic field itself: each of them has a number of dimensions, or 'semantic features' (they have many more names: semes, semantic components, semantic markers or semantic primes), which are useful for distinguishing among the different members. So, for example, *girl, woman, sister, wife* and *queen* all share one semantic feature, which could be called 'gender', with the value [FEMALE], while *boy, man, brother, husband* and *king* would share a contrasting version of this feature, with the value [MALE]. There is also the possibility of having words in which this feature is unspecified, as in *child, person, sibling, spouse* and *monarch*.

The feature values [MALE] and [FEMALE] are also **complementary**: that means that we do not need them both, since the presence of one of them implies the absence of the other. We could also say that these features are *binary*. We only need one of them and add a '+' or '−' sign to indicate one or the other. Therefore, [+MALE] is the same thing as [−FEMALE], and [+FEMALE] is the same as [−MALE]. Which of the two features one uses is, to a certain extent, arbitrary. Nonetheless, it is often the case that theories try to decide which is the most basic feature by applying the notion of 'markedness'. The most 'normal' or 'basic' one is the less marked one, and that is the one chosen; in the case of [MALE] vs. [FEMALE], the 'default' option is the male one. For example, in words such as *lioness, goddess* or *waitress*, the feature [+FEMALE] must be indicated by adding a special or extra morpheme; also, the male gender frequently subsumes both the male and female variants in sentences like *lions are fierce, man is mortal* or *boys will be boys*.

One of the advantages of feature analysis is that it supplies an easy and transparent method of capturing the meaning structure (similarities and differences) of groups of words by combining the use of several semantic features. The result is called a semantic matrix. This is what we see in Table 2.1.

Table 2.1 *Feature Matrix for Six Person Terms*

	[HUMAN]	[ADULT]	[MALE]
Child	+	−	
Girl	+	−	−
Boy	+	−	+
Adult	+	+	
Woman	+	+	−
Man	+	+	+

Componential semantic feature analysis thus allows us to capture in an economical, compact and highly explicit way the basic meaning of words, and some semantic relationships (e.g., hyponymy). Semantic features can also be used to formulate *selectional restrictions*, that is, to specify the semantic constraints of the arguments of a given predicate (we will deal with these issues a bit more precisely in Chapter 8). Thus, the semantic anomaly of *John drinks rocks* can be captured by saying that the verb *to drink* imposes a selectional restriction on its object: it must be [+LIQUID]. We can describe many selectional descriptions with the binary feature approach, though there are certain limits, and for this task, features would have to be combined with a more complex and structured analysis of the meaning of the verb itself, which goes beyond the binary features of individual words (e.g., Dowty, 1991; Jackendoff, 1990).

As we have mentioned, different semantic fields will use different sets of semantic features to distinguish among their members; for example, kinship terms will use dimensions such as age, gender or degree of relation (Bierwisch, 1971); cooking terms could be distinguished by features such as heat source, utensils involved and materials cooked (Lehrer, 1974), colour terms by features such as hue and brightness, etc.

2.2.1 Some Problems of Binary Semantic Features

Though the general approach is quite commonsensical and its method and goals are clear, there are quite a few problems with analysing meaning in this way. The first and most immediate one is that only certain types of words can be fruitfully analysed using this method. We have seen how it works with kinship terms, terms referring to male/female or young/adult animals or humans, but there are a great number of words that are hard to analyse in this way: how would we establish the semantic features of *light* (as in *Light is entering through the window*), or *intelligence* or *hunger*? It is easy to come up with words that cannot be analysed in any straightforward way using this system.

Next in line, we have the problem of subjectivity: the features that one analyst proposes for a word may be different from those of some other analyst. And that is indeed the case: there are studies that show that the degree of intersubjective agreement on the number and name of semantic features for a given word is quite low: in one study (Wu and Barsalou, 2009), only 44 per cent of the features mentioned by one subject were mentioned by another one. Even intrasubjective agreement is not very high: if you compare the features that one person comes up with for a given word with the features the same person comes up with for the same word on a different occasion, there are great differences to be found. The problem is also that if we have two sets of features to explain the same set of words, we have no way of deciding which of them is the one we should settle for. These analyses always remain somewhat idiosyncratic.

Yet another problem of semantic features is that they capture a very incomplete portion of the meaning of words. This method is valid for distinguishing among related items within a semantic field. However, this leaves out a great deal of what we know about a word. We could try to apply this approach to the analysis of a word until we have extracted *all* its semantic features. We would then have an exhaustive and complete feature list of its meaning, and such a list would be *the* meaning of the word, which would ideally capture all the relevant semantic aspects and characteristics of the word. This is, obviously, an impossible task: as Murphy (2002: 174) mentions 'It is not too controversial to say that any object could be thought of as having an infinite number of features'. No matter how many features we list for a given word, there will always be a remnant of meaning that escapes us.

We could also ask ourselves what qualifies as a semantic feature: can we propose anything? For example, we could propose features such as [FOR SITTING], [WITH ARMS], [WITH BACK] for *chair*. If we admit this, should we admit features like [FOR LYING] for *couches*, or [FOR PUTTING YOUR FEET ON] for *footstools*? Initially, there seems to be no restriction on what type of thing a semantic feature should be. Thus, another issue in semantic feature analysis concerns the nature of the semantic features themselves. What is a semantic feature? Are they *primitives* or can they be decomposed into finer distinctions? What is the level of granularity that will prove adequate for semantic analysis? This is a controversial issue and different answers are supplied by different scholars; authors such as Wierzbicka or Goddard think that there is a universal set of 'atomic' semantic features which can be combined to form the meaning of any possible word in all languages; this approach is called Natural Semantic Metalanguage (e.g., Goddard and Wierzbicka 1994; 2002).

Finally, some authors suggest (as we will see in the next chapter, when we discuss embodiment effects in language) that certain bits of knowledge cannot be captured with a feature, but need something more 'imagistic' in nature. In other words, we could say that the animal *duck* has the feature [+feet], but that does not capture what we know about the feet of ducks, their shape and structure.

Table 2.2 *Summary of Problems of Binary Semantic Features*

- There are many words that cannot be easily analysed with this method
- Semantic feature analyses are sensitive to the subjectivity of the analyst
- There are meaning 'residues' which cannot be analysed (i.e., you cannot capture *all* aspects of a word using binary features)
- It is difficult to agree on what a semantic feature should be
- They cannot capture imagistic information (e.g., shape)

Before ending, a small disclaimer is, however, necessary: in this section, we have focused mainly on *binary* semantic feature analysis. Nowadays, most analysts agree that meaning must be componential in nature (the hard part is to agree on what those components are). Many authors nonetheless do use semantic features, of different types, which often are useful to explain certain phenomena.

2.3 Statistical Methods: HAL and LSA

With the advent of computers, methods that were quite complex before the 1980s are becoming common practice. For example, any standard computer can nowadays process very large collections of texts containing millions of words and extract information about the statistical co-occurrences of the different words. Methods based on this have provided a firm empirical base for an idea that has been around for more than a century: the belief is that precisely this type of information, how words co-occur with each other, is enough to construct a representation of the meaning of a word. Although this proposal (finding out about the meaning of a word just by looking at combinations with other words and disregarding any connection to an outer world), might seem a bit shocking at first, it nevertheless resonates with many theoretical proposals in the past history of semantics and linguistics.

For example, the philosopher Wittgenstein believed that the meaning of a word or expression was basically dependent on the use we make of that word/expression. This is the approach to meaning known as '*meaning as use*'. For him, the meaning of a word is like the meaning of a tool or a piece of chess: the meaning of a knight in chess is the type of movements you can make with it; the meaning of a hammer is the type of things you can use it for. In structural linguistics this idea has also been popular; for example, Saussure famously said, 'Language is a system of interdependent terms in which the value of each term results **solely** from the simultaneous presence of the others' (Saussure, 1916: 114; emphasis added). Another famous quotation that fits nicely here comes from the field of corpus linguistics: 'A word is characterized by the company it keeps' (Firth, 1957).

The concept is fairly straightforward: if you know the meaning of the word *flower* and you know that you can *grow a flower, water a flower* or *cut a flower* (and you know also about the relationship between flowers and bees and pollen, for example), once you meet a new word, say *rose*, and realize that it appears in very similar linguistic expressions (you can also grow it, water it, cut it, etc.), you would then guess that they must be pretty close in meaning, thereby forming an adequate notion of the meaning of *rose*.

We can now use the power of computers to come up with mathematical models that can extract the meaning of a given word from its context. Models that build semantic representations directly from lexical co-occurrences (from untagged corpora) are called **high-dimensional models**, for reasons that will become clear presently. There are a number of different versions of this approach, such as Hyperspace Analogue to Language (**HAL**; Lund and Burgess, 1996), Latent Semantic Analysis (**LSA**; Landauer and Dumais, 1997) and most recently, the **Topics** model (Griffiths et al., 2007). All these approaches can be considered computational models of human semantic memory. Though similar, they do not work in exactly the same way: LSA essentially counts the frequency with which a word appears in a given context (which can be a sentence or a paragraph) while HAL moves a ten-word window across a text base and computes all pair-wise distances between words within the window at a given point.

As we have mentioned, the whole idea behind these approaches is quite simple: words that are similar in meaning will tend to appear in the same contexts. So the words *doctor, nurse, medicine* or *prescription* will tend to appear in similar contexts and more or less next to each other, and the same will happen with words such as *restaurant, waiter, menu* or *food*. What these approaches do is to provide a numerical measure of this vicinity and use it as a surrogate of semantic similarity. In the next section, we are going to examine how one of these approaches, **Latent Semantic Analysis**, carries out this process.

2.3.1 An Example of a High-Dimensional Vectorial Model: LSA

Historically, LSA originated from the need for computer scientists to find the most effective way to retrieve documents by using a number of keywords (Deerwester *et al.*, 1990). This is a tougher problem than it might seem at first. Thus, if in your search you type keywords such as *film* and *Tom Cruise*, you are interested in retrieving documents that do mention *film*, but quite probably you would also be interested in other documents that include some related words and synonyms, such as *movie, Hollywood* or *motion picture*. At the same time, you are not interested in other senses of *film* which are not coherent in the context provided (*Tom Cruise*), as would be the case of a cooking document that included the instruction *to cook this dish, you begin by spreading a thin film of oil on the wok*.

To solve this, LSA starts by analysing a large corpus of texts, seeing how often a given word appears within different 'chunks' of this corpus; these chunks are called 'documents'. What LSA does is construct a table in which the rows correspond to all the different words in the corpus and the columns to the different documents (i.e., it divides the corpus into different segments). For example, a 100-million-word corpus may have about 100,000 different words and could be divided into 50,000 documents. So, initially what we have is a gigantic matrix, a table of 100,000 x 50,000 cells. In each cell we can see how many times a given word appears in a given document. Thus, the word *table*, for example, would consist of a gigantic list of 50,000 numbers (this is roughly what we call a 'vector': a list of numbers). Each of the numbers in the row for *table* would correspond to the number of times that this word appears in Document 1, Document 2, Document 3, etc. All words would have their corresponding 50,000 vector, specifying how frequently that word appears in each of the 50,000 documents.

Most of the numbers in this vector will be zero: we cannot expect the word *table* to appear in all of the sentences of the corpus, much less a more unusual word such as *serendipity*. Thus, what we have is technically known as a 'sparse matrix', a matrix in which most of its cells contain the value '0'. That is why after having constructed this gigantic table, LSA applies a number of mathematical transformations so that the table is simplified, and the dimensionality of the vector (its length) can be reduced without losing information. We do not have to fully understand how this process is carried out in order to get a grasp of how the system is working (the specific technique used by LSA is called Singular Value Decomposition, or SVD).

Once we have a final vectorial representation for each word (a typical number after this simplification process could be about 300 dimensions, thus the name 'high-dimensional semantics'), a number of quite interesting things can be done. For example, we can see how close in meaning two words are, just by comparing their two vectors. Since the mathematical technique for comparing vectors is quite simple, we can obtain a numerical measure of the semantic closeness of two words. In the next section, we review some of the applications of these models.

2.3.2 Pros and Cons of High-Dimensional Models

Besides its many practical applications (ranging from document retrieval from the Internet, automated scoring of written essays, e-mail filtering or automated tutoring, to name just a few), everybody acknowledges the 'impressive ability of LSA to predict psychological phenomena' (De Vega *et al.*, 2008: 339). The adequacy of these models as a reflection of human knowledge has been established in different ways. For example, a standard exercise in the Test of English as a Foreign Language (TOEFL) asks students to choose among four options for the one closest in meaning to a given item. This test was submitted to an LSA-trained computer, and the results obtained compared to those obtained by a sample of foreign students applying to an American University. Not only were the results numerically similar, but the pattern of results also resembled that of the students (Landauer *et al.*, 1998). The results of LSA also mimic human word sorting and category judgments, and quite accurately simulate word–word lexical priming data (we explain priming in the next section). Word and discourse meaning representations extracted by LSA have thus been found capable of simulating a wide variety of human cognitive phenomena, from the acquisition of vocabulary to judgments of essay quality.

Not all aspects of LSA work equally well; supporters of these approaches acknowledge that these systems have problems capturing polysemy and homonymy. The system puts together all the co-occurrences of a word, regardless of whether they belong to sense 1 or sense 2 of a word. That is, they sum up the 'animal' sense of *seal* with its 'stamp' sense. Also, LSA treats texts as 'bag of words': word order and other syntactic issues are completely ignored by the system, thus disregarding relevant information. Finally, some scholars complain that the dimensions of the words cannot be interpreted; it is hard to 'read inside' the vector to see how the meaning of a given word is structured. There is no obvious way of knowing what a given dimension (or group of dimensions) stands for: is it capturing the distinction between the animacy of two given words, or their shape, or any other aspect?

Nonetheless, the success of these representations has entered semantic theorizing with great force. It should be noted again that these models induce their representations of the meaning of words exclusively from the co-occurrence relations with other words: none of their knowledge comes directly from perceptual information about the physical world. In this way, these meaning representations have entered the debate between the two main approaches to semantics: the amodal, symbolic camp, which says that meaning stems from the combination of abstract symbols, and followers of embodiment, who opt for a sensorimotor basis for meaning.

Symbolists argue that the fact that the measures produced by these statistical methods correlate so well with human cognitive phenomena implies that they are indeed capturing the same type of representation of meaning that people use when carrying out these tasks. In other words, these models are so successful because they are using the same method that the human mind uses when computing meaning: they combine symbols. There is in fact research that shows that congenital blind children, who have never experienced colour, can say that the colour of the sky is blue and that orange is closer to red, gold to yellow, turquoise to green and purple to violet (Shepard and Cooper, 1992; Marmor, 1978), which means that they must extract this information from the language patterns they hear. On their part, followers of embodiment argue back that it is true that the co-occurrences found in language are meaningful, but that is due to the fact that we use language to describe the world, and things in the world also co-occur: in the real world, when you *see* a hamburger, it usually goes with tomato, onion and ketchup, so when you *talk* about it, your linguistic description will normally include these words (the same could be said of paper, pencil and staplers, or doctors, nurses, patients and hospitals, etc.). Therefore, language does capture information of the world in its word co-occurrences but only indirectly, as a reflection of the structure of the world that we perceive: LSA captures information because words correlate with experience. This debate still goes on; our next chapter will review these two approaches to meaning, the symbolic and the embodied in more detail.

2.4 Psycholinguistic Methods

Psycholinguistic methods examine the cognitive processes at work when people understand or produce language. The basic idea behind all of them is to try to relate some change in the behaviour of subjects to the key concept being investigated, typically by means of a controlled experiment. As long as a relationship can be established with the theoretical concept being investigated (be it causal or just correlational), any change in behaviour can be valid. Quite often they focus on the time it takes to carry out some task (e.g., how quickly you decide whether something is a word of your language or not, or how long it takes you to read a given text); other times they examine the type of things you remember after a given task (a list of words, a text, a situation). These methods are sometimes separated into two different classes. A group of them, called **online measures**, examine the activity that goes on as participants are actively processing the experimental stimuli; this is the case of lexical decision tasks, naming tasks or reading times. On the other hand, **offline measures** are based on the information that can be collected once the processing of the stimuli has been completed; this would be the case of memory measures or feature listing.

In this section we are going to examine some of the more typical tasks used in these experiments. Specifically, we will look at lexical decision and naming tasks, memory tasks and self-paced reading tasks. We will complete the section with a more sophisticated type of measure: the movements we make with our eyes as we are performing a linguistic task.

2.4.1 Lexical Decision Tasks and Priming

In a **lexical decision task**, the participants are presented with a string of letters on a computer screen and they have to decide as quickly as possible whether they correspond to a word in their language or not, typically by pressing a key. Normally, half of the letter strings correspond to real words (e.g., *boat*), and the other half to non-words (e.g., *loat*), so that the task is not automatic (if all letter strings corresponded to real words, subjects would start pushing the 'yes' button automatically after a little while). The interesting part in these experiments comes from the existence of an incredibly useful phenomenon known as **priming**. This effect was first discussed in a series of experiments conducted by Meyer and Schvaneveldt in the early 1970s. In these experiments, people were shown pairs of letter strings and had to decide whether both of them were words (e.g., *doctor–nurse*, or *bread–butter*) or not (e.g., *bread–marb*). People were much faster at recognizing pairs of real words when they were related (e.g., *doctor–nurse*, *bread–butter*) than when they were not (e.g., *doctor–butter*, *bread–nurse*). The explanation for this is normally attributed to a mental connection between both words: *doctor* and *nurse* are connected in our mental lexicon, while *bread* and *nurse* are not. Thus, when we encounter the word *doctor*, it becomes active, and part of that activation is passed on to words connected to it, in what is known as a **spreading activation model**. This is quite a useful and objective method to postulate connections among words. Such connections can be of different kinds; synonyms, antonyms, hyponyms and words belonging to the same category (e.g., *apple* and *orange*) can prime each other; *doctor–nurse* is an example of *associative* priming. We will talk about this at more length in Chapter 5 when we discuss relations among word meanings. The terminology used in these experiments refers to the item seen in the first place as the **prime**, and the one whose recognition is facilitated, the **target**. The prime is typically compared with a **control** word, which provides a base-level comparison: if the prime elicits a quicker reaction time of the target than a control (also called a distractor), then priming can be said to occur. Experimenters can also manipulate the temporal separation between prime and target to find out when certain connections become available for the subject, or the order in which the different sources of information come into play (Figure 2.2).

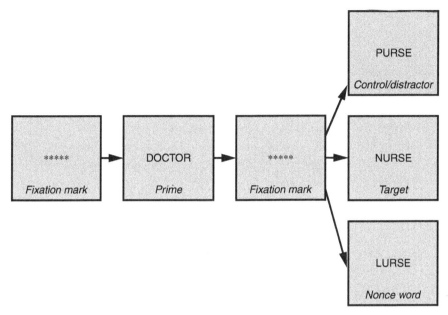

Figure 2.2 Structure of a Lexical Decision Priming Task

Priming techniques can be used to test any type of connection between structures in the mind, not just between words; we will see some variants of this paradigm in Chapter 7, applied to the connection of different domains in metaphor studies. As an example of priming in lexical decision tasks, in Chapter 5 we will examine how this technique has been applied to the study of polysemy. Swinney (1979), for example, used it to investigate the effects of context on the retrieval of the different senses of ambiguous words. His subjects heard sentences with the word *bug* (which has at least two different meanings, the first one corresponding to *insect* and the second one to *spying device*) and then were shown letter strings corresponding to words related to the first of these meanings, to the second one, or an unrelated meaning. Swinney further manipulated the temporal point at which the target word was presented in order to find out at which point the contextual effect of the sentence 'kicked in' and selected only one of the meanings. We will review this type of effect in Chapter 5.

2.4.2 Memory Measures

Another task that can be useful for semantic studies is **memory measures**: examining what type of information people remember after having encountered a given word or text. The idea is that this can inform us about how people represented the meaning of the expression when they committed it to memory. These tasks typically have a learning phase, in which participants are shown a given stimulus, and then a test phase, in which they are tested about the things they remember. Both phases are normally separated by a time interval long enough to eliminate any effects of working memory, and thereby ensure that the effects are solely due to the way in which the stimulus was codified in semantic memory. An example of how memory measures can be informative for semantic studies will be presented in Chapter 6. In order to examine the possible influences of language on cognitive processing (which we will introduce as the Sapir-Whorf Hypothesis), Boroditsky *et al.* (2002) showed Indonesian and English speakers a number of pictures with actors carrying out tasks in different tenses (past, present and future). They later tested their subjects' memory for specific pictures, in order to find out whether the fact that the Indonesian language has no tense (while English does) would influence the precision with which both groups of speakers remembered the pictures shown, thereby revealing a cognitive influence of language on memory. We will review this in more detail in Chapter 6.

2.4.3 Reading Times

In another type of task, the time that it takes to read a text can be informative about the type of processing that is going on during the comprehension of the text. These experiments typically compare the reading times of a text that contains one given feature against another one that does not have it; since participants control (by pressing a key) the speed with which they read the different chunks of the text, these tasks are also known as **self-paced reading tasks**. An example of a study that uses this methodology is Gentner *et al.* (2001). These authors wanted to find out whether the comprehension of a metaphorical expression necessarily entails the activation of the source domain of the metaphor; for example, are we really thinking about wars when we hear expressions such as *he demolished my argument* or *he attacked my point of view*? With this end in mind, they constructed two types of texts: both ended with the same metaphorical statement, which was consistent with the metaphor A DEBATE IS A RACE. However, while the first type of text presented several other previous statements consistent with this final metaphor, the second type of text contained expressions from a different metaphor: A DEBATE IS A WAR. The results showed that people read the last sentence more quickly when the metaphor used was the same throughout the text than when the sentence introduced a new metaphorical mapping (though in both cases the target domain was still the same, DEBATE). This was taken as evidence that people use a general mapping schema from a source to a target domain when understanding a text, which helps them integrate information smoothly. It must be noted that a second experiment with a more conventional type of metaphor did not yield the same effects, which was only found with novel or creative metaphors. We will examine the issues of metaphor processing in Chapter 7.

2.4.4 Eye-Tracking Methods

More recently, psycholinguistics has incorporated more sophisticated equipment in the attempt to measure how people process different cognitive events. One of these new technologies allows **eye-tracking**: dedicated devices (known as eye-trackers) follow the gaze of subjects as they are performing a given task and record different parameters of their eye behaviour (Figure 2.3). This is interesting because humans do not look at scenes in a fixed, steady way (as birds do, for example), but instead perform rapid eye movements, called **saccades**, which stay on a specific spot during 200–300 milliseconds approximately, and then move to a different part of a scene. We must do this because although our eyes can cover a perceptual field of 200 degrees, only 2° can be surveyed with complete sharpness and precision: to cover the rest of the visual field we have to move our eyes performing these saccadic movements. Eye-trackers are able to register different parameters in our saccadic movements that can be informative about cognitive processing. For example, they can detect the **fixations** of our eyes, that is, the exact spot where our eyes stop temporarily; we can also check the amount of time spent looking at a specific location or area (**fixation duration**), the path that the eyes follow as they fixate on the different spots (**scanpath**), or the time lapse between a stimulus and the moment the saccadic movement starts (**saccade latency**).

Eye movements are especially useful because they can give us clues as to on-going processes (not just the end result of a process); they are also a very

Figure 2.3 Eye-Tracker

ecological measure, that is, they are quite natural and do not interfere with the task.

We know a good deal about the typical eye movements we perform when processing language, especially when reading. For example, we know that the chances of an individual word being fixated vary according to whether it is a content word (around 85 per cent) or a function word (35 per cent). Another very informative measure refers to **backtracks**: the occasions in reading when our eyes move backwards, normally due to some problem in the processing of an individual word or the meaning structure of the sentence. Thus, semantic problems such as pronoun resolution, co-reference or lexical ambiguity can be fruitfully studied using these eye-movement patterns.

An example of a study that has used eye-tracking to evaluate whether people construct a mental image when understanding language (or instead go for the amodal, abstract representation advocated by followers of the symbolic view of language) is that of Spivey and Geng (2001). These authors recorded the eye movements of participants who were listening to sentences while facing a large white projection screen that took up most of their visual field. These are some examples of the stories they heard:

Upward story
Imagine that you are standing across the street from a forty story apartment building. At the bottom there is a doorman in blue. On the tenth floor, a woman is hanging her laundry out of the window. On the twenty-ninth floor, two kids are sitting on the fire escape smoking cigarettes. On the very top floor, two people are screaming.

Downward story
Imagine you are standing at the top of a canyon. Several people are preparing to rappel down the far canyon wall across from you. The first person descends 10 feet before she is brought back to the wall. She jumps again and falls 12 feet. She jumps another 15 feet. And the last jump, of 8 feet, takes her to the canyon floor.

While listening to each of these passages, the saccades of subjects coincided with the motion descriptions supplied in the stories: that is, they made more upward saccades in the 'upward' story and more downward saccades during the 'downward' story. Thus, although they were really looking at nothing, their eyes were doing something similar to what they would have done if the scene being described were actually right there in front of them, which was taken by the authors as a proof that they were constructing imagistic representations of the text, rather than a symbolic representation. As we have mentioned, we will discuss these issues in Chapter 3.

More recently, Kamide *et al.* (2004) have demonstrated that when participants hear a sentence such as *The boy will eat the cake*, they start looking at a picture of a cake *before* hearing the word *cake*, something that does not happen when they hear the sentence *The boy will move the cake*. What this shows is that understanding the verb *eat* entails the activation of a detailed schema with 'thematic knowledge' of possible elements that can be eaten; that is why participants start looking at potential candidates for this role as soon as they encounter the verb *eat*, before actually hearing what is coming next. We will discuss this more deeply in Chapter 8.

2.5 Methods from Neuroscience

Neuroscience is also contributing to the discipline of semantics; there are currently a variety of methods that can be used to measure the activity that is going on in the brain as subjects are understanding or producing language. This can help us to confirm or disconfirm hypotheses of how meaning works (and how meaning relates to brain structure, of course).

For example, there is an area of research that studies people who have lost their ability to speak correctly due to some brain impairment. There are cases of patients who lose their ability to name living things, such as animals, while their knowledge about objects remains intact. For some others, it is the other way round; they will have trouble naming a screwdriver (or any other tool), for example, but will easily identify any animal or plant (see Capitani *et al.*, 2003, for a review). This is known as the study of **category-specific deficits**. Researchers use these selective impairments to make educated guesses about how conceptual knowledge could be represented and structured. These cases could help elucidate whether semantic information is localized 'discretely', in specific parts of the brain, or is instead perhaps 'distributed' across different neural areas. The rest of this section will, however, be devoted to examining several popular techniques that are becoming increasingly more familiar to anybody interested in language and semantics.

2.5.1 Event-Related Potentials (ERPs)

The study of Event-Related Potentials, or **ERPs**, tries to link language use to the patterns of neuronal firing in our brains. As is well known, when neurons communicate, the signals that travel through the networks are both chemical (with the interchange of different chemical substances from neuron to neuron in synaptic connections) and electrical: a synapse between two neurons generates a change in the electrical potential of these cells, which go from a resting state to a quick negative charge, followed by a positive one, to finally reach a resting state again. These small changes in

45

voltage can actually be measured: two electrodes are placed close to each other on the scalp of the subject, and the small voltage difference between both electrodes is amplified and registered. Since the activity recorded is so small, a given experimental event is normally repeated several times and the activations are added up and averaged. However, the interesting thing is that the way in which these changes in potential are produced is related to the cognitive event (perceptual, motor, etc.) that elicits them; hence its name, **event-related potentials**. The number of electrodes used can range from twenty to sixty, in order to achieve a topographic map of the activity of the brain. Since electricity travels so far, this method is also really effective in capturing phenomena with great temporal precision (Figure 2.4).

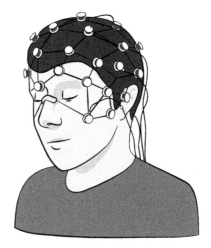

Figure 2.4 Recording Event-Related Potentials

The way in which ERPs are informative is due to alterations of the typical shape or waveform of positive and negative voltage changes. There are several 'components' of this waveform, negative or positive 'peaks' in the waveform, which are named with a letter (N for negative; and P for positive) and a number (which corresponds to the time in milliseconds of appearance of peak after the event). Two of these components are especially revealing for language studies: P600 (that is, the peak in positive charge which is typically produced 600 milliseconds after the eliciting event) and N400 (the negative peak typically produced 400 milliseconds after the event). These components are sensitive to different linguistic components; thus, the typical shape of the N400 is altered when the subject detects a semantic anomaly. On the other hand, the P600 is affected by syntactic or grammatical alterations. For example, Kutas and Hillyard (1980) discovered that the N400 elicited by the sentence *the pizza was too hot to eat* had a normal, small amplitude; when the sentence was changed to *the pizza was too hot to drink*, the N400 shape was affected and became larger, and when the sentence was *the pizza was too hot to cry*, the N400 component become even bigger.

2.5.2 Hemodynamic Methods (MRIs and PETs)

As we have seen, neurons communicate by means of electrochemical signals; these signals need energy to be produced, and that energy is supplied by oxygenated blood, which flows to the area where brain activity is taking place. There are now methods that can detect the amount of oxygen consumption in specific areas of the brain. They are imaging methods known as **positron emission tomography (PET)** or **functional magnetic resonance imaging (fMRI**, Figure 2.5). These methods are, of course, much more expensive and complicated than ERPs; however, they are able to locate with much more precision the specific area in the brain where activation is taking place. The downside is temporal resolution: these methods depend on blood flow, which is of course much slower than electric signals. This is why ERPs are useful for telling us *when* and fMRIs for telling us *where*.

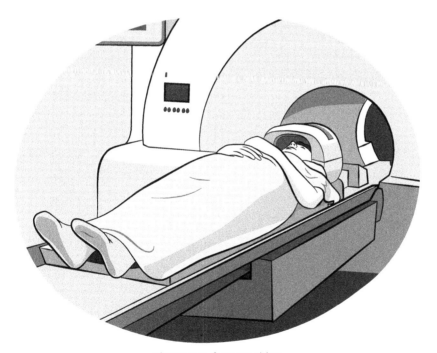

Figure 2.5 fMRI Machine

Brain imaging studies have been instrumental in advancing the embodied view of cognition; we are now able to see which parts of the brain are active as we are understanding language, informing us of how meaning activation is produced in the brain. For example, Pulvermüller *et al.* (2005) showed

47

how understanding action words such as *pick, lick* or *kick* activates areas of the motor cortex which are responsible for the real movement of fingers, lips and feet, respectively; González *et al.* (2006) showed that the olfactory areas of the brain are activated automatically when recognizing words with strong olfactory associations, such as *cinnamon, lemon* or *perfume*; brain regions involved in colour perception are also active when retrieving colour knowledge about objects (Hsu *et al.*, 2011; Simmons *et al.*, 2007). We will review many of these examples in Chapter 3, when discussing the embodied view of meaning.

2.5.3 Transcraneal Magnetic Stimulation (TMS)

One of the latest additions to the arsenal of neuroscientific techniques is the method known as TMS, for **transcraneal magnetic stimulation**, whose main use has until very recently been therapeutic (as a complement in depression therapies, helping the rehabilitation of lesioned areas after brain strokes or for migraine treatment). Nowadays, TMS is also being used to find out how the brain carries out certain cognitive tasks. This method consists of supplying a mild electric shock to a highly localized area of the brain, creating what could be called a 'reversible temporary lesion'. In this way, the function of this area in a given cognitive operation can be effectively tested; sometimes, applying TMS to a certain area will cause the impairment of a given function; sometimes it can also 'prime' the area, bringing about improved performance. What is important with TMS is that, while with fMRIs all

Figure 2.6 Transcraneal Magnetic Stimulation (TMS)

one can say about a given experimental result is that there is a certain correlation between the activation of a given brain area and a given cognitive process, with TMS we can test the *causality*: whether that brain area really is involved crucially in the process being investigated. For example, Pulvermüller *et al.* (2005) applied TMS to hand and leg motor cortex areas just 150 milliseconds after presenting subjects with words of these types (e.g., *pick* and *kick*) in a lexical decision task; it was found that subjects recognized these words faster and more efficiently, as would be consistent with a theory that proposes the involvement of the motor cortex in the understanding of action words.

2.6 Methods from Computer Science: Computational Modelling

The term **computational modelling** refers to the construction of a computer model that captures the main features of a theory or explanation and that can be run on a computer so that the behaviour of the program can inform us about how well the model fits with reality (what is known as the 'goodness of fit' of the model). Computational **modelling** is an extremely useful tool when studying complex systems; it is currently used in many 'hard' sciences, such as physics (e.g. fluid dynamics), biology (e.g, protein folding, gene regulation), neurology, chemistry, astrophysics or engineering.

A carefully designed computational model can be of great help to theoretical proposals, providing clues about their limitations and their internal contradictions, and generally speaking, allowing us to better understand their intricacies and implications. It is also accompanied by the extra requirement of forcing theories to provide completely explicit, detailed and precise explanations.

One specific example of the benefits of computational modelling in linguistics can be found in what has been termed 'the past-tense debate'. In English, the past of some verbs is formed by means of a 'general rule' (i.e., by adding '-ed' to the stem), while some others, the so-called 'irregular' or 'strong' verbs, have to be learned by rote (e.g., *sing-sang-sung*). In order to explain this phenomenon, two different types of mechanisms had been proposed for the two different cases. However, Rumelhart and McClelland (1986) presented a computer simulation that could learn to solve this problem using just a single mechanism, thus providing an 'existence proof' against dual-route theories. The impact of this work was enormous; it spawned an enormously active area of research, and created what can truthfully be called a 'sub-genre' in the debate over the architecture of the human mind. The debate has been going on for more than two decades now; in this case, the introduction of a computational model has been able to spark a lively discussion in which arguments and counter-arguments have had to be increasingly precise and accurate, thus greatly refining our understanding of the psychological status of grammatical rules and the differential roles of computation vs. storage in language processing.

The LSA approach we presented at the beginning of this chapter could also be considered as a computer model of human semantic memory. Its theoretical usefulness is also evident, since it shows how the symbolic account of meaning can indeed explain a substantial number of phenomena, and thus can be taken as proof of the possible appropriateness of the symbolic hypothesis. Embodied computational models are less frequent, but they also exist. Luc Steels (Steels, 2001, 2003, 2010) has used pairs of 'embodied agents' (i.e., robots), who have to play a 'language game' (Figure 2.7).

For example, the robots may have to guess the referent of a given utterance (typically by pointing), describe an event with a set of words, act out the physical motion conveyed by a given utterance or differentiate between different objects in the world in order to arrive at a shared ontology. These robots can build their own embodied representation of the world and are also given some basic cognitive abilities, such as the ability to learn from experience, to detect problems in communication or to invent new strategies to solve linguistic problems. Pairs of robots, chosen randomly from a population of robots, propose different alternatives in their interactions, trying out options until a solution to the problem is (hopefully) found and becomes stabilized across the population by means of group dynamics. This setting allows researchers to

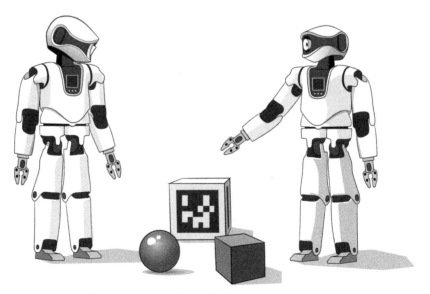

Figure 2.7 Two Robots Playing a 'Language Game'

see, on the one hand, which communicative pressures have to be present in the environment (pressures which are embedded in the requirements of the type of language game to be solved) and on the other, which cognitive capacities the agent must possess in order for a given communicative strategy to emerge. If the combination of a particular set of functional pressures with a particular set of cognitive capacities is enough for a given communicative solution to emerge within the system shared by the community of agents, this can be taken as an existence proof for any theoretical explanation along those lines.

2.7 What Lies Ahead: Future Work

As we have seen, there are many methods that are complementing the traditional linguistic methods and can provide an empirical base to semantic theories; the list we have presented here is partial, and other methods have indeed been used, in the introspective arena (e.g., Osgood's Semantic Differential Technique, which we will cover in Chapter 4 when talking about connotation), in psycholinguistics (e.g., feature listing, which will appear when talking about prototypes in Chapter 4) or in neuroscience (with new methods such as Diffusion Tensor Imaging and Tractography, which allows us not only to see which area of the brain is active, but also how one area is connected to another). The era of computers has brought along a myriad of methods that were previously only available to few laboratories. Today, anyone with a computer can set up experiments in which reading times and priming are studied, or perform sophisticated processing of large corpora. Other methods, such as eye-tracking or ERPs, remain more expensive and therefore more restricted, though their cost has also come down. Yet other methods, such as neural network modelling, have proved useful, but the extent of their usefulness must still be tested more thoroughly, since there are disagreements on the validity of the conclusions we can draw from such a methodology.

The request to back up theoretical explanations empirically also pushes theories in the direction of an increased level of explicitness; only a theory that is explicit enough to make predictions that can be falsified can be submitted to experimental/empirical verification. Some theorists complain that this is too stringent a requirement; there are theories which are accepted as scientific, and yet they do not make predictions or are difficult to falsify. Perhaps the most popular example would be Darwin's theory of natural selection and the origin of species. As the evolutionary biologist Waddington observed:

> Natural selection, which was at first considered as though it were a hypothesis that was in need of experimental or observational confirmation, turns out on closer inspection to be a tautology, a statement of an

inevitable although previously unrecognized relation. It states that the fittest individuals in a population (defined as those which leave most offspring) will leave the most offspring (Waddington 1960: 385–386).

Even if some of the constructs in semantics are not directly observable, it should be pointed out that there are in fact many theoretical constructs used in science that do not stem from direct observation. For example, you cannot see electrons (or quarks or genes, for that matter); in this sense, electrons are also 'theoretical entities'. They can however be observed 'indirectly': we could say that they are inferable from a carefully thought explanatory model. That is, once we assume that these explanatory constructs exist and behave in a specific way (that is, in the way that scientists say they do), we can explain a whole range of natural phenomena much more appropriately, and we can also make predictions about how the world will behave. It is thus their important role in the explanatory schemes we construct that convinces us that they are 'real'. One example of this is the recently discovered Higgs Boson, whose existence was predicted only for theoretical reasons. Once its existence was assumed and its role in an explanatory model of reality (the Standard Model of particle physics) laid out carefully, an experiment could be set up to decide its 'reality' (or usefulness); such an experiment was finally successful (after fifty years!) according to the results reported at Geneva's CERN in July 2012.

In semantic studies, the movement we seem to be witnessing at this point in time is towards the use of a mixture of methods. The notion of *converging evidence* seems to be a key notion. As a matter of fact, we could say that cognitive science as a discipline depends on this notion; the idea that by using different types of methodologies we can advance step by step in the incredibly complex area of human cognition and meaning.

2.8 Chapter Summary

In this chapter, we have looked at some of the methods that have been traditionally used in semantic theorizing, as well as some of the more recent ones, which are being incorporated from the area of cognitive science. After introducing the need for some type of empirical method in Section 2.1, we started our review with a discussion of an example of the classic introspective methodology: binary semantic feature analysis (Section 2.2). We examined the rationale behind it, and then discussed some of the problems that these approaches face, especially the possible subjectivity inherent in the analyses, as well as some of the limitations of the approach. We moved on to examine one of the more influential methodologies in recent times: high-dimensional vectorial semantic approaches, presenting some examples of how Latent

Semantic Analysis works (Section 2.3). Section 2.4 was devoted to a review of the most popular methods used in psycholinguistics, and explained how lexical decision tasks, memory measure tasks and reading times work, supplying some examples of their application to semantic theory. The section closed with a special discussion of eye-tracking, a technique that allows us to use eye movements as clues about the mental processing taking place while people process language. The next section (Section 2.5) dealt with methods from neuroscience, explaining the workings of Event-Related Potentials (ERPs), Functional Magnetic Resonance Imaging (fMRIs) and Transcraneal Magnetic Resonance (TMS). The final group of methods reviewed was the use of computational models in order to check the adequacy of different semantic explanations. The chapter closed with a short reflection in Section 2.7 on the limitations and the proper place of empirical data in semantic theorizing.

Exercises

Exercise 2.1   Analyse the semantic features of the following groups of words so that their meanings can be distinguished:

    a. *whisper, speak, shout*

    b. *open, close, ajar*

    c. *nail, finger, hand*

Exercise 2.2   Do the same with these groups:

    a. Mathematical objects (*triangle, square, pentagon, hexagon*)

    b. Fruit (*orange, lemon, apple, pear, watermelon, pineapple*)

    c. Types of drink (*milk, water, coffee, whisky, rum, gin, vodka*)

    d. Types of clothes (*trousers, skirt, socks, gloves, bikini, hat*)

    e. Verbs of walking (*stride, amble, stroll, limp, stomp, tiptoe, parade, strut, shuffle*)

Exercise 2.3   Compare the results you have found for the previous exercises with those found by your classmates. Do they overlap? Can you decide who got closest to a good result?

Exercise 2.4   In this exercise, we will try to create a very simplified LSA analysis of four words. Suppose that you have a corpus consisting of eight sentences:

    A1. *Some doctors work in an office, others in the hospital and some in laboratories where they develop new medicines.*

A2. *Doctors see patients, run and interpret tests, prescribe medicines or treatments, talk to patients about how to stay healthy and respond to emergencies.*

A3. *Most doctors work very long hours and have to be available for emergencies.*

A4. *They are helped by nurses, who may take temperatures, give shots, administer medicines and check patients' blood pressure and pulse, among other things.*

B1. *The job of a chef is to manage a kitchen, such as that in a restaurant or bakery.*

B2. *Sometimes, a chef is in charge of developing menus or finding food vendors.*

B3. *Other times, a chef is involved in the direct cooking and preparation of the food being served on a daily basis, depending on the restaurant.*

B4. *A chef has to be very creative, using his or her knowledge of food and cooking techniques to create something delicious that people will enjoy!*

Try to calculate the vector for the words *chef, food, restaurant, doctor, medicine* and *patient* given this corpus and this division into documents. To give you a head start, just note down how many times these words appear in each of the documents (A1, A2, etc.) listed above.

	A1	A2	A3	A4	B1	B2	B3	B4
chef								
food								
restaurant								
doctor								
medicine								
patient								

Can you tell by looking at the resulting vectors which words are more similar in meaning?

Exercise 2.5   There are many opportunities for performing on-line experiments on the web. To give you a feel for how these experiments work, you can go to the following site and perform one of the Implicit Association Tasks they propose:

https://implicit.harvard.edu/implicit/takeatest.html.

Key Terms Introduced in this Chapter

cognitive science
converging evidence
high-dimensional models of semantics
latent semantic analysis
priming
lexical decision task
self-paced reading task
eye-tracking
saccade
fixation
gaze duration
backtrack
event-related potentials
N400
P600
functional magnetic resonance imaging
transcraneal magnetic stimulation
computational modelling in semantics

Further reading

Gonzalez-Marquez et al. (2007), *Methods in Cognitive Linguistics* is a very complete compilation of methods that can be applied to semantic studies. Three of its chapters are especially informative: the one on psycholinguistic methods (by Hasson and Giora), the one on eye-tracking (by Richardson, Dale and Spivey) and the one on ERPs, by Seana Coulson. A good complement to neurological methods in semantics is Kutas and Federmeier (2000) and more recently, Hauk and Tschentscher (2013). The classic introduction to Latent Semantic Analysis is Landauer and Dumais (1997). A more thorough revision of computational models is found in Valenzuela (2010).

CHAPTER 3

Language and Thought

In this chapter . . .

In this chapter, we take a look at the relationships between language and thought, examining the two competing proposals that exist nowadays: the formal and the cognitive approach. After situating both of them historically in Section 3.1, we explain the main tenets of the formal viewpoint in Section 3.2, including the idea that the format of thought is language-like (the Language of Thought Hypothesis). Then, we review some criticisms levelled at formal approaches, especially the one known as 'the symbol grounding problem'. The next section of the chapter is devoted to the cognitive or embodied approach; after introducing the approach in Section 3.3 and explaining the concept of embodied simulation (Section 3.3.1), we review the parameters that have been shown to be simulated in the literature (Section 3.3.2) and also examine Glenberg's Indexical Hypothesis (Section 3.3.3), which articulates all these assumptions into a specific model of how we understand language. This block closes with some criticisms of the embodied approaches, in particular the problem presented by abstract thought. The chapter concludes with a final reflection on the interactions of both approaches (Section 3.4).

3.1 Language and Thought: the Formal vs. Embodied Split

In Chapter 1, we drew up a list of basic questions about meaning. Two of the most basic ones were concerned with the nature of meaning itself, on the one hand, and its relationship with thought, on the other. How do we think? Do we think directly in language? Do we think in images, or perhaps is there another mode of thought? What actually goes on in people's minds (or brains) when they understand some linguistic object? How should the 'meaning' that is created in the mind of the hearer be conceived of?

Unsurprisingly, there are different opinions on these matters. There is a classic (and on-going) debate in cognitive science concerning the format in which information is represented, stored and manipulated in our brains. We can distinguish two opposing views, which can be described as the **formal semantics** view (also known as the **symbolic** or **amodal** view) and the **embodied semantics** view (also known as the **cognitive** view).

Formal semantics tries to describe the meaning of language using the descriptive apparatus of formal logic. Attempts to apply the tools of logic to natural language started with Aristotle and continue today. The twentieth century saw a great surge of interest in this topic; philosophers and logicians such as Alfred Tarski, Rudolf Carnap, Saul Kripke, Hilary Putnam, Richard Montague or Donald Davidson, to name but a few of them, devoted themselves to this endeavour. One of their main goals was to describe natural language in a formal, precise and unambiguous way.

This type of semantics is often called **truth-conditional semantics**, because it assumes that the goal of semantics is to describe the conditions that would have to be met for a linguistic expression to be true. Formal semantics is thus concerned with how words are related to objects in the world (that is, the connection between language and external reality), which is why it is also known as 'referential' semantics (we will see more about this in Chapter 4, when we discuss the notion of reference). Formal semantics is also interested in how combinations of words preserve the truth-conditions of their components. It studies, for example, the logical inferences or entailments that can be drawn from a given statement.

However, this long tradition on how to approach meaning started to be challenged by the mid-twentieth century. A number of scholars grew dissatisfied with the formal approach, doubting its suitability for the analysis of real, common natural language. For example, the philosopher Paul

Grice observed that the logical devices used in formal approaches (e.g., ~, ∧, ∨, ⊃, (∀x), (∃x), etc.) cannot be taken as equivalent to their analogues in natural language (e.g., *not, and, or, if, all, some*, etc.). In addition, some authors pointed out that logicians are not really interested in the sentences as uttered in real-life situations, with all their complexities and nuances. Rather, they are interested in an idealized version of them, their 'propositional content' (we will examine the notion of **proposition** more closely in Chapter 8), which can be manipulated and subjected to a number of logical operations. In this way, a movement within philosophy emerged, led by scholars such as Ludwig Wittgenstein, John Austin, Gilbert Gyle and Peter Strawson, who were known as 'ordinary language' philosophers. These scholars advocated a study of language closer to its everyday use, and not in the 'idealized' or 'distilled' state of formal semantics (which is sometimes known as 'analytic' or 'ideal language philosophy'). Wittgenstein acknowledged this real-world complexity when he said that 'to imagine a language means to imagine a form of life' (Wittgenstein, 1957: 19).

From the 1980s onwards, a second wave of scholars, coming from linguistics, psychology and philosophy, felt that meaning goes well beyond what logic can capture, and decided to eschew the notion of truth in semantic theorizing, exploring new avenues of research. They began treating language less as a formal product that can be analysed mathematically and focused on the relationships between language and its biological, psychological and social functions. Instead of looking at the direct connections between language and external reality, they became more interested in the connections between language and mental representation. This alternative approach to semantics eventually coalesced around a view of semantics that can be termed 'psychologically oriented' semantics or cognitive semantics (we will also refer to this view as **embodied**, for reasons that will become clear presently). This approach does not consider the logical structure of language to be important for the description of the meaning in language and tends to disregard notions such as truth-values or strict compositionality. Cognitive semantics tries to explain semantic phenomena by appealing to biological, psychological and even cultural issues. Its proponents try to propose explanations that fit in with what we know about cognition, including perception, memory, attention, categorization and the role of the body in how meaning is structured.

In the following sections, we will examine in more detail the assumptions of these two approaches regarding the relationships between language, meaning and thought. Our next section deals with the formal approach.

3.2 The Formal Approach: Meaning as Amodal Symbols

As mentioned above, the formal approach is based on the notion of **truth-condition**. The idea is that to understand a sentence like *It is raining*, you have to know which conditions must obtain in the world for this sentence to be true: if you know these conditions, you know the meaning of the expression. These truth-conditions, therefore, are said to capture the meaning of the expression (Figure 3.1). Once you know these conditions and you represent them in your mind, they become 'symbols', since they 'stand for' the thing they represent. The interesting point is that then we can operate with these symbolic representations, combining them and using them in our thought processes. Formal semantics follows **Frege's principle of compositionality:** the meaning of the whole is a function of the meaning of the parts. Syntax is therefore very important to this type of analysis.

Figure 3.1 Truth Conditions of *It's Raining*

According to many scholars, minds are 'symbol systems'. Concepts or ideas in our minds are symbols, connections between a form (a brain state, i.e., a given configuration of neuron connections) and a given content (what those connections stand for). Collections of symbols connected in the appropriate way correspond to ideas. As we have seen, these symbols can be combined and manipulated using explicit rules in order to derive new ideas, which is what thinking is about. It is important to note that, in these systems, the rule operates on the 'form' of the symbol; its content (what it stands for) is irrelevant for the computation of the rule. Let us illustrate this with an example.

A syllogism can be seen as a 'rule' that operates over arbitrary symbols in order to arrive at new ideas. For example, if you know that 'X is a Y' and you further know that 'all Y are Z', there is a symbolic rule that tells you that 'X is Z'. You can replace X, Y and Z by anything, and the appropriate conclusion will still hold. For example, if X is *Socrates is a man*, and Y is *all men are mortal*, you automatically infer Z, i.e., that *Socrates is mortal*. The same can be done with *my Volvo is a car, all cars are expensive*, and thus, *my Volvo is expensive*, or *you are a student of semantics, all students of semantics are smart*, and therefore, *you are smart*. As can be seen, you can insert anything in X and Y and the conclusion Z will automatically follow; it is the *syntax*, the combination of symbols, which leads to the conclusion, regardless of the content of X, Y or Z.

The idea is that what people do when they understand a sentence is to perform operations with an internal representation of the linguistic expressions included in the sentence. Once those representations (which, as we saw, are the truth conditions of their referents) are activated, we can work with them, performing the combinatorial (i.e., syntactic) operations that we call thought. These representations are **amodal**, because they are not connected to any perceptual or motor modality, like sight, hearing, etc. No matter which perceptual modality is involved in the perception that activates the given concept (smell, sight, taste, etc.), the end result in our mind/brain is an *abstract* representation, which is the same for all types of words. As in any symbol, the connection between form and content is *arbitrary*, and you have to memorize it.

For example, you may have a mental amodal symbol representing the meaning of *kick*. Since it is not modal, it is detached from the perceptual or motor systems; its form is arbitrary. In the brain, it would probably correspond to some arbitrary pattern of activation of a network of neurons. We also know that this symbol involves two participants: a kicker and 'kickee'. So, a convenient way of writing the symbol could be kick (kicker, kickee). This is completely different to what it would look like in the brain, but that is of no concern here: the interesting part is the abstract representation. The meaning of this symbol resides in the fact that it stands as a 'representation' of a type of thing in the world, in this case, kicking events; once we have established the arbitrary connection between form and meaning, and we have the symbol in place, we can use it in mental operations.

According to proponents of this model of mind such as Fodor (1983) or Pylyshyn (1981, 1984), this symbolic level (which, for them, corresponds to the mental level) is a natural functional level of its own; cognition operates over conceptual representations of this type, not over analogical representations. In order to carry out mental operations such as categorical inference or conceptual combination, the representations of reality needed are just that: explicit, discrete, abstract and amodal.

As we have mentioned, the description and functioning of these symbolic structures is completely independent of their specific physical realizations. We can illustrate this with the example of the concept of 'money': if you want to understand this concept, looking at neuron firing is of no use; you need a 'higher' level of representation, namely, the symbolic level. Analogously, to explain the meaning of a bank note, details about its size, colour, material or any other chemico-physical feature will not help you to understand its real significance as a piece of money with a certain value in a society; this can only be understood at a higher level, which is independent of the particular implementation details. Bank notes would function in the same way if we decided to have them made in plastic or any other material, instead of paper. In the same way, linking the meaning of a concept to some specific brain state is equivalent to linking the same meaning to any other physical implementation, like a specific combination of 1s and 0s in a computer program.

For symbolists, this implementation-independence (also called 'multiple realizability') is very important; to describe cognition (or intelligence) you do not have to focus on implementation details, neurons and synapses, but on its logical structure, the combinations of abstract symbols. In this sense, human cognition is seen like a computer program, which can be implemented in different physical formats. This is what classic artificial intelligence (also called Symbolic AI) tried to arrive at: an inventory of our mental software, which can be implemented in human brains or in artificial ones (e.g., in computers or robots). This is in fact a very exciting enterprise: if we can work out the rules governing our thought processes then we can write computer programs simulating them, thereby achieving artificial intelligence. The overarching metaphor here, which has permeated much of classic cognitive science, is that our minds are computers, since they do basically the same thing that computers do, namely, manipulate symbolic structures according to syntactic rules; this view is also known as computationalism or the computational theory of mind.

3.2.1 The Language of Thought Hypothesis

Closely associated with this view is the complementary idea which holds that thought must then be basically 'language-like'; in other words, the format of thought is basically linguistic in nature, even if it does not correspond exactly to any actual language. In this view, when we understand a sentence (in any language), what we actually do is translate the words we hear into an internal language of thought, also known as **mentalese**. Probably, the best-known champion of the **Language of Thought Hypothesis** is Jerry Fodor; cognitive scientists such as Steven Pinker are firm followers. Mentalese is thus an inner 'universal' language that allows us to express any meaning in any language on Earth. Mentalese has 'mental words', so to speak, that express concepts that can be combined to form true or false mental sentences.

There are some characteristics of thought that are also found in language; the fact that they are shared by both is what makes proponents of the hypothesis claim that cognition must be language-like in nature. These features are the following:

(1) Thought is *productive*: we are able to entertain an indefinitely large number of semantically distinct thoughts, just as we are able to produce and understand an infinite number of sentences.

(2) Thought is *systematic*: it is impossible to imagine a person who is able to entertain the thought that *John loves Mary*, and fails to do the same with *Mary loves John*.

(3) Thought is *compositional*: if you know the meaning of *John*, the meaning of *Mary* and the meaning of *loves*, then you can combine them in a meaningful way; we understand complex thoughts because we understand the components and know how to combine them.

3.2.2 Problems of the Formal Approach: the Symbol Grounding Problem

The symbolic view of cognition has met many opponents. One of the major criticisms is called the **symbol grounding problem** (Harnad, 1990): the problem of explaining how the symbols in our mind are connected to the external world. In the symbolic view, symbols are 'semantically interpretable'; that is, a given form is arbitrarily or conventionally assigned to a given meaning. But the key question is how is this connection between words and the things to which they refer established? Who does that? Is there an 'inner agent' within our minds that establishes the relevant connections? And how does this inner agent do it? Does it have another 'inner agent' within that does it? This is known as the homunculus problem, an infinite regression loop. If meaning works by the combination of arbitrary symbols and content is irrelevant, how do you get off the ground? How can you learn the meaning of any symbol at all? It is rather like trying to learn a foreign language from a monolingual dictionary: when you try to look up the meaning of an unknown word in the dictionary, you are referred to other unknown words, in a vicious circle from which there is no escape (rather like we see in Figure 3.2). Symbols cannot be grounded on other symbols, because this leads again to the problem of infinite regression.

Finding a direct link between symbols and referents is thus a thorny issue; there is no obvious way of establishing meaning from *within* the system (without an external agent). This has been offered as a criticism of strong

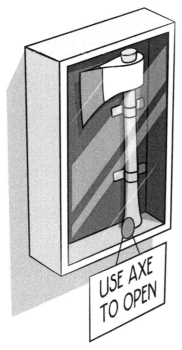

Figure 3.2 A Problem of Circularity

artificial intelligence (AI). For example, a computer that processes language (translates or summarizes texts, answers questions, etc.) does this by processing arbitrary symbols: groups of 1s and 0s in its internal implementation. All it has is a series of very elaborate rules telling it how to combine groups of bits. Without the possibility of real perception and interaction with the world, the computer cannot hope to achieve true understanding. To grasp the problem, we can look at one of the best-known criticisms, the thought-experiment proposed by the philosopher John Searle, known as the 'Chinese Room Argument':

> Consider a language you don't understand. In my case, I do not understand Chinese. To me Chinese writing looks like so many meaningless squiggles. Now, suppose I am placed in a room containing baskets full of Chinese symbols. Suppose also that I am given a rule book in English for matching Chinese symbols to other Chinese symbols. The rules identify the symbols entirely by their shapes and do not require that I understand any of them. The rules might say things like 'Take a squiggle-squiggle sign from basket number one and put it next to a squoggle-squoggle sign from basket number two'.

Imagine that people outside the room who understand Chinese hand in small bunches of symbols and that in response I manipulate the symbols according to the rule book and hand back more small bunches of symbols . . .

Now suppose that the rulebook is written in such a way that my 'answers' to the 'questions' are indistinguishable from those of a native Chinese speaker. For example, the people outside might hand me some symbols that unknown to me mean, 'What's your favorite color?' and I might after going through the rules give back symbols that, also unknown to me, mean, 'My favorite is blue, but I also like green a lot' (Searle, 1980: 26).

In this case, though Searle is answering the question is a way that makes sense to the people outside, he still doesn't speak Chinese: he has no clue of what the question (or the answer) was about and there is no true understanding involved. What is implied here is that the Chinese Room is the computer; the person inside the room (Searle) is the computer program that manipulates arbitrary symbols according to a syntactic rule without grasping the meaning of the computations he is performing. This example is used to criticize classical AI approaches and to show that the understanding that goes on in natural language comprehension cannot be based solely on symbol manipulation. Syntactic combination is not enough for comprehension; something else is needed.

3.3 The Embodied Approach: the Embodied Cognition Thesis

More recently, a growing number of scholars has opted for an alternative view of how meaning and cognition works, known as the **embodied cognition thesis**. Though there are several ways of understanding what an embodied approach to cognition really entails (Wilson, 2002), we will stick here to one of the most popular and relevant for semantic studies. This approach focuses on the relationships between the meaning structures that are activated in our mind when we understand language and our bodily, biological characteristics. The idea is that understanding the meaning of a sentence entails the activation of **simulations** in our brain. These simulations re-enact the sensorimotor, proprioceptive and introspective information gathered in our interactions with the entities to which the linguistic expressions refer. Let us see in more detail how this could work.

Our bodies have means of informing us about different aspects of our environment, via our different senses; we can also act on that environment via our motor skills. So, we have sensory cells that are sensitive to

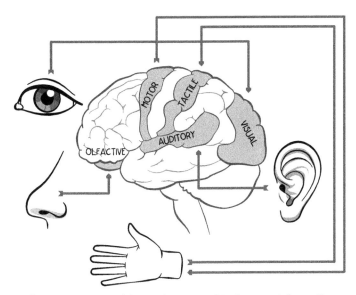

Figure 3.3 Areas of the Brain Devoted to Sensory Information

information about light (sight), about sound waves (hearing), about pressure (touch) or about different chemicals in our food or in the air (taste and smell). We also have motor neurons that activate our muscles and create action. The different cells register all this information about the world and about our own bodies and send it to our brain.

These different types of information are processed in different parts of our brains, which have specific areas devoted to registering and processing them (see Figure 3.3). This distribution is species-dependent and the result of our evolutionary and biological history; for example, due to our past as apes, a great deal of brain tissue is devoted to sight.

The amount of information registered is vast and can be very complex; for example, the cells in the retina of our eye register very different and nuanced types of information about light variations in the world. We have cells (called 'cone' cells) that are specialized in capturing variations in the wavelength of the light: they only fire when the wavelength falls into some specific range. As is well known, there are three types of cone cells, which are sensitive to short, medium and long wavelengths, and their combined function is what supports our perception of colour. There are also visual cells specialized in detecting movement, contrasts in light, edges, certain spatial orientations, etc. The slight difference between the images we capture from each of our two eyes allows us to perceive the world in 3D (this is called 'stereopsis', one of the main cues that allow us to construct perception of depth). All these messages travel through our neuronal pathways and are represented in their corresponding brain areas.

Our brains also register information about our body, or *proprioceptive* information. For example, you don't have to look at your feet to know where they are or how they are positioned, because you 'notice' them; information about their position and orientation is represented in your brain. Another source of information comes from *introspective* states: if every time you see a snake you feel afraid, this emotional information is represented in your brain along with external details about the snake. Thus, emotional and other introspective states (e.g., pain, pleasure, motivation) can also form part of your information about a given object in the world.

3.3.1 Language as Simulation

The idea behind embodied approaches is that these neuronal activations from different informational sources are accumulated over repeated experiences with the world and they become associated and bound together to form 'concepts' or 'categories'. Our concept of chair, for example, corresponds to the different neuronal networks that are active when we see a chair, touch a chair or sit on a chair. Any aspect of experience that our attentional system focuses on and that is encountered frequently enough can form part of this bundle of associated activations. In the course of both storing and recalling these structures from memory, the sensory and motor information can become somehow 'bleached' and we lose some details. This is why we are able to group slightly different exemplars into the same category (we will examine categorization processes in more detail in Chapter 4). When this concept is activated, part of this information is 're-enacted' and we come to think of a chair. The perceptual, motor and introspective information that these neural networks bring about the chair is a big part of what we could call the meaning of chair. The exact process by which these heterogenous neural activations in different parts of the brain are 'joined' together to form concepts is still not well known. Probably the two most popular stories are (1) the 'rhythmic solution': a synchronization in the firing pattern of these different areas: all of them fire in unison and thus a 'unified concept' emerges, and (2) the existence of 'convergence zones' (Damasio, 1989): areas in the brain that link together all these activations (that is, they become active when they receive input from a set of different perceptuomotor areas).

These multimodal mental simulations are then used to deal with high-level cognitive tasks, such as memory, language or reasoning. Therefore, the format in which we store meaning is not amodal or abstracted away from reality but instead always remains modal: related to the different perceptual, motor or introspective systems of the brain. There is considerable evidence that this is indeed the way in which the brain represents both words and concepts. For example, Barsalou and his colleagues found that when you ask people to verify certain modal facts about objects, their answers are quicker when the questions belong to the same perceptual mode (e.g., eyesight, hearing, taste) than when they have to switch between modes. In other words, they are quicker to agree that *lemons are sour* after having been told that *coffee is bitter* (since both belong to the taste modality) than after having heard *the motorbike is loud*, which belongs to another modality, the auditory one (Pecher *et al.*, 2003); the same was found with changes from other modes (e.g., sound: *television–noisy* and *microwave–beeping*, and then sight: *aubergine–purple*).

Concepts can be activated in different ways: any of the parts that form the concept can act as a cue or a link to the general concept: the sight of a cat, a meow, or other related concepts (like DOG or MOUSE) can activate the concept CAT. Needless to say, another way of activating the concept is by hearing the sounds to which a concept is linguistically linked: [kæt] in English. For proponents of this view, language in fact evolved to control simulations: language directs our attention to specific areas of simulations, specifies how to combine them (via grammar) and facilitates the coordination of simulations in the different members of a social group. The relationships between language and simulation can become very complex; the role that each of the different linguistic mechanisms plays in the reconstruction of a complex simulation is a question still under study (Bergen, 2012).

3.3.2 What is Simulated?

What features of an object or situation are present in its mental simulation? There is an abundance of experimental work that has examined the different types of information that can be present in these simulations. Unsurprisingly, many of them have to do with visual or motor details of the object or scene.

For example, we know that people simulate **shape:** the image of an eagle with its wings stretched is recognized faster after having heard *the ranger saw the eagle in the sky*, than a picture of an eagle with its wings closed. The opposite happens after hearing *the ranger saw the eagle in the nest* (Zwaan *et al.*, 2002).

The specific **orientation** of objects is also simulated: people recognize the image of a horizontal nail faster after having heard *he hammered the nail on the wall*, as compared with the picture of a vertical nail. The opposite happens after hearing *he hammered the nail into the floor* (Stanfield and Zwaan, 2001).

Perspective is also part of the simulation. In an experiment, subjects were told to imagine that they were 'driving a car', and then asked to answer as quickly as possible which objects belonged to a car (Borghi *et al.*, 2004). They provided quicker answers to parts that were inside the car (e.g., steering-wheel, accelerator pedal, stereo) than external parts (e.g., antenna, wheel, door-handle); the opposite pattern emerged when they were told to imagine that they were 'washing a car'. This is why this type of view is also called **situated**: it places you in a given situated setting (we will have more things to say about situated conceptualization in Chapter 4).

Direction of motion has also been shown to play a part in people's simulations. Zwaan *et al.* (2004) presented two images of a baseball in rapid succession; one of them was bigger than the other one, so that depending on the order of presentation, the impression was that the ball was getting bigger (if the small version was presented first) or smaller (in the other case). This interacted with the comprehension of sentences such as *he hurled the ball at you* or *you hurled the ball at him*, showing that people were simulating the direction of motion when understanding them.

In some sentences, **colour** can also be part of the simulation; for example, people recognized red more quickly after hearing *Jane tasted the tomato when it was ready to eat* than after hearing *Jane tasted the tomato before it was ready to eat* (Connell and Lynott, 2009).

A great number of words are associated with a very specific **sound**; to name only a few, this is the case of *motorbike, telephone, bell, ambulance, rain, typewriter, machine gun, helicopter*, all sorts of animals (*roosters, dogs, lions, birds* and *bees*) and of course, musical instruments like *trumpet, banjo* or *piano*. Kiefer *et al.* (2008) compared these types of words to another group of words not associated with any specific sounds (e.g., *table, apple* and *sock*) and found that hearing a burst of white noise just before identifying a picture of an object slowed the naming of the picture in the first group (sound-related) but not the second.

Smell can also play a role in people's simulations. González *et al.* (2006), for example, had people recognize a number of words with strong olfactory associations (e.g., *lemon, cinnamon, garlic, perfume, stink, coffee*, etc.) and compared their brain activation in an fMRI scan with more neutral words. The mere fact of recognizing the words belonging to the first group activated the subjects' olfactory brain centres. Thus, we can say that part of the meaning of *cinnamon* is its smell.

Simmons *et al.* (2005) showed that **taste** can also be a part of what is simulated in understanding. In their experiment, they showed people a number of pictures of food (cheeseburgers, spaghetti, chocolate cookies, etc.) or pictures of locations (different types of houses, a shopping mall, a school, etc.). Their task was to detect when two pictures were repeated. While they were doing this, an fMRI scan of their brains showed that their gustatory area was activated automatically in the case of food pictures.

Motor information is also simulated: when asked about the grammaticality of sentences such as *open the drawer* or *close the drawer*, people answered more quickly when the response motion mimicked the movement implicit in the sentence: thus, a quicker answer for the 'open' sentence was produced when subjects had to move their hand towards their bodies (instead of away from their body), and the opposite pattern was found after having heard the 'close' sentence. This has been called the effect Action-Compatibility Effect (ACE).

As mentioned above, introspective or **emotional** states can also be included in the simulation. Strack *et al.* (1988) carried out an experiment in which subjects had to hold a pencil in their mouths using only their teeth (and not their lips), which forced them into a partial smile, or using their lips, which inhibited their smile. Having your face in a particular configuration is part of the bodily state corresponding to a given emotion. In this experiment, participants rated cartoons as funnier when holding the pen in their teeth than when holding the pen in their lips; this is a robust effect, that has been replicated many times. Some researchers have even experimented with Botox injections, provoking a temporary paralysis in the face area where frowning takes place; they found that this reduced the ability of their participants to recognize emotions in other people, and in another study, it reduced their speed when reading angry and sad sentences.

It is important to remember that simulations are always partial; they do not re-enact everything that we have gathered about the elements activated. What is activated depends heavily on the current contextual situation and the task at hand. Depending on the case, they can be a bit sketchy or more detailed, containing more elements or fewer. In this sense, simulations are dynamic and constructed on the spot more than stored in a static and fixed way in long-term memory. Also, these simulations do not occur in the vacuum; they typically form part of situations, which serve them as 'background contexts'. Thus, a bicycle, a bottle or a hammer are simulated within their specific typical situations or scenes.

There are different specific theories that try to base their explanation on this type of embodied approach. Barsalou's *Perceptual Symbol System*, Lakoff's *Embodied Construction Grammar*, or Glenberg's *Indexical Hypothesis* can be mentioned as examples of theories that opt for this vision of cognition and language. All these theories endow language with a crucial role; linguistic structures can be considered to be a set of instructions that guide the construction of complex simulations. Language directs our attention to relevant areas and tells us how different elements in the situation we must simulate are to be combined; in this view, the main function of language is to direct and control the construction of simulations. In the next section, we review briefly one of these theories, which has an initial proposal of how this process takes place: Glenberg's **Indexical Hypothesis.**

3.3.3 A Concrete Case: Glenberg's Indexical Hypothesis

The **Indexical Hypothesis** (IH) proposes that meaning is mainly based on action (Glenberg and Robertson, 1999; 2000). It claims that people understand language by simulating the actions described in phrases and sentences. The IH relies heavily on one key notion in embodied approaches: the notion of **affordance**, which originated in ecological psychology (Gibson, 1979). **Affordances** are the possible actions that a given object offers to a given organism. For example, well-designed objects provide clear clues about the types of affordances they invite: a handle in a door affords pulling, a knob affords turning and a button affords pushing. An interesting fact of affordances is that they are not a property of the objects themselves or of the organisms, but rather stem from the interaction between both. Affordances are body-specific and thus species-specific; for example, a chair affords sitting for humans but not for other animals, such as mice or elephants, whose bodies cannot interact with normal chairs in this way. At the same time, the affordances that an object offers may be different depending on our current goal. For example, besides sitting on a chair, we can also stand on it in order to reach something high, or we can use it to lock a door, or as a weapon in a saloon fight, as shown in Figure 3.4. Creative affordances can be derived from objects quite easily; for example, a cup normally affords the transfer of liquid to our mouths, but if it is empty, we can use it upside down to capture a bug. It is actually difficult to think of some concepts, especially tools, like scissors, hammers, bottles or keys, and not think of the typical actions associated with them, which are only accessible for humans, who have the right type of bodies.

Figure 3.4 Different Affordances of a Chair

According to the IH, sentences are transformed into action-based meaning in three stages. First, words are mapped to their perceptual symbols (Barsalou, 1999). Second, affordances are derived from these symbols. Since perceptual symbols are embodied, that is, they are modal (i.e., dependent on the mode of perception) and non-arbitrary (i.e., based on the brain states underlying the perception of the referent and therefore related to them), we can flexibly derive new affordances from them as required by the contextual situation, something that is not possible if we connect objects to their abstract symbolic representations. The final stage involves the smooth combination or **meshing** of the affordances of the different words, following the instructions provided by the grammatical constructions. As we saw in Chapter 1, grammatical constructions often convey information about the interaction of their elements; this is what we saw in the case of the transitive construction (X acts on Y) or the ditransitive construction (X transfers Y to Z; see Section 1.6.4 in Chapter 1). A construction then guides how the affordances of the different elements should be meshed. If the meshed set of affordances corresponds to a doable action, something that makes sense, the utterance is understood.

For example, Kaschak and Glenberg (2000) included an example of how constructions provide instructions on how to mesh creative affordances. A sentence such as *She crutched him the ball*, which includes the novel verb *to crutch*, would be interpreted as 'she transferred the ball to him using a crutch'. We are able to build a coherent scene from these words because the transfer meaning of the construction and the affordances of *crutch* can be meshed. Something similar would be found in the sentence *she crutched him*: the meaning of the transitive construction tells us that the subject (*she*) acts on the object (*him*) and given the affordances that we can derive from a crutch, the end result is that we imagine a scene in which she hits him with a crutch. We can use the novel verb *to crutch* in any other grammatical construction that stipulates a meshing of affordances compatible with those derivable from crutches (e.g., *she crutched out of the building*). However, look at the sentences in 1 (adapted from Glenberg and Kaschak, 2002):

1. a. *Hang the coat on the back of that chair*
    b. *Hang the coat on the tea cup*

1a is interpretable and makes sense, because we know that the back of a chair can afford the action of hanging something from it (especially, a coat). However, 1b would not make sense in most contexts, because we know that cups do not offer the type of affordances that would allow us to hang a coat on them. That is why it does not make sense, even though it is perfectly grammatical: because the affordances of its components cannot be meshed correctly.

3.3.4 Problems of the Embodied Approach: the Case of Abstract Words

So far, the case for embodied representations seems quite clear, but there is a final catch. What happens when we understand abstract words/concepts, which have no clear sensory-motor representation? That is, how do we understand concepts like INTELLIGENCE, PEACE, JUSTICE, IMPORTANCE, LUCK, TRUTH, FUN or TIME? Abstract concepts like these pose a serious theoretical challenge to the embodied cognition thesis because, by definition, they leave no sensorimotor trace in the brain. Since we do not see them, smell them, touch them or feel them in any way, there is no sensorimotor memory to re-enact. Abstract concepts are thus the 'Achilles' heel' of embodied theories.

There are different answers to this question; some supporters of embodied views state that we also understand these cases by simulating scenes. The difference is that, instead of focusing our attention on concrete and well-defined parts of the scene (bounded objects or simple events), as we would do to understand *hammer* or *to hammer*, for example, in a case such as *truth*, our attention focuses on the mental states of participants and also involves more complex events, related to different types of situations. Barsalou and Wiemer-Hastings (2005), for example, found that people reported more introspective features (e.g., emotional states, or states related to beliefs, to events, etc.), and more social features in their simulations of abstract concepts in contrast with concrete words, which involved more action-related and physical features.

Some other authors within the embodied camp think that we do activate simulations of specific domains in these cases, and that we 'transfer' this type of specific information to help us conceptualize abstract domains. Thus, to conceptualize the abstract domain of IMPORTANCE, which does not activate directly any sensory-motor areas, we use concrete, sensory-motor domains, such as physical SIZE to help us deal with it. That is why we have linguistic expressions such as *a big day*, or *a small matter*. One of the main theories supporting this view is **Conceptual Metaphor Theory**, which will be examined more closely in Chapter 7 of this book.

Yet another group of scholars thinks that the way we deal with abstract words is by looking at their relationships with other words in the system; that is, we deal with them in a completely amodal, symbolic way. There have been some advances in understanding how this would take place, and even how to simulate this computationally; this is in fact what we saw in Chapter 2, when we talked about **Latent Semantic Analysis**. This is one of the main points of contention between modal and amodal theories of meaning: if amodal symbolic processing can be shown to be necessary in order to process abstract words, then why should we have two different systems, one for concrete words and a different one for abstract ones, when we can just get by with one, the symbolic one?

3.4 Formal vs. Embodied Approaches to Meaning: a Tentative Conclusion

It is not yet completely clear which of the two approaches to language and cognition is the correct one. Embodied approaches have received a great deal of support from experimental cognitive science, but there remain a number of reasonable doubts about whether they can explain everything (especially regarding the problem of abstract concepts, where they are less convincing). The key question in the embodied-vs.-symbolic discussion is which of these explanations is really *necessary* to account for language meaning, and also whether only one explanation is *sufficient*. Some scholars have expressed doubts as to whether embodied representations are sufficient to explain all the intricacies of high-level cognitive processing or whether they have to be supplemented with symbolic, amodal operations. Certain cognitive operations seem to depend on more 'symbolic' operations, such as counterfactuals or reasoning with superordinate level categories (a broad type of category that we will cover in Chapter 4).

Figure 3.5 Different Representations of *Duck*

At present, some researchers are trying to reach some sort of consensus. For example, most supporters of amodal approaches acknowledge that some degree of embodiment or simulation must be present in cognition at some level: an encapsulated system, made of only arbitrary, abstract symbols combined with syntactic rules and with no connection to its environment, cannot possibly capture linguistic reference. And for their part, even firm supporters of embodied approaches have conceded that not all mental representations have to be grounded; some tasks can be carried out in a more symbolic way. The general idea is that in order to achieve true, deep semantic understanding, you do have to perform an embodied simulation, but in other cases, the so-called 'shallow' tasks, this is not necessarily the case. For example, in lexical decision tasks (which we presented in Chapter 2), where you are given a string of letters and have to decide whether they correspond to a word (e.g., *lemon*) of your language or not (e.g., *nemon*) you can take your decision just by reviewing the combinations of phonemes that are listed as words in your mental lexicon; there is no real need to perform an embodied simulation in this case.

Barsalou found something similar in one of his modality-switching experiments (Solomon and Barsalou, 2004). Subjects had to judge whether one concept/word was part of another (e.g., 'Is *leg* a part of *table*?'), and a modality-switch cost was found: subjects were quicker to decide that *mane* is a part of *horse* when they had previously been asked a 'same-modality' question, such as *elephant–tusk*. However, this effect depended on the 'no' answers supplied in the experiment: in experiments like these, there must be a number of 'no' answers, because otherwise, participants would just press the yes-button all the time. If the 'no' answers were pairs such as *bathtub–fruit*, or *airplane–cake*, that is, words that are not normally associated in language use, subjects did not perform any modal simulation. In those cases, people could just solve the task by checking whether the words in the pair were linguistically associated or not, and no simulation was needed. When the 'no' answers included words that were linguistically associated, things changed. Thus, when supplied with word pairs such as *banana–yellow* or *fish–river*, they had to answer 'no' (because *yellow* is not a part of *banana*, and *river* is not a part of a *fish*), but these words are nevertheless linguistically associated. In these cases, they were forced to perform the full simulation and check whether one concept was a part of the other or not, and the modality-switch effect was found again.

Thus, many scholars are now assuming that meaning and cognition is both embodied and symbolic, and the task right now is find out *when* and *for which tasks* each of these strategies is used by our mind (Arbib *et al.*, 2014; Barsalou, 2008; Dove, 2011; Louwerse and Jeuniaux, 2008, 2010; Meteyard *et al.*, 2012; Zwaan 2014; *inter alia*). There are even earlier precursors of this explanatory pluralism: in the 1970s (actually, before the appearance of embodied cognition),

Paivio's **Dual Code** theory already proposed that we deal with concrete words using both imagery *and* the linguistic system, while we deal with abstract words using only the linguistic system. For him, this explained the differences in recognition time and memory for concrete vs. abstract words; concrete words are recognized faster and remembered better because two different systems are involved in their processing (Paivio, 1971).

In his Language and Situated Simulation (LASS) theory, Barsalou proposes that both approaches can work in parallel, and that one task may start resorting to one strategy (e.g., computing the associations of a word symbolically), followed closely by the other (simulating something using the associations found), followed by another wave of symbolic associations and so on.

High-dimensional approaches such as LSA have had a great impact on this debate, showing the great deal of information that can be extracted from the statistical co-occurrences of words (a purely symbolic operation). The combination of perceptual grounding and symbolic processing gives language an added power. Thus, once we have grasped the embodied meaning of a number of words, new words can be added just by learning about their relations with other words. That is, we go from word–world association to word–word association. Since language patterns capture information about correlations in the world, we can use that information to learn other words, which achieve 'embodied' powers in this indirect way. We can thus learn about the world from word combinations. This is quite frequent; a great amount of our knowledge of the world does not stem from our direct experiences but from these 'recycled conceptual representations' encoded in language statistics. If you do not know what the word *spork* means, and I tell you that it is '*a hybrid piece of cutlery that combines the round bowl of a spoon and the pointy tines of a fork*', you can recognize a *spork* as soon as you see one. Neurologist Friedrich Pullvermüller calls this process 'parasitic semantic learning'; Pulvermüller (2002) is an explanation of the neurological mechanisms that would enable this. Computational theorist Angelo Cangelosi calls this 'symbolic theft'; Cangelosi *et al.* (2002) explains how this could be implemented computationally. Other scholars agree that this process of 'indirect learning of embodied structures by linguistic association' is a big part of how we learn the meaning of words. For example, Louwerse's *Symbol Interdependency Hypothesis* defends this use of language as a 'conceptual shortcut' (Louwerse, 2011; cf. also Boroditsky and Prinz, 2008).

Table 3.1 *A Summary of Some Characteristics of Symbolic vs. Embodied Approaches to Cognition*

Symbolic Approaches	Embodied Approaches
Symbol systems: symbols as amodal, abstract and arbitrary	Perceptual Symbol systems: symbols as modal and embodied
Classical Artificial Intelligence	Connectionism and neural networks
Digital treatment of information	Analogical treatment of information
Language of Thought Hypothesis	Linguistic relativity
Software matters; hardware doesn't (multiple reliability)	Hardware is also important; implementation details are important
Syntax matters; semantics is less important	Syntax is not enough; semantics is also needed

3.5 Chapter Summary

In this chapter, we have looked at the two main approaches to language and meaning: the formal and the cognitive. We have learned about the historical roots of both approaches and have looked at their main tenets and assumptions about language and meaning. Section 3.2 was devoted to the formal approach, where we examined the idea of symbolic processing, based on syntactic combinations of conventional, arbitrary symbols that can be implemented in a variety of physical formats. The idea that thought itself is language-like in nature (that is, the Language of Thought Hypothesis), was explained in Section 3.2.1. We also reviewed one of the more popular criticisms addressed at symbolic approaches: Searle's Chinese Room exemplifies the Symbol Grounding Problem in a thought experiment, which shows that pure syntactic manipulation is not enough to give meaning to symbols. The embodied approach was then introduced in Section 3.3 with the notion of embodied simulation: the proposal that understanding the meaning of a linguistic expression entails the re-enactment of the sensory-motor information elicited by the referents of those expressions. We have seen what type of parameters have been shown to be present in mental simulations in the experimental literature (Section 3.3.2) and also looked at Glenberg's Indexical Hypothesis, which makes use of a crucial concept in embodied approaches, the notion of affordance (i.e., the possibilities for physical interaction offered by a given object). The problem posed by abstract words for embodied approaches was examined in Section 3.3.4). Finally, one last reflection on how both approaches could possibly work in tandem depending on the task at hand was presented in Section 3.5.

Key Terms Introduced in this Chapter

formal semantics
cognitive/embodied semantics
truth-conditional semantics
amodal symbolic systems
Frege's principle of compositionality
computational theory of mind; computationalism
Language of Thought Hypothesis; mentalese
symbol grounding problem
embodiment; embodied cognition thesis
simulation
affordances
affordance meshing
Indexical Hypothesis

Further reading
There are quite a few good introductory books on formal semantics; Chierchia and McGonnell-Ginet (2000) is quite detailed and presents all the main aspects; a more gentle introduction is Bach (1989). Reviews of the embodied approach are Barsalou (2008; 2010) and Zwaan (2009). Bergen (2012) is a recent book that reviews the findings and methods of simulation-based approaches to language in an engaging and yet rigorous way. De Vega *et al.* (2008) is a book devoted to the discussion between symbolic and embodied approaches, with chapters of supporters of both camps that include direct discussions among the different authors.

CHAPTER 4

Word Meaning

In this chapter . . .

In this chapter, we introduce the main mechanisms by which words can be said to convey meaning. We start with two of the more classic notions in semantics, reference and sense, examining different types of reference. Since words typically refer to 'classes of things', we devote some time to the notion of 'category'. We will discuss what categorization is, how it has been treated since classical times (e.g., Aristotle) and how this view has been called into question by scholars like Wittgenstein. We then introduce one of the prevailing theories of categorization, namely the prototype theory of categorization established by Rosch and her colleagues. The chapter also presents for the first time a construct that will show up in several places throughout the book: semantic frames. We will show here how frames can be extremely useful in characterizing the meaning of words. The chapter closes with a discussion of connotation, an important part of meaning that is sometimes overlooked, reviewing the ways in which it can be measured and analysed.

4.1 The Meaning of Words

> I wanted to utter a word; that word I cannot remember, and the bodiless thought will now return to the palace of shadows (*The Swallow*, by the Russian poet Isap Mandelstam; cited in Aitchison, 2012).

When talking about how meaning is expressed with language, our gut feeling is that linguistic meaning resides mainly in words. Words are the key to a great part of the information we store in our heads. According to some estimates (e.g., Aitchison, 2012: 7) an educated adult speaker of English knows between 50,000 and 80,000 words (the numbers vary according to the individual, the method of measuring, etc.). However, in spite of the great number of words we store, we can use a word in no time at all. Native speakers can recognize a word 200 milliseconds after its onset, well before it has been completely pronounced. It is no wonder that psychologists are trying to elucidate in what ways words are organized in our minds (e.g., Aitchison, 2012; Altmann, 1997).

The highly efficient organization of the thousands of words we store is no doubt a very interesting issue (which we will examine in Chapter 5), but for semantics there are questions that come before that: how do words mean? How do we use words to convey meaning? A basic, common-sense view would assert that we normally use words to point to objects or events in the world (or in our minds). In this way, the word *table* is meaningful because we can use it to refer to a given object in the world. However, the isolated word *table* is not used for just one particular object, but rather for a 'class' of them: there are many objects in the world that we can call *table*. Most words are used in this way, to refer to classes of objects (*types* rather than *tokens*). Of course, we also have single words that 'point' to individual instances: such is the case of proper nouns. Normally, in order to refer to a concrete, specific entity, we need a combination of words (e.g. '*the book page that you are reading right now*'). We can even have words that do not point to anything concrete: what does the word *if* pick out from the world? We can start then by considering the possible relationships between words and the objects they point to.

4.2 How Words Mean: Reference

As we have just mentioned, if we can communicate meaning at all, it is because we can use words to 'pick out' things from the world, so that our hearer knows what we are talking about. A word, it seems, is a 'pointer' to something (Figure 4.1). The word *duck* has meaning because we can use it to refer to an object in the world (or, a bit more inclusively, to direct the hearer's attention towards that object). This would be, then, the first way in which words can be said to 'have' meaning.

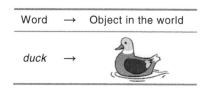

Word	→	Object in the world
duck	→	

Figure 4.1 Basic Reference

The object in the world picked out by a particular word is called its **referent**. This general function of words, of picking out objects from reality, is accordingly called **reference**. Reference is normally related to other similar technical terms, namely, **denotation** and **extension**. They mean almost the same, but their use is different. For example, the word *chair* can be used to pick out an object in the world, so we say that the word *chair* **denotes** a specific type of object. **Denotation** is thus a relationship that exists between a word and a set of objects, its potential referents. **Reference** is the act that speakers carry out when they pick out objects in the world by using words. Finally, all the objects in the world that can be picked out by the word *chair* form its **extension**. Extension is the total number of things that can be referred to by a word (Table 4.1).

Table 4.1 *Some Terms Related to Reference*

Reference	The action by which a speaker picks out an object (the referent) in the world; it can be variable, depending on context, user, etc.
Denotation	The relationship between a linguistic expression and the objects out in the world; it is stable and not user-dependent
Extension	The set of all objects in the world that can be picked out by a word

So, probably the most immediate function of language is to facilitate the establishment of reference. In fact, reference is present even in animal language: vervet monkeys have specific calls that signal the presence of a predator (e.g., an eagle or a snake). In order to start the process of understanding, we must first identify the referents mentioned in a sentence, and then place them in a given relationship, such as who did what to whom, or what is a property of what, etc. From the point of view of production, we start by representing objects and actions in our mind (the referents), and then we have to convert this structured scene into a linearly organized series of speech sounds.

4.2.1 Referring and Non-Referring Expressions: Types of Reference

Do all words have reference? If so, what is the reference of words such as *maybe, the, very, if, but* or *not*? It seems clear that 'grammatical' words cannot be used to refer to objects in the same way as lexical words, which of course does not mean that they have no meaning at all. Nouns, on the other hand, are essentially referring expressions. But not always: sometimes nouns can be used in non-referring ways. Consider these two examples:

(1) a. *A **chair** is the most basic piece of furniture in today's homes*
     b. *I bumped into a **chair** this morning*
     c. *I have to buy a **chair** for my office*

Though we are looking at the same noun, *chair*, and even the phrase in which it occurs is the same (*a chair*), we would like to say that example (1a) does not make reference to any particular chair, but rather to a class of things, and, in this way, includes all chairs. In this case, we are dealing with a **generic** reading of *chair*. That is not the case in (1b), in which the speaker is definitely referring to some particular chair; we would call this **specific** reference. Some scholars introduce another distinction, which can be seen in (1c): the reference of *chair* in that case is not generic (we are not referring to all chairs), and is not specific either (as it would have been if we had said *I have to buy that chair for my office*). In this case, we are referring to one instance of the class, just one exemplar, but its precise identity is not important; what is important is the inclusion of the object I will buy within the category of chairs. In this case, we are talking about **indefinite** reference. These three options are not so easy to tease apart, and frequently, we find sentences that are ambiguous in this regard, such as (2):

(2) *John wants to marry <u>a blonde</u>*

In example (2), we could think that John has a specific blonde person in mind, his fiancée, or alternatively, that John really likes blondes and is willing to marry *any* blonde (Figure 4.2).

There are languages that indicate this distinction grammatically, with the indicative/subjunctive alternation; this is the case of Spanish, as shown in (3):

(3) a. *Busco a un hombre que* habla *inglés*
     b. *Busco a un hombre que* hable *inglés*.

Sentences (3a) and (3b) can both be translated as 'I'm looking for a man who speaks English'; but (3a) uses the indicative version of the verb 'speak' (*habla*) and thus indicates specific reference (one concrete man), while

Figure 4.2 Definite vs. Indefinite Reference of *John Wants to Marry a Blonde*

(3b) has the subjunctive version (*hable*), and thus has a generic reading (any man who speaks English is equally valid). French behaves in a similar way: Cruse (2000: 309) shows this with the sentences in (4):

(4)   a. *Marie cherche un homme qui* peut *lui faire l'amour douze fois par jour*

      b. *Marie cherche un homme qui* puisse *lui faire l'amour douze fois par jour*

which can both be translated as 'Mary is looking for a man who can make love to her twelve times a day'. They establish the same distinction we have just seen; *peut* is in indicative mood (and thus, Marie is referring to a specific man) and *puisse* is subjunctive, indicating that Marie is just hopeful (or as Cruse says, overly optimistic).

4.2.2 Constant vs. Variable Reference

Another variation related to reference concerns its scope. Some words or expressions always refer to the same object: *America* is one case. In principle, no matter who utters the word, when, where or to whom, the reference is always the same. But what happens with the underlined expressions in the following example?

(5)   *I* want to go *there tomorrow in your car*

If you picked up a random piece of paper and found this sentence, not knowing about the participants involved in the communicative exchange, you would not be able to identify the referent of any of the underlined elements. Expressions that depend on contextual information are called **deictics**; depending on who says them, to whom, when, and where, they change their referent. We will deal with deictics and how they work more extensively in Chapter 9. Also, some words or expressions can be just slightly deictic: think about the referent of *the British Prime Minister*: if nothing out of the ordinary happens, it tends to remain stable during a period of five years after the election.

4.2.3 Denotational theories of meaning

For many authors, this is the way in which the study of meaning should be approached: by examining how words are mapped to the objects they refer to. Theories of meaning that opt for this type of approach are accordingly known as **denotational**. We should warn that the situation is of course much more complex than what we have described here so far. For a start, there are many words for which there is no physical referent in the world. For example, what is the referent of the English noun *unicorn*? What about *Santa Claus, the Loch Ness monster* or *God*? This makes it necessary to widen the scope of the theory so that these words can be included. Denotational theories have solved this by creating the notion of **possible world**: hypothetical versions of reality that can be used as a background for the meanings of a word. For most denotational theories, the meaning of an expression is based on its **truth-conditions**, that is, the set of conditions under which the sentence is true in any possible world, and that is what theories in formal semantics strive for. However, as we commented in the first chapter, there is a 'schism' in the field of semantics, and the opposing theories (e.g., cognitively oriented semantics) tend to be sceptical about this enterprise. These theories think that it is more advantageous to approach meaning and reference from a 'mentalistic' point of view; in their opinion, words mean by activating concepts in hearers' minds. Therefore, notions such as conceptual organization or categorization or even the intentionality of the speakers, as we shall discuss in Chapter 9, are more interesting for semantics than truth conditions. As Cruse (2000) puts it:

> The approach to meaning which promises to be most fruitful is to regard it as conceptual in nature. This is not to deny that there are (presumably

important) relations between linguistic forms and extralinguistic reality. Our approach is, however, based on the assumption that the most direct connections of linguistic forms are with conceptual structures, and until these are sorted out, there is little hope of making progress with the more indirect links with the outside world (Cruse, 2000: 127).

4.3 How Words Mean: Sense

We have seen one aspect of how words can activate their meaning: by pointing to an element in the world (be it a 'possible' world or a 'mental' world). But this cannot be all that there is to meaning; meaning must be something more than reference. For example, what happens when two words or expressions have the same reference? Is their meaning the same? We could use many different linguistic expressions for exactly the same referent, such as *Bill Clinton, William Jefferson Clinton, The former President of the United States, Hilary's husband* or *Chelsea Clinton's dad*. But these expressions, in spite of having the same referent, are not equivalent at all: each of them has a slightly different meaning; each of them highlights different parts of information, and, of course, their contexts of use are not the same. For example, some of these expressions would be appropriate as a way of introducing Bill Clinton at a NATO press conference, while others definitely wouldn't. Additionally, having many different expressions that are exactly equivalent would not make sense psychologically: why should we overload our minds learning and storing many different labels for the same thing? Surely each of them must be there for some specific reason.

The first person to address this problem was **Gottlob Frege**. He was the one who realized that two expressions could have one and the same reference and yet have a different meaning. The example that is normally used to explain this distinction involves the expressions *the Evening Star* and *the Morning Star*. Both expressions have the same referent: the planet Venus, but seen at different times of the day. He argued that their meaning was different, since to someone who did not know that both objects refer to Planet Venus, we could meaningfully say:

(6) a. *The Evening Star is the Morning Star*
     b. *The Morning Star is the Evening Star*

On the other hand, example (7) sounds tautological and absurd:

(7) *Planet Venus is Planet Venus*

What distinguishes Evening Star and Morning Star is something different from its reference, and this is what we call **sense** (see another example in Figure 4.3). The **sense** of a word or expression is normally related to two different things: (i) its relation to other words in the system (e.g., Lyons, 1977); (ii) our knowledge of the word itself. Let us see both aspects with some examples.

Figure 4.3 Dr. Jeckyll and Mr. Hyde: Two Senses, One Reference

How can we know the precise meaning of the word *large* as an indicator of size in a clothes store? How big is a '*large*' size? To answer this, we should know what other sizes are available. If the options are *small, medium* and *large*, then *large* corresponds to the largest size available. However, if the choices are *medium, large* and *extra-large*, we would say that the meaning of *large* is different (in that case, it would correspond to *medium* in the previous set of labels). Another example could be colours: the meaning of the word *blue* depends on other distinctions in the English colour system. In Russian, for example, there are two words for blue: *siniy* (dark blue) and *goluboy* (light blue); a similar distinction is found in Italian (*blu* and *azzurro*). Thus, in order to know about the meaning of a word, we have to take into account other words which are available and which could delimit their precise range of meaning.

The second aspect with which **sense** is normally associated concerns the knowledge we have about a word or how we use it; put in another way, the 'conditions' that must be met in order to use a word with a given referent. That is, the sense of the word *table* is related to our knowledge about tables, the conditions that some object must meet to be able to be called *table*. So, sense could also be defined as the 'defining properties' of a word. Knowing what *table* means, then, involves having information in our minds about what type of things tables are, or the criteria, conditions or properties that must be met by something to be called a table. We can see, then, how these two notions work together: **reference** is the operation that identifies which object we are talking about; the rest of the information we have about it is called **sense.**

There is another terminological variant that relates **sense** to **intension** (so that we have the almost equivalent pairs *reference-sense* and *extension-intension*). Again, this term is not exactly the same as **sense**, but it is very close: **intension** has been defined as 'the set of properties shared by all members of its extension'. An additional definition states that intension is 'the set of criteria for identifying the category together with the properties which relate it to other concepts' (Saeed, 1997: 49). We will talk about this aspect of sense (the relationships between words or between concepts) in Chapter 5.

4.4 Categorization and Prototypes

Something that has already been mentioned is that isolated words do not point to specific objects: the most typical meaning of a word refers back to a 'class' of things (if we wanted to be more precise, we could say that a word 'denotes' a class of things). Thus, words like *dog, table* or *dance* do not point to just one specific entity or event, but rather to a class of things out there in the world that can be rightfully identified using these words. If the meaning of a word corresponds to a class of things, that is, to a category, then in order to examine the way that words express meaning, we need to look at categories, their structure and their behaviour. This is what we turn to in the next section.

4.4.1 What is a Category?

> If it looks like a duck, swims like a duck, and quacks like a duck, then it probably is a duck (attributed to poet James Whitcomb Riley).

When we interact with objects or events in the world, we notice their similarities and differences and group them accordingly in a way that will be useful for us. These collections are what we call **categories.** **Categorization** thus corresponds roughly to 'chunking of experience' (Figure 4.4). For example: entities that are animate, of medium size, furry, with whiskers and long tails, that walk silently and say 'meow', are grouped together under one category, that we call CAT. This is quite useful, since by ascribing a particular entity to a category, we can generalize and transfer to the particular entity the knowledge we have about its class. To continue with our feline example, if X is a cat, then we know that probably X chases mice, likes fish, purrs, and may scratch you if you annoy it (even if we have not witnessed any of these facts from the particular X we are categorizing). In this way, we can ascribe any characteristic typical of the 'type' (the category) to the 'token' (the concrete exemplar).

Figure 4.4 We Organize the Objects of the World into Categories

Categorization is an essential activity for survival, since it helps us predict the future to a given extent and put some order in the infinite variations found in experience. If you encounter some piece of fruit hanging from a tree, you eat it, and the experience is positive, it is quite useful to build a category (you can call it, for example, *apple*), so that if in the future you encounter any other piece of fruit similar to this one, you know it will be good to eat. If on one occasion you see a really big yellow cat with black stripes attacking someone, the next time you see an animal similar to that one, you will run for cover; in this way, having the category TIGER will help you survive. This ability to transfer inferences from one member of the category to another is the most important function of categorization. All animals are capable of categorizing, though of course, their categorical systems can be completely different. Categories are driven by functional needs; they make sense as tools to enhance survival, or at the very least, facilitate life.

Categorization can be trickier than it seems. First of all, as we have said categories are not 'out there' in the world; they are, like beauty, in the eye of the beholder. Two objects will probably be assigned to different categories by different animals, because each animal has different needs and goals. Second, all objects are inherently multifaceted, and we can select any of their features as a basis for the categorizing. Often, perceptual features will be in charge; sometimes, more functional ones. For example, going back to our apple example, the same apple can be grouped within the category of FRUIT (along with other items such as bananas and pears), or with the category of HEALTHY FOOD (along with whole-wheat and omega-3-fish), within the category SUPERMARKET ITEMS (along with chicken, milk, coffee and all sorts of house cleaning material), within ROUND OBJECTS (along with tennis balls or eggs), within RED OBJECTS (if the apple is red; see Figure 4.5), or in a possibly open-ended list of *ad hoc* categories (we will focus on *ad hoc* categories at the end of Section 4.5).

Each of these categorizations imposes a different viewpoint on the element, highlighting some facets while leaving some others in the background. Thus, placing an element within a category implies that the

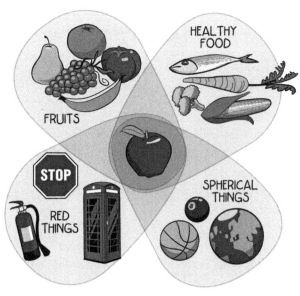

Figure 4.5 Different Ways of Categorizing an Apple

similarities with other elements within the category will be enhanced as will be differences with items belonging to different categories. A more terse definition would be that categorizing maximizes both within-category similarities and between-category differences. That is why using a word for a given object alters our perception and experience of the object to a certain extent.

In our experience, we encounter tokens on repeated occasions and build a 'generic' representation in our minds that is somehow simplified or idealized. Depending on our purpose, some characteristics of a given item may be less important for their categorization than others; for example, the colour of a table is probably not that important for its categorization, so it is not included in its categorical representation; in the case of lemons, colour *is* an important factor, and so it would figure in its categorical representation.

Lupyan (2008a, 2008b) has shown that *linguistic* categorization is special in many regards. To start with, it changes the representation of an element in our minds. In one of his experiments, he asked participants to examine a number of familiar objects (e.g., chairs, lamps and tables) and then sort them using a 'preference' rule (by pushing a 'like' or a 'don't like' button) or using a linguistic label (by pushing a 'chair' or a 'table' button). In the second phase of the experiment, they were shown again a number of objects that could be either the same ones they had previously seen or slight variations of them (e.g., a chair with a slightly different height or colour or material). This time they had to press the buttons 'new' or 'old' to indicate whether they had already seen them or not. People remembered more accurately the elements they had seen in the blocks they had categorized according to the 'like/don't like' rule than those they had categorized using a linguistic label. The explanation is that when you categorize an object using a linguistic label, the mental representation of the element is 'shifted' in your memory, since linguistic labelling is an invitation to focus on the similarities with other members of the category and so individual differences are not as important, and thus less remembered. In another study by this team (Boutonnet and Lupyan, 2015), they also showed that hearing the word *dog* allowed people to recognize more quickly the image of a dog than other equally informative non-verbal cues, such as the bark of a dog.

All this gives us some clues about the specificity of word meaning: using a specific label for a given object not only categorizes the object (with all the associated conceptualization effects we have just seen), but also somehow 'congeals' its meaning and presents it from a specific perspective. The metaphor used by some authors is that words are something like 'photographs of three-dimensional objects from a single angle' (Malt and

Wolff, 2010: 9). Words direct our attention to the features that are diagnostic of the category labelled, and which do not have to be necessarily perceptual (they can be functional, for example); babies can then focus on the similarities shared by objects with the same linguistic label and in this way, group together things which do not have to be perceptually similar. We will discuss specific cases when we talk about the acquisition of meaning, in Chapter 6.

Given the great relevance of the process of categorization, a number of questions crop up: How do we categorize things? Are all categories the same? How do categories work? How do we store them?

4.4.2 The Classical Version

Since Aristotle, categories have been seen as 'containers'; you can consider the category TABLE as a container into which you can put things; things that can be called tables are found inside this container and the rest fall outside. In a way, when we categorize the world, we divide it into TABLES and NON-TABLES.

The way to decide whether something belongs to a category or not is by looking at the features that it should have. The common sense view holds that there are certain features that all the members of the category share; it is this list of features that members have and non-members do not have which define the category in question. If you have them, you belong to the category; if you do not have them, you do not: as simple as that. This list of features ideally defines the **necessary and sufficient conditions** (that is, neither more, nor less) that an object must satisfy to enter the category.

For example, a BACHELOR is somebody who:

a. is human
b. is a male
c. is adult
d. is not married

If someone meets all these conditions, then we can classify this person as a bachelor. If someone meets all these conditions except for one (the person is married, is a child or is a woman), such a person cannot qualify as a bachelor, and would have to stay outside the category (all of them are *necessary*). And it doesn't matter if this person has other features, like being tall, rich or blonde; this set is *sufficient*, we do not need the rest. From this state of affairs, several facts follow (Taylor, 2004: 82):

a. There is a fixed set of necessary and sufficient conditions defining the membership to each category

b. All members of a category have equal status
c. All non-members of a category have equal status
d. All necessary and sufficient features defining a category have equal status
e. Categories have clear and well defined boundaries

The first one, (a), is assumed as a given: things that are classified within a category must surely have something in common, and that something is what we state in the form of necessary and sufficient conditions. (b) and (c) stem from the fact that something either belongs (if it has all the features) or does not belong to the category (if at least one is missing); there is no place for 'in-betweens', and thus members and non-members share the same status. (d) is another logical conclusion: all conditions have the same status; there is no more important condition, since you have to meet all of them, and if you fail to meet just one, no matter which, you do not qualify. All this takes us to conclusion (e): categories have clear boundaries, with things falling either inside or outside. It is a black-or-white duality; something is either a cat or not a cat, but cannot be only 'partially a cat'.

For a long time, this was the picture everyone followed and believed. During the twentieth century, however, this view was challenged by several scholars from different fields.

4.4.3 A New View on Categories: Wittgenstein and Labov

This rather clear and intuitive view of categorization was called into question by different people coming from fields such as philosophy, sociolinguistics or psychology. The first one was the Austrian philosopher **Ludwig Wittgenstein**. He examined the case of the category GAME. When you try to look for the common features of activities that can be called games (e.g., tennis, cards, roulette, rope-skipping, football, chess, etc.) you find features like these:

a. they are done for entertainment (they are amusing)
b. there is somebody that wins (or at least, competition)
c. they end when somebody wins
d. they require training or practice
e. they involve more than one person

However, there is a problem with the list: not all games share all these attributes, and it is in fact very difficult or even impossible to find something common to all of them. This is how Wittgenstein expressed it:

> Consider for example the proceedings that we call 'games'. I mean board-games, card-games, Olympic games, and so on. What is

common to them all? Don't say: 'There must be something common, or they would not be called 'games' – but look and see whether there is anything common to all. For if you look at them you will not see something that is common to all, but similarities, relationships, and a whole series of them at that. To repeat: don't think, but look! Look for example at board-games, with their multifarious relationships. Now pass to card-games; here you find many correspondences with the first group, but many common features drop out, and others appear. When we pass next to ball-games, much that is common is retained, but much is lost. Are they all 'amusing'? Compare chess with noughts and crosses. Or is there always winning and losing, or competition between players? Think of patience. In ball-games there is winning and losing; but when a child throws his ball at the wall and catches it again, this feature has disappeared. Look at the parts played by skill and luck; and at the difference between skill in chess and skill in tennis. Think now of how many other characteristic features have disappeared! And we can see how similarities crop up and disappear.

And the result of this examination is: we see a complicated network of similarities overlapping and criss-crossing: sometimes overall similarities, sometimes similarities of detail.

I can think of no better expression to characterize these similarities than 'family resemblances'; for the various resemblances between members of a family: build, features, color of eyes, gait, temperament, etc. etc. overlap and criss-cross in the same way. And I shall say: 'games' form a family (Wittgenstein, 1952: 31–32).

Wittgenstein's notion of **family resemblance** had a considerable impact on categorization studies. Many scholars nowadays agree that this is what we should expect when trying to characterize all the members of a category: we are going to find distributed, partial and sectorial similarities rather than universal and across-the-board necessary and sufficient conditions. If we apply this view to the meaning of words, we see its great relevance: this entails that words do not have a common core that is always activated; that is, that the distinction between semantics and pragmatics is blurred.

Another scholar who contributed to the new view on categorization was **William Labov**, a scholar investigating sociology and language. He performed some experiments aimed at finding out how people categorized objects into two similar and contiguous categories: CUPS and VASES (Labov, 1973). In one experiment, participants were presented with a list of objects, ranging from very clear cup-like objects to very clear vase-like objects, and were told to group them in one of these two categories. After this, he repeated the experiment a couple of times, but providing the participants with some additional information: that these were objects in which you would put flowers or you would put coffee. Depending on what they were told, subjects divided the objects in different ways, moving the dividing line to one side or the other: they tended to see more vases in the 'flower' condition and more cups in the 'coffee' condition. This experiment showed very clearly that context does affect the way in which we categorize objects, a fact that cannot be easily explained by the necessary and sufficient theory of categories, which predicts that context should have no effect on categorization.

4.4.4 Prototypes: Rosch

The scholar who has provided the most convincing and influential case against classical categories has been **Eleanor Rosch**. She carried out a great deal of experiments that showed that we do not necessarily classify things into categories by checking whether they strictly follow a list of criteria (Rosch, 1973, 1975, 1978).

She performed a number of experiments around the same activity of categorization, using different experimental paradigms. In one of them, she asked a group of subjects to rank examples of a series of categories; the categories tested were FURNITURE, FRUIT, VEHICLE, WEAPON, VEGETABLE, TOOL, BIRD and SPORT. Participants were asked to what extent a list of items could be regarded as a good example of the category. Thus, for example, in the sixty furniture items used in Rosch (1975), elements such as *chair, sofa, couch* or *table* consistently received the highest 'goodness-of-exemplar' ratings; objects such as *bookcase, footstool* or *bench* were found in the middle position, and items such as *ashtray, fan* or *telephone* were judged by most participants as the less typical members of the category. The level of consistency in the pattern of results was really high and it agreed in a seamless way with the results from other experiments in a number of ways. For example, she asked her subjects to list as many examples as possible of a category in a limited time. She found that the first examples mentioned were always the ones that were judged as 'better' examples of the category; also, the number of times that an exemplar was mentioned correlated to a high degree with goodness-of-exemplar ratings. In some other experiments, she used more sophisticated methods, measuring the amount of time it takes to decide whether something belongs to a given category or not (e.g., 'is this [showing a picture of a penguin] a bird or not?'). She found that subjects did not always answer with the same speed: they tended to respond very quickly in very clear cases (which coincided with those that had received very high goodness-of-examplar ratings and that had been mentioned earlier and more frequently in listing tasks); in less typical cases, the responses were slower.

Her results were clear and consistent: there are good and bad examples of categories. For example, *robin* is a better example of the category BIRD than *penguin*. This contradicted everything we thought was true about categories; it was clearly shown that categories had a graded-structure. The best example is called the prototype, and the rest of the category is organized around it. Central members are the ones that share many features with the prototype; more peripheral members (such as penguins or ostriches in the case of BIRD) share fewer features with the prototype.

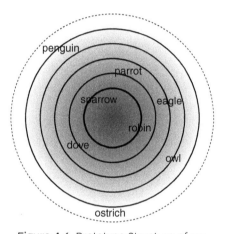

Figure 4.6 Prototype Structure of BIRD

Summarizing, the idea is that when we categorize, we compare the object under scrutiny to the prototype. If it shares a substantial number of features with the prototype, we include it in the category; if it shares some, we can still consider it a peripheral member or, if the number is too low, we exclude it. It must be added that not all features are equally important in this approach; some features are more useful for identifying an exemplar as a member of a given category. When the presence of a feature makes it very probable that the exemplar belongs to the category, we say that that feature has a **high cue validity**; in opposite cases, we speak of **low cue validity** features. This is sometimes known as **cue strength**.

A very important consequence of this view is that categorization is normally not a matter of 'black or white', but rather of 'better or worse'. This does not exclude the possibility that in some cases, categories *do* have fixed boundaries. Such is the case of ODD-NUMBERS, for example. However, the fact that some categories may have fixed boundaries does not necessarily imply that we follow the criterial approach. For example, geometrical figures (e.g., a triangle) do have fixed boundaries; however, rather than applying a list of necessary and sufficient features, we probably use Gestalt principles of overall perceived shape.

The psychological status of prototypes is unclear for some authors. For example, is there a *specific* dog which we take as our 'prototypical' dog, or do we abstract away and have a less concrete dog in our minds, a kind of abstract, under-specified, non-existent concept which can be considered as 'the essence of dogness'? Some versions of prototype theory believe that the prototype is best understood in this way, as a fairly schematic notion; yet, other theories think we compute categorization by comparison with concrete, specific members of the category (the so-called **exemplar theories** of categorization).

Whatever the answer is, what everybody accepts is the existence of **prototype effects**, which are clearly observable. We have mentioned some of them (*order of mention* and *overall frequency in recall* as well as *speed of verification*); to this list, we could add *order of acquisition* (since prototypical members tend to be acquired first).

Finally, languages also have ways to allow speakers to indicate whether an expression is to be construed as a central/prototypical member of a category, or as a more peripheral one. Such is the case of **hedging constructions** or, more simply, **hedges**. Consider the following sentences:

(8) a. *Loosely speaking, an ashtray is a piece of furniture*
     b. *??Loosely speaking, a chair is a piece of furniture*
     c. *Technically speaking, a tomato is a fruit*
     d. *??Technically speaking, an apple is a fruit*

Loosely speaking is an expression that warns the hearer about the peripheral nature of a given member of a category. That is why (8a) sounds natural, but (8b) sounds less natural, since we are asking the hearer not to be too strict about the boundaries of the category; this makes sense for the case of peripheral members but not for prototypical ones. Something similar happens with *technically speaking* in (8c) and (8d): the speaker is using this hedge to convince the hearer that the entity mentioned does belong to the category, which, again, makes sense if we are talking about a peripheral member, but becomes unnecessary when talking about prototypical ones. Other English hedges are *sort of* and *kind of*, which are so frequent they are sometimes fused to become a single word (*he's kinda cute*).

Table 4.2 is a summary of the prototype model of categorization.

Table 4.2 *Some Characteristics of the Prototypical Approach*

- **The prototype is the best example of a category**. It is the member that is judged as the most representative of the category.
- **Categories have a graded structure**. Members of a category are more or less central depending on their similarity to the prototype; category membership is thus a matter of degree.
- **Fuzzy boundaries**. Categories do not have clear boundaries.
- **There is no set of necessary and sufficient conditions**. Not all members can be defined by the same set of conditions; central examples share more features with the rest than peripheral members.
- **Cue validity**. When the presence of a feature makes it very probable that the exemplar belongs to the category, that feature has a high cue validity.

4.5 Semantic Domains and Frames

In all the cases we have seen so far, we group together objects depending on some perceived similarity. If the objects share a number of features, they can be grouped under the same category. Different types of dogs do share a good number of features, and so do birds, or just animals, for that matter (though the category ANIMAL is slightly different; it is more inclusive and more general than the category of DOG; we will deal with this type of category, called **superordinate-level** category, in Chapter 5). However, this is not the only way in which we organize objects in our mind; we form other types of 'chunks' in which objects that do not share any perceptual similarity are grouped together. This is what happens when we put together *car* and *garage*, or *water* and *glass*, or *chalk* and *blackboard*. Elements that are associated because they show up as different elements of the same scene, elements that co-occur in space or time or that are related by some interactional property are linked by **thematic relations** (which, again, we will examine more closely in Chapters 5 and 8).

What is interesting at this point is that thematically related elements create structures known as **schemas** (also known as **frames**; Fillmore, 1985). A word can form part of different schemas, and thus, acquire different meanings. For example, consider the following list of sentences (adapted from Ungerer and Schmid, 2006):

(9). a. *The hunter took his rifle, called his dog, and went out.*
b. *The dogs started chasing the rabbit right from the start of the race.*

c. *The sleigh raced across the snow, pulled by the dogs.*

d. *She took her dog to the beauty parlour to have its curls reset.*

e. *The policemen lined up with the dogs to face the rioters.*

In each of these cases, the type of dog that would spring to mind is different (probably, a retriever in (9a), a greyhound in (9b), an Eskimo dog in (9c), a poodle in (9d) and a German shepherd in (9e)). The fact that a different type of dog is evoked in each case cannot be properly predicted by any feature-theory of meaning; no matter how we consider categorization in a narrow sense, we are not going to get these effects. This is where the concept of schema or frame comes in handy, providing a simple answer to this puzzle. By considering the role of schemas, we can see how concepts can be stored along with their role in a typical context, which is quite often cultural and even user-dependent. This makes sense if we consider how prototypes work: if we replicated the experiment on the typicality of, say, BIRDS or FRUIT in different countries, the results would very probably be different (a prototypical fruit in England could be *apple*; in Spain, *orange* and in New Zealand, *kiwi*). The meaning of TABLE in England or in Japan is different, because a prototypical Japanese table is different (owing to differences between Japanese and British culture and society, that is, in the different schemas of both cultures).

This view in which we store concepts, along with a thematic schema that provides an underlying context, is thus a very nice complement to the theory of categorization; we do not represent concepts in isolation, but in relevant situations (hence the name 'situated simulation' we mentioned in Chapter 3). Frames thus capture recurrent regularities in the world. This helps us explain facts like the rather unpredicted denotation of words such as *bachelor*. Though intuitively, a criterial definition of bachelor includes features such as '+human', '+male', '+adult' and '–married', this list cannot explain why we feel reluctant to classify certain people as bachelors, for example the Pope, Tarzan, a widower or an Arab who can have four wives but only has three. To fully understand the notion of BACHELOR, we have to take into account a background of cultural expectations, and only then is the classification of people into prototypical and non-prototypical bachelors correctly understood. Thus, in Western culture, male members of a certain age are supposed to get married unless there is a cultural reason for not doing so (as in the case of priests).

As a matter of fact, the context that is stored along with the concept is quite often completely necessary to explain the meaning of the concept itself. For example, how could you explain the meaning of a word such as *Tuesday* without making reference to the notion of WEEK?

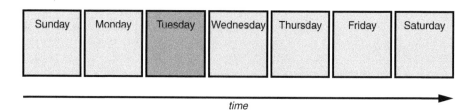

Figure 4.7 TUESDAY and the WEEK Frame

The same would happen with many other concepts; to understand BREAKFAST, you need a bigger context which we might call THE DAILY MEAL SYSTEM, in which there are three meals a day and the first one is called *breakfast*. Finding cross-cultural equivalents of words thus depends not only on the word itself, but also on the underlying schema. It would be quite difficult, if not just impossible, to translate the word *Tuesday* to a language that lacks the notion of WEEK, or the word *breakfast* to a culture in which there is only one meal a day.

The way in which words get their meanings, then, is by activating one of these structures (cognitive domains or frames) and then focusing on some part of it. This is analogous to what happens in **figure/ground** perception. In Gestalt psychology, figure and ground segregation is one of the most basic laws of perception: whenever we perceive something, we impose this figure/ground organization. So, when we see something, we 'highlight' it from the rest of its surrounding context; the same happens with hearing or other perception modes. For example, in order to hear somebody's voice,

Figure 4.8 Some Figure/Ground Reversals

you have to concentrate on it and 'isolate' it from other background noises. In some cases, we find objects that can be viewed differently depending on what we choose as figure or as ground. Four of them are included in Figure 4.8 (going from left to right, a young or an old woman, a duck or a rabbit, a cube with two possible shapes (upper or bottom face closer to us) and two faces looking at each other or a vase).

In our example of TUESDAY, what that word does is to highlight one specific day as **figure** against the **ground** of the WEEK frame; other days of the week highlight different parts of the same structure; in this sense, it is a bit like the duck/rabbit trick: you focus on some part of the same structure and perceive different things. Another very clear example is the notion of HYPOTENUSE. From the domain of a RIGHT TRIANGLE, we highlight the **figure** (also called **profile**), which corresponds to one of the lines that form it, and leave the rest as **ground** (or **base**); as can be seen in Figure 4.9, the underlying base is completely necessary for a correct characterization of its meaning.

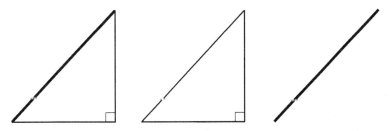

Figure 4.9 HYPOTENUSE as Figure and RIGHT-ANGLED TRIANGLE as Ground

Sometimes (and this is probably the most frequent case), words can highlight facets of several different cognitive domains at the same time. Consider the case of *knee*. On the one hand, the concept of KNEE must have as a base the cognitive domain of LEG (which in turn, will have as its cognitive domain BODY; we can see how concepts are embedded into each other, following a sort of fractal structure). But what we know about knees is not only that they are a certain part of a leg; we also have other types of knowledge, such as flexibility (i.e., a quality it possesses), that it is a joint, along with elbows or wrists (i.e., its taxonomic domain) and that it plays a part in locomotion (i.e., its function). All these different cognitive domains can probably be activated or invoked when we say *knee*.

This is very similar to the view proposed by psychologist **Lawrence Barsalou** for the difference between **category** and **concept**. In his opinion, all the information that we have about a concept forms our **categorical** information. Each time we use a word, certain parts of this information become activated, depending on context. So, the concept PIANO contains features belonging to different domains, the domain of MUSICAL INSTRUMENTS (and thus, we know it is used to produce sound), the domain of FURNITURE (and we know that they are expensive and heavy), etc. Not all this information is active at the same time. Therefore, Barsalou (1987) proposes that we keep the notion of *concept* for this on-line construction of the elements that become active in a given context. In this way, one category can give rise to many different concepts (Figure 4.10). Thus in each of the following sentences, the concept of *piano* evoked would be slightly different; (10a) activates the sound-producing features of pianos, (10b) relates it to the furniture category and (10c) highlights the material pianos are made of (wood):

(10)   a. *Every afternoon, a piano can be heard from my kitchen window*
       b. *This piano is really heavy; it took five burly men to get it here*
       c. *During the war, people were so cold that they used pianos to build fires*

Another useful distinction provided by Barsalou is that of **ad-hoc categories** (Barsalou, 1983). These categories have several distinguishing features. Their main characteristic is that they are not well established in long-term memory, as would be the case of conventional categories, but are instead created on-line for a specific purpose (they are also called 'goal-directed categories'). They also tend to hold members that have little in

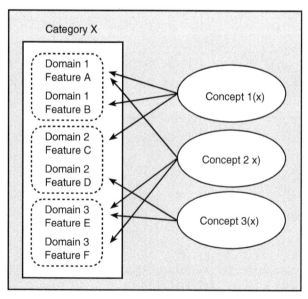

Figure 4.10 Different Arrays of Features Forming Different Concepts of the Same Category

common. Some *ad hoc* categories are WAYS TO ESCAPE BEING KILLED BY THE MAFIA, THINGS TO PUT IN A SUITCASE FOR A ONE-WEEK STAY AT THE BEACH, or THINGS THAT YOU WOULD TAKE OUT OF YOUR HOUSE IN CASE OF FIRE. Though we do not have a list of members of these categories stored in our minds, we can create the category quite easily, and such a category would exhibit the same graded structure of standard categories, with prototypical and peripheral members, etc.

These notions introduced by Barsalou, the flexibility inherent in our use of concepts and the 'ad hoc' character of many categories, can be quite useful to explain many effects in language and in cognition. As we mentioned before, all categorizing is a bit 'ad-hoc' and dependent on contextual factors (as we exemplified with the many ways of categorizing an apple). The basic idea is that, more than things we *have* in our minds, concepts are things we *create* with our minds. Exactly the same can be applied to the meaning of words: instead of being retrieved from memory, as stable form-meaning pairings, word meanings are constructed on-the-fly, always modulated by context and thus slightly different every time we use a word in a different sentence or a different context. This is related to the problematic distinction between semantics and pragmatics that we discussed in Chapter 1. Lebois *et al.* (2015) review a great body of evidence which argues against the existence of a central core of context-independent information in word meanings, claiming that 'even the most salient features in a word's meaning are not activated automatically' (Lebois *et al.*, 2015: 1), a notion that goes back to Wittgenstein at least and the 'family resemblances' we discussed in Section 4.4.3. We will discuss again this idea with some more detail in Chapter 9.

4.6 Denotation and Connotation

As we saw at the beginning of this chapter, **reference** and **sense** have their related notions (**extension** and **intension**, respectively); to these, another notion can be added, this time related to **denotation**: **connotation** (Table 4.3). Roughly speaking, **denotation** is equated with **reference** (and **extension**), while **connotation** is more related with **sense** (and **intension**).

Table 4.3 *More Terminological Relations*

reference	extension	denotation
sense	intension	connotation

A common way to explain the difference between denotation and connotation is to link denotation to the 'primary' meaning of a word and connotation to other 'secondary' meanings. Let us look at some examples. Think of colours. Colours have one primary meaning, the chromatic one, which points at a specific range of light wavelength, which is 'isolated' from the rest: red, yellow, blue, etc. However, most colours have other secondary meanings associated with them. Thus, the primary meaning of *red* is the chromatic one (roughly, 'the hue of the long-wave end of the visible spectrum, evoked in the human observer by radiant energy with wavelengths of approximately 630 to 750 nanometres'). However, it is clear that this is not the only meaning evoked by the word *red*. For example, we associate *red* with the idea of danger on the one hand, and of passion, on the other (also with anger). In this case, these connotations are almost universal, and probably based on biological facts: anger is physiologically connected to the colour red, since when we are angry, blood rushes to the neck and face areas. Many other connotations, however, are highly cultural; still within the domain of colours, in India, the colour of mourning is white, while in Western cultures, the colour of mourning is black; Chinese brides wear red, while Western brides wear white. Table 4.4 provides a list of some colours and their connotations:

Table 4.4 *A Partial List of Connotations of Some Colours*

red	danger, passion
yellow	scandal (press)
black	depression
blue	sadness; obscenity
green	envy; environment
pink	homosexuality

Connotation is often difficult to apprehend; the connotation of the word *lady*, for example, could link this word to things such as elegance, class, politeness or civility. It is probably easier to associate this word with skirts and dresses than with trousers. On the other hand, for some speakers, especially those closer to feminist ideas, this word can also evoke not-so-positive connotations, such as meek, submissive and outdated. The connotations of words are a highly sensitive area, always in constant social evolution. Another fact that should be noted is one of the *leitmotifs* of this book: context has a pervasive influence on all factors related to meaning, and both denotation *and* connotation are of course included. *Chicken* has different connotations when talking about food or when talking about somebody's behaviour.

Additionally, connotation is frequently linked to a narrower sense: the emotional overtones of a word or expression. One of the most basic ways of categorizing objects in the world is the division between dangerous things, that we should avoid, and pleasant or useful things (that is, we need a quick answer to the question asked by the rock band The Clash: 'Should I stay or should I go'?). In this sense, words are associated with two types of connotational information, positive or negative, depending on whether they elicit a pleasing emotional reaction or a negative one. Words such as *baby, mummy* or *love* would have positive connotations, while words such as *death, violence* or *dirty* would have negative ones. Back in 1969, Boucher and Osgood stated, in true Monty Python fashion, that human languages look on (and talk about) the bright side of life. This became known as the 'Pollyanna hypothesis': the idea that humans show a universal tendency to use positive words over negative ones. A more recent study, using a 'big data' approach (i.e., using statistical methods) has apparently confirmed this (Dodds *et al.*, 2015). Of the sample of ten languages included in this 2015 study, Spanish turned out to be the happiest language, followed by Portuguese and English; the least positive one in the list (or the most balanced, if you prefer) was Chinese.

Emotional connotations can be measured with a number of techniques, ranging from pupil dilation to skin conductance (skin becomes a better conductor of electricity when we are emotionally aroused). Another way to measure connotation is Osgood's **Semantic Differential Technique**. This technique is used to find out about the attitudes towards objects, events or persons. To do this, participants are asked to rate a given word according to a number of scales, which are framed by bipolar opposing adjectives (e.g., *good–bad, nice–awful, useful–useless*). Any type of scale that suits the thing being described can be thought of. For example, to describe a book we could use scales such as *good–bad, entertaining–boring, fast–slow, deep–shallow, up-to-date–outmoded, well-organized–messy, attractive–unattractive, dynamic–static, reliable–unreliable*, etc. However, Osgood and his colleagues decided that all could be boiled down to three dimensions: potency (e.g., *strong–weak*), activity (*active–passive*) and evaluation (*good–bad*). After running questionnaires with many participants, they found that words can achieve their own 'profile'; for example, *war* and *danger* would be both 'strong', 'bad' and 'active', while *death* would be 'strong', 'bad' and 'passive', *calm* and *sleep* would be 'passive and 'good' and so on.

Swear words are expressions which are linked to very strong emotional connotations, which is why they are uttered in emotional situations, normally in related to anger, frustration or pain (though we curse in many other situations, including joy and surprise). The usefulness of swear words in providing relief has even been tested experimentally. Stephens *et al.* (2009) measured how long a group of students could keep their hands submerged in cold water; one group was allowed to swear, while the other group could say only a neutral word. The group that was allowed to curse endured the pain for a longer time and reported less pain than their non-swearing companions (it was later found out, however, that this analgesic effect was smaller for people who swore more frequently in their daily life, showing a 'habituation' effect of swearing: cf. Stephens and Umland, 2011). **Euphemisms** are attempts at neutralizing the connotations of some expressions using an alternative. Some authors think that the current use of euphemistic expressions is a way of providing a different world-view, thereby bringing together the study of connotations and linguistic relativism (which we will cover in Chapter 6). A very similar notion is what is known as 'politically correct language': the negative connotations of *garbage man* can perhaps be avoided if we replace it by the term *sanitation engineer*.

Connotation can be explained more or less naturally by the embodied view of language. Remember that we said that concepts (and also words) are formed by 'amalgamation' of different embodied experiences, including sensorimotor and introspective experiences. Thus, if every time we encounter a snake or a cockroach we experience a certain emotion (fear or revulsion), those negative emotions leave their traces in the brain and are activated along with the rest of the information when we encounter the word that activates the concept. Our concept of DOG, for example, could include not only sensorimotor information about its shape, motion, feel, smell and sound but also introspective: our personal feelings about dogs, which could be positive or negative depending on our specific experiences with dogs. Emotional experiences are in this way also part of the embodied simulation associated with words. In this sense, connotation has been linked to episodic memories; it has been related to the brain's right-hemisphere function (in charge of more holistic aspects of language) and the limbic system, the oldest and inner part of the brain, in charge of emotional processing. In fact, some scholars talk about an 'Affect Primacy Hypothesis' (e.g., Murphy and Zajonc, 1993) which claims that affective information is processed before the remaining information by a non-conscious mental system: when you encounter a snake or a dangerous animal, it is important to be able to react as quickly as possible. This is a bit tricky, because in order to elicit an appropriate response, you have to be able to identify the object you arc looking at, so researchers are still debating whether there is an affective primacy or a cognitive primacy. The latest views seem to opt for different possibilities depending on each particular circumstance (in true 'ad-hoc cognition' style). On the other hand, the notions of frame and schema also help us explain other types of connotative association (as in the case of *lady*: you just have to imagine the underlying schemas for this word).

Finally, it should be noted that connotation is a hot topic today and is bound to become even hotter. People who create commercial products are quite aware of this: how you name your product affects how people conceptualize it. For example, the microchip *Pentium* was named in this way because of its connotations: 'Pent-' sounds powerful and strong (e.g., the *Pentagon*), while '-ium' sounds scientific and technical (e.g., *actinium*). We will encounter this notion in other chapters of the book; for example, we will see in Chapter 5 how connotation can sometimes be 'spread out' over a text, in a phenomenon known as **semantic prosody**; in that chapter we will also talk about **sentiment analysis**, a new computational technique that uses connotation to extract the attitudes of speakers towards a given product or event; WordNet, the well known lexical database, has a version called, Q-WordNet, which classifies WordNet senses automatically by positive and negative polarity.

4.7 Chapter Summary

In this chapter we looked at the main ways in which words convey meaning, introducing two of the most basic notions in semantics: reference and sense. We saw that, roughly, reference is concerned with the relationships between words and some external object (in the real world, in a possible world or in a mental world) while sense is concerned with relationships within language. We also examined the different types of reference (indefinite, definite and generic) and saw the ways in which sense can be related to the relationships between one word and other words in the system and also with our knowledge of the word itself. The following section was devoted to categorization: we reviewed how categorization was approached in the classical version (i.e., trying to find the 'necessary and sufficient conditions' common to all members of the category) and how this vision was challenged by scholars like Wittgenstein (who thought that it is often impossible to find necessary and sufficient conditions that hold for all members of a category, which are related by more partial 'family resemblance' links) and Labov (who showed how context can alter the way in which we categorize elements). We also explained the prototypical theory of categorization, established by Eleanor Rosch and her colleagues, in which categories have fuzzy boundaries and graded structure, with central and peripheral members. We went on to introduce the notion of 'semantic frame', which serves as background to the meaning of words and expressions, and also presented the notion of 'ad hoc category'. The chapter concluded by reviewing aspects related to connotation, that is, the secondary meanings we attach to words.

Exercises

Exercise 4.1   Look at the following sentences and try to decide whether they contain expressions with definite reference, indefinite reference or generic reference. Is that distinction possible for all of them or are some of them ambiguous?

    a.   *Yesterday I saw* a movie *that completely horrified me*
    b.   *If you are bored you should go and see a movie*
    c.   *Filming* a movie *is always an expensive business*
    d.   *The door to the cave opens when you say a word*
    e.   *As soon as I utter a* word, *people know I'm from Texas*
    f.   Words *can be dangerous weapons*
    g.   A dog *is the best type of pet you can have*
    h.   *There was* a dog *barking last night and I couldn't sleep*
    i.   *Our neighbour has a very scary* dog

Exercise 4.2   Riemer (2010: 26) mentions that sometimes we can have sentences that apparently have no reference, such as '*Robin Hood's private helicopter*' or '*the highest number in the world*'. Can you come up with more examples of sentences like these?

Exercise 4.3   How many subcategories can you find in the following list of objects:

    (1) a cigarette   (2) a bottle of wine   (3) a tennis sock
    (4) a hat   (5) an apple   (6) an egg

    Try to find at least five (clue: think of colour, shape or function).

Exercise 4.4   Do the categories 'DEAD/ALIVE' have fixed boundaries? What about TRIANGLE? What about MALE/FEMALE? How many categories with fixed boundaries can you think of?

Exercise 4.5   Think about the features that would define the concept CHOCOLATE. Now compare it to the different types of chocolate: A MARS BAR, WHITE CHOCOLATE, COOKING CHOCOLATE, COCOA. Do they all share the same attributes?

Exercise 4.6   What is the underlying semantic frame we need to understand the meaning of the following words:

a. Nail   b. Finger   c. Hand   d. Arm
e. Knob   f. Belt   g. Sail   h. Roof
i. Menu   j. Port and starboard

Now, the word *fridge* can be characterized by several underlying frames, as we saw in the case of *piano*. How many frames can you think of that could be used to characterize it? What types of information would each frame highlight?

Exercise 4.7   Try to think of ad hoc categories, such as WAYS OF MAKING NEW FRIENDS, PEOPLE YOU WOULD INVITE TO YOUR WEDDING IF YOU HAD AN UNLIMITED BUDGET or POINTED OBJECTS YOU CAN USE TO DEFEND YOURSELF.

Exercise 4.8   Try to classify the following list of words into positive and negative connotations. Do you agree with your fellow students? What does this tell you about the connotations of these words?

beauty, cancer, champion, cheat, death, disease, divorce, doctor, enemy, failure, family, fountain, fraud, freedom, garden, happy, hate, health, loser, music, peace, pleasure, poison, poverty, sex, snake, truth, violence, war, wealth

Can you do the same with this list of synonyms?

determined   dogged   firm   headstrong
inflexible   obstinate   persevering   persistent
resolute   rigid   single-minded   stubborn
tenacious   unswerving

Exercise 4.9   Think again of the connotations for colours; which of them can be traced back to experience (and thus should be more universal) and which seem to have a more cultural basis?

Key Terms Introduced in this Chapter

reference
denotation
extension
referring vs. non-referring expressions
generic, indefinite and specific reference
constant vs. variable reference
deictics
possible world
denotational theories of meaning
truth conditions
sense
intension
categorization
classical view of categories
necessary and sufficient conditions
family resemblances
prototype; prototype structure
prototype effects
(high and low) cue validity; cue strength
exemplar theories
hedges; hedging constructions
thematic relations
frames
schemas
figure and ground
profile and base
ad hoc category
connotation
semantic differential technique

Further reading

The classic treatment of reference and sense is Lyons (1977); Cruse (2000) includes a very enlightening discussion of reference in Chapter 15; for a treatment of reference from the point of view of truth-conditional semantics, see Chierchia and McConnell-Ginet (2000). Löbner (2013, chapter 11) and Riemer (2010, chapter 7) discuss prototypes and categorization; Löbner's chapter also offers a very critical view of prototypical categorization and its role in semantics. Another classic work for the description of prototypes in linguistic theory is Taylor (2004). The exemplar theory of categorization is described in Rouder and Ratcliff (2006). Semantic frames are discussed in Löbner (2013), who dedicates a whole chapter to them (Chapter 12). The original paper on ad hoc categories is Barsalou (1983). Finally, connotation is examined in Riemer (2010, Chapters 1 and 11) and Löbner (2013, Chapter 2); a classic reference for the Semantic Differential Technique is Snider and Osgood (1969).

CHAPTER 5

Meaning Relations

In this chapter . . .

In this chapter, we consider the topic of the different relations among the meaning of words. After reviewing the importance and centrality of meaning relations in accounts of word meaning, we first distinguish between two broad types of relations: semantic relations, which are held by words based on an overlap in their meaning, and associative relations, which are established by the co-occurrence of words in discourse. We also introduce a third type of relation: thematic relations, in which items that appear together in a scene become associated (as in *hammer* and *nail*). Before diving into semantic relations, we review the central but complex notion of polysemy (the different but related senses associated with a single word), and distinguish it from homonymy (in which the meanings of a word are not related). We also review the mechanisms by which a word can be connected to a number of related meanings in a principled way, introducing the notion of **regular polysemy**, which is contrasted with the more contextual meaning adaptations present in **irregular polysemy**. Next, we review synonymy and antonymy, distinguishing between canonical and non-canonical antonyms and other sub-types of antonymy. We also look at hyponymy and hyperonymy, introducing the distinction between basic-level, superordinate and subordinate categories. The chapter ends with a brief discussion of associative relations, examining how combining two words can alter their meaning, and reviewing the notion of collocation and some relatively new notions coming from corpus linguistics: semantic preference and semantic prosody.

5.1 The Structure of the Lexicon: a Network of Words

Words are not isolated things. We know this from many sources. When people are given one word and they are asked to respond with any word that comes to mind (an exercise known as a 'word association test'), the responses are not random at all: in fact, depending on the type of word, they can show a surprising degree of overlap. For example, in response to the word *canary*, a majority of people will answer *bird* (other options normally supplied are *yellow* or *sing*); when given the word *furniture*, the most frequent answer is *table* or *chair*; adjectives like *hot* or *wide* typically evoke their opposing pairs, *cold* and *narrow*, respectively. There are now huge databases that supply a concrete measure of the probability with which one word will evoke another in a word association test, an index known as the **word association strength** (e.g., Nelson *et al.*, 1998).

Another clear proof of the existence of these connections among words is the phenomenon of lexical **priming** that we saw in Chapter 3: words are processed more quickly when a related word has been shown before. Again, we can also quantify the amount of 'facilitation' that one word exerts on another (usually, this is measured in milliseconds). Priming measures can be taken as an index of how closely related in our mental lexicon words are, and are frequently used to hypothesize about the structure of our mental lexicon. There is also evidence that children start learning word associations at very early stages of their language acquisition process (starting from 18 to 24 months old; cf. Arias-Trejo and Plunkett, 2009).

So, there is all sorts of evidence to show that links among words do exist in our minds. These links are especially interesting because, for most authors, they provide useful clues about the way our conceptual system is structured. It is safe to say that for most scholars, the meanings of words are greatly influenced and constrained by their connections to other word meanings in the system. In fact, for structuralists, this would be the *main* way in which words acquire their meaning: by contrasting with other items in the system. As we saw in Chapter 3, Latent Semantic Analysis (LSA) is a great proof of how far you can take this approach.

5.1.1 Types of Relations: Semantic, Associative and Thematic

The next thing we would like to know is whether all the connections among words are of the same type. There is growing evidence that there are several types of relationship at work within the lexicon. One of the most basic distinctions found in the literature is that between **associative relations** and **semantic relations** proper.

Associative relations are those that connect word forms to each other; that is, those based on co-occurrence. For example, *dog* and *cat* tend to co-occur in speech (for example, in the idiom *to fight like cat and dog*), and in this way they become associated in our memory. This is actually what explains many of the results in word association tests: if people answer back with *Stones* after hearing *Rolling*, it is because of this associative relation in discourse, based on the popularity of the rock band the *Rolling Stones*.

On the other hand, some words are connected to other words because of an overlap in their meaning. This shows up in 'slip-of-the-tongue' mistakes, in which we typically replace one word by another one related in meaning (Garrett, 1992). Considering words as 'bundles' of semantic features, two words are perceived as similar when they share a significant number of those features. This would be the case of relations such as **synonymy, antonymy, hyponymy** or **category co-membership**, as we will see below. These relations receive many names in the literature: *taxonomic, semantic* or *similarity-based*. Thus, an initial difference between these two types of associations could be summarized as follows: we establish *semantic* relations among words that share a common core (what we could call 'intra-word' similarities); we establish *associative* relations between words that are found together in discourse.

To these two types, another type of relationship among words can be added: sometimes, two word meanings are associated because they refer to elements that co-occur in a given event or situation. Such would be the case of *hammer* and *nail*: their connection is established through a scene in which both items appear together and interact. A **thematic relation** is '*a temporal, spatial, causal, or functional relation between things that perform complementary roles in the same scenario or event*' (Estes *et al.*, 2011). We see how these relations are different from the previous, because they are 'language-external': they are based on the complementary roles that two different items play in a common scene. In the case of a restaurant scene, for example, thematically related items might include food, menus, waiters and wine. If we look at the meaning of each of these items, they do not share many features, but they are nonetheless linked by their participation in the common EATING-AT-A-RESTAURANT event (which can be considered as a *frame* or *schema*). We introduced the notion of frames back in Chapter 4 when we discussed their function, which was to provide a background for the meaning of words (as in *Tuesday*-WEEK); we will see them again in Chapter 6, when discussing the 'interactive social routines' that children learn, and that help them guess the structure of the events they participate in and thus facilitate the learning of words. The discussion about thematic relations will be taken up in Chapter 8, where we shall see their key role in the organization of sentences; finally in Chapter 9, we will see how many discourse inferences are actually based on this type of relations.

Thematic relations have a completely basic organizing function in cognition; they convey knowledge about events and scenarios and, to a great extent, it can be said that conceptual knowledge is organized around them as we mentioned. Some of these relations can be spatial (a *roof* is typically on the top of a *house*), functional (a *key* is what we use to open a *door*), temporal (*bills* come after you have eaten in a *restaurant*), or causal (*electricity* is what makes a *bulb* light up).

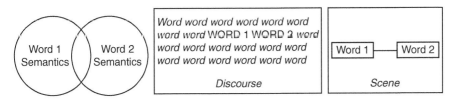

Figure 5.1 Semantic, Associative and Thematic Relations

5.1.2 Differences among the Different Types of Relations

There are numerous studies showing that these different types of connections are not processed in the same way. For example, studies from priming have shown that *semantic* priming starts very early when hearing a word, while *associative* priming takes a bit longer; semantic priming also lasts less time than associative priming, whose effects can be active more than one second after listening to the word. Neurologically, they also seem to be different (they alter the N400 component in different ways; see Chapter 3). Thematic relations also seem to be distinct: they tend to elicit much bigger priming effects than other semantic relations. Many authors suggest that this is due to the centrality of these relations in word meaning (Tyler and Moss, 1997); some other studies have shown that their neurological processing is also different (Schwartz *et al.*, 2011).

Once this has been said, it nevertheless seems to be quite difficult to really tease apart these relations in concrete cases: for example, when two words have an associative relationship, they also tend to have some type of semantic relationship. Distinguishing empirically between associative and semantic relations has proved a very complicated task; association is normally built *on top* of the other relationships. For example, do *lion* and *tiger* have a semantic relationship, an associative one, or a thematic one? Or perhaps all of them are present at the same time? On the other hand, you could also say that, roughly, semantic relations pertain more directly to word meanings, associative relations to word forms and thematic relations to objects.

5.1.3 Difficulties in Studying Relations among Word Meanings

Finally, yet another problem for the analysis of semantic relations is their sensitivity to the specific way in which they are studied. Word relations seem to display different characteristics depending on the task used for their analysis (e.g., a priming study, an elicitation technique, a corpus study or an acceptability rating). It is well known that context can have a great influence on how word meanings are judged to be related. This should not come as a surprise; in this book we have been suggesting that words do not really 'have meaning' by themselves. Rather, they can be seen as prompts for the construction of meaning by speakers in a given contextual situation, which is why we said before that almost every meaning is a bit ad hoc (as we saw in our *coffee* example in Chapter 1 or in the study of ad hoc categories in Chapter 4).

If this is so, it is no wonder that the relationship between two words can also be construed dynamically to a certain extent. This applies to words that are opposed in meaning, like antonyms, or words that are related, like synonyms, hyponyms or meronyms: quite often it is context that puts them in such an opposite or a similar position. For example, it is not clear what the antonym of *owl* might be, but in the question *Are you a lark or an owl?* (taken to mean 'Are you a morning person or an evening person?'), both items become two opposite extremes of a continuum. In the on-going controversy about whether these connections are established at a pure *lexical* level (and are thus more 'form-based'), or are rather of a *conceptual* nature, these contextual modulation effects seem to point in the direction of their conceptual basis (e.g., Murphy and Andrew, 1993), but, as we have said, this issue is still unresolved.

In the rest of this chapter, we are going to examine some of the most prominent relations among word meanings. However, before that, we have to pay attention to yet another problem that is logically prior: how to establish how many different meanings (or 'senses') a word may have. Typically, word meanings do not apply to a single, quite specific situation, but instead allow a certain amount of flexibility, so that they can also be used for similar objects or situations. When this 'stretching' process is continued, we can end up with words that refer to distinct, but related referents: this is what is called **polysemy**. Sometimes, these senses can grow far apart and become less and less related; on some other occasions, we find different words etymologically, which happen to share a form, but which are associated with completely different meanings: this would be the case of **homonymy.** We will examine the problems derived from polysemy and homonymy in the next section.

5.2 **Words and Senses: Polysemy and Homonymy**

> There's a sign on the wall, but she wants to be sure
> 'cause you know sometimes words have two meanings
> > (from the song 'Stairway to Heaven' by Led Zeppelin)

5.2.1 Polysemy

As we mentioned in the previous section, words do not refer to completely fixed and specific objects or events. In *Funes the Memorious*, the Argentinian writer Borges describes a boy with an extraordinary memory who remembers every single minute change in the objects of the world: for example, he can remember the different shapes of every cloud at different moments, and is sometimes puzzled that things so different can be given the same name. In the tale, this boy cannot generalize or abstract away and is locked up in the details, and thus cannot reason properly. Clearly, this is not how words function: normally, there is a certain 'slack' in the meaning of words. Speakers allow a certain variation of meanings when they use a word. This 'stretching' process can go on for a while, with the result that often different, but related concepts are grouped together under the same name. This phenomenon has received the name of **polysemy** (Breál, 1987). Polysemy makes sense in terms of storage and memory: we do not have to store a different word form for every different meaning; we can store only one form and remember that it can have different (and related) meanings, which is 'cheaper' than having to store a different word-form for each meaning. Most words in English (or in other languages, for that matter) are polysemous. Polysemy is extremely frequent in language, and actually there is a correlation between the frequency of a word and the number of its senses: the more frequent a word is, the more senses it tends to have (compare the many meanings of the word *head* compared to the word *cranium*, for example). Children incorporate polysemy in their speech quite early and naturally; by age 4, they will use the word *book* both in its sense as a material object – *this book is yellow/heavy* – and in its content sense – *this book is interesting*.

Polysemy is an interesting notion for many reasons. Linguistically, polysemy helps explain many phenomena, such as the diachronic evolution of the meaning of words. Words typically change their meanings over time, and that evolution proceeds incrementally, by polysemous links. Also, many authors suggest that polysemy is what allows the great flexibility of language combination, the almost limitless meanings that can be achieved when two words are put together (we will see an example of this at the end of this chapter, in Section 5.4). Polysemy is also interesting for more practical reasons: ambiguity in meaning has been called the 'bane of Natural Language Processing' (Koster, 2004). While human speakers effortlessly choose the correct possibility when a word points at different meanings, computers have real problems dealing with this. Quite often, a word in one language corresponds to different translation equivalents depending on its different senses: this is a serious complication for machine translation software, for example. The word *light* changes its meaning depending on whether we are talking about a *light suitcase, a light dinner, light coffee, light rain* or *light blue*, to give a few examples. And of course, psycholinguists would be interested in knowing exactly how we choose the appropriate meaning of a word and how we process it.

All types of words can be polysemous, not just nouns and verbs. For example, prepositions turn out to be one of the most polysemous word categories. Brugman (1981) investigated the different meanings that a preposition such as *over* could have, and found more than twenty (and other authors have suggested an even higher number). In Table 5.1, we see polysemy at work with different grammatical categories.

Table 5.1 *Polysemy in Different Grammatical Categories*

NOUN	ring	I don't like wearing rings	The rings of Saturn
VERB	grow	My son grows quickly	I grow daisies
ADJECTIVE	high	This is a high building	He's high on dope
ADVERB	quietly	He lives quietly in the country	He left the room quietly
PREPOSITION	over	They were walking over the hill	The war is over
CONJUNCTION	but	He's tall but she isn't	I like all fruit but apples
DETERMINER	the	The tall building I saw yesterday	The lion is an animal

So far, we have only mentioned **lexical polysemy**. Since polysemy is such a basic notion of language, it is not surprising that other levels of language can be polysemous too:

- There is polysemy in *morphology*. We already mentioned the polysemy of derivational morphemes in Chapter 1, when we saw the different meanings of morphemes such as -ful in examples like *wonderful, spoonful, forgetful* or *grateful*. Another case is the past tense morpheme -*ed*. Taylor (1995) augments the basic temporal meaning with a few additional ones:
  - **past**, that is, that the event is before the time of speaking or telling;
  - to indicate **unreality** or **counter-factuality**, that is, that something is not real (cf. *If I went there tomorrow, would you come with me?* or *I thought this book would be more boring* (but it isn't);
  - as a **pragmatic softener** (cf. *I wanted to tell you something*, which is softer than the more direct *I want to tell you something*).
- Grammatical constructions can be polysemous. For example, yes/no questions can mean several things. The meaning of the sentence in (1) would be different depending on the continuation we think of:
  (1) *Can you play the piano?*
       a. *Yes or no?*
       b. *Come on, please, do!*
       c. *I didn't know you did!*
- We can find polysemy in *intonation*; Taylor (1995) again shows how the same intonation contour can be applied to a variety of sentences to convey different types of meaning. For example, uttering the word *coffee* with a rising intonation can mean several things, depending on context: an invitation to share a coffee, an offer to make somebody a coffee, a feeling of incredulity that your interlocutor should have a coffee at this time of the day, a suggestion to add this item to a shopping list, etc.

So, the importance of polysemy cannot be overstated; however, its study is exceedingly complex, for a number of reasons. To start with, it is not very clear how to determine whether we are dealing with a distinct, separate meaning or just a contextual variant. Therefore, even agreeing on how many meanings a word has is a complicated issue (e.g., Geeraerts, 1993; Tuggy, 1993). Dictionaries quite frequently disagree on this issue: the *Collins English Dictionary* lists thirteen senses for the verb *open*, while the Longman's Dictionary of Contemporary English lists only five. And it is not just a question of more or less granularity: quite often the senses identified in one dictionary do not overlap at all with those found in another dictionary (an example of this is what Fillmore and Atkins (2000) found in their study of the verb *crawl*). There are a number of 'linguistic tests' to distinguish among polysemous senses (e.g., Geeraerts, 1993), but they are complex and mostly inconclusive.

5.2.2 Homonymy

Up till now, we have been only mentioning polysemy: a word 'develops', so to speak, a number of different but related senses, like *foot* for part of the leg (*My left foot is bigger than my right one*) and *foot* as a unit of measure (*He's six foot tall*). But there is another related phenomenon: **homonymy**, when two words happen to arrive at the same form (so, they look like only one) but each of them has a different meaning. In this case we have two (identical) word forms with completely unrelated meanings: *ball* can be a round object to play with, or it can be a dance; *bat* can be a flying animal or an object used in baseball; *bass* has a musical sense and a fish sense (Figure 5.2).

Figure 5.2 Weird Readings of *Baseball Bat* and *He's a Great Bass Player* due to Homonymy

In dictionaries, the different senses of polysemous items are typically listed within the same entry, while homonymous senses are listed as separate entries. The distinction we have established between polysemy and homonymy thus looks simple enough: in polysemy, the senses of a word are related and in homonymy they are not related. However, the 'relatedness' of meanings that distinguishes polysemy can be a tricky notion. When are two senses related and how can we tell? This is actually a problem that makes many cases of polysemy quite hard to distinguish from homonymy. Two traditional ways to tease apart polysemy and homonymy are (1) reliance on speakers' intuition and (2) etymological information.

However, both are problematic: speakers' intuition is known to be very subjective. Lyons (1977: 550) phrases this in very precise words: 'Relatedness of meaning is a matter of degree. Those lexical items which one person might regard to be semantically related to a certain degree, the other person might see them to be very far apart'. And then, checking the etymology of words (two homonymous words should have different etymologies) can help, but not always. Take the case of polysemous links: imagine a word with Sense 1, which evolves towards a related Sense 2, which then gives rise to a related Sense 3. All of them can be perceived as polysemous, but if Sense 2 is historically lost, what was a polysemous chain suddenly becomes homonymous.

On the other hand, their distinction seems to be necessary: polysemy and homonymy are processed psycholinguistically in different ways: it seems that polysemous words are processed faster (because their related senses share a common core and somehow 'help' each other) while homonymous words take some more time (because the different senses compete with each other and delay the choice of the right one). The idea seems to be that polysemous senses are represented in a similar way in our mind, while homonymous senses have distinct representations.

So, how can we reconcile these contradictory issues? On the one hand, the distinction between polysemy and homonymy seems to be real and have processing consequences; on the other, it is a very hard distinction to establish. What some authors have opted for is to treat this distinction as a continuum, going from closely related meanings, to medium or distant related meanings to completely separate meanings, thus treating the distinction as graded more than binary. This allows us to treat polysemes in different ways when they are closer to homonyms (Figure 5.3).

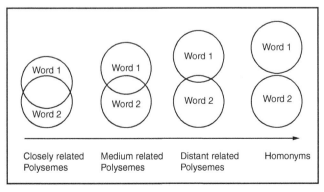

Figure 5.3 Different Degrees of Overlap between Polysemy and Homonymy

There is one final issue: how the different senses are represented in our minds. The representation of homonymy is not problematic: they are just different senses (attached to the same word form), so we store them separately in our minds. But the case of polysemy is not so clear. There are two possibilities: perhaps, as in homonymy, we keep different meanings separately or, alternatively, we might store only a general, under-specified meaning and the remaining senses are generated on-line. If this latter possibility is correct, how do we do this? Do we extend the meaning of words in a principled way, that is, are there 'rules' for creating poly-semous extensions? As sometimes happens, both options seem to be correct.

On the one hand, there are general mechanisms to extend meanings in predictable ways: this is what is known as **regular polysemy** (Apresjan, 1974). In regular polysemy, the meanings of words are extended in a systematic way, by means of a more or less concrete extension pattern. This pattern can be conceptualized as a sort of 'lexical rule' (e.g., Jackendoff, 1976; Pustejovsky, 1995; Copestake and Briscoe, 1995), as a metaphorical or metonymic extension (Lakoff and Johnson, 1980; Kövecses and Radden, 1998) or perhaps involve some sort of analogical reasoning (Gentner *et al.*, 2001). For example, in many languages of the world, including English, the name of an animal can also be used as the meat of that animal: *I saw a duck* vs. *I ate some duck*. This is a productive strategy and can be applied to new cases that would be understood with no problem: you can say *I ate some crocodile/kangaroo/ostrich* and people will under-stand it, even if they are not typical foods. An example of a metaphorical extension would be the two senses of *long*: the spatial one (*a long line*) and the temporal one (*a long time*). We will review some of the extensions based on metaphor and metonymy in Chapter 7. On the other hand, in **irregular polysemy**, we have patterns of extension that apply only in certain cases. For example, the round objects we find on shirts are called *buttons*; this word can be extended to a round object of a similar size, like in *emergency button* (or any other *button* you can push), but this extension does not apply 'across the board', as we saw in the 'animal for food' pattern: we can only use this extension in this particular case, but we cannot use it for other round objects, like, say, a coin, a monocle, a disk, a frisbee, a hockey puck or a smartie. To be clear, irregular polysemy is also applied to cases in which a word has many meanings, but these meanings do not seem to follow any type of predictable criteria; that is, it is not easy to come up with something like a 'rule' which would somehow 'generate' those new readings. Another example that comes to mind is the word *paper*, which has many different related meanings (writing material, sheet of paper, newspaper, a scholarly essay, an oral presentation, etc.), but some of them are not so easy to predict, as they are rather 'idiosyncratic' extensions.

On the other hand, sometimes a given polysemous sense becomes very conventional and is stored separately: people learn that extension and keep it in mind. This can explain why we keep polysemous senses that originated a long time ago. For example, *iron* is a metal; this material was used in the devices used to take out the wrinkles of clothing, and thus the extension *material > object*: nowadays irons are not made of iron, but still, we have these two senses associated with the word *iron*. Thus, depending on the case, polysemy and homonymy can function in the same way.

5.3 Semantic Relations

5.3.1 Synonymy

Sometimes two different words may have a very similar meaning. Such is the case of *car* and *automobile*, for example. When two words or expressions have the same meaning, they are called **synonyms.** In the opinion of many authors, though, **total synonymy** does not exist: that is, no two words or expressions have *exactly* the same meaning. In a way, total synonymy would make less sense in terms of storage. If we have one meaning A associated with form X, why bother learning another form Y for exactly the same meaning? So, what we find normally is **near-synonyms** or **partial-synonyms**; synonyms that are different in some small aspect, either in formality (register), or in syntagmatic relations, or that offer some different nuance of meaning. Take the example of *quick* and *fast*. They look very similar, but it is easy to find a difference. Take the examples in (2):

(2)   a. *a fast walk*
      b. *a quick walk*

(2a) would describe a walk that proceeds at a quick pace, walking quickly, and (2b) would correspond to a walk that takes a short time to complete (even if you walk slowly). In order to be considered total synonyms, two words would have to comply with these strict conditions:

i.   They should be synonymous across all contexts, that is, they should have the same collocational range. Ideally, if two words are total synonyms, you could use either of them in any context you may find. *Big* and *large* are synonyms, but it is easy to spot differences in meaning depending on their collocations: we say *a big mistake*, but not a *large* mistake; there is also a difference between *Ann is my big sister* (i.e., older than me), and *Ann is my large sister* (i.e., physically bigger than the rest; see Figure 5.4).

LARGE SISTER   BIG SISTER

Figure 5.4 Different Meanings of *Large* and *Big*

ii. They should be semantically equivalent on all dimensions of meaning, including their register, their intended style, their connotations, etc. This is what would distinguish *bike* from *bicycle* or *boy* from *lad*.

iii. They should be equivalent in all their senses. In the case of a polysemous word, a total synonym should have exactly the same list of senses and should be equivalent in all of them. *Dark* is the synonym of *obscure* in one of its senses, but it could be a synonym of *sinister* in another one.

Synonymy can be a really useful way of relating words; it is the most typical relation we find when we want to know the meaning of a word (in dictionaries or thesauri). The lexical database *WordNet*, a very popular tool in computational linguistics and natural language processing, uses synonymy as the main type of organizational relation. WordNet groups nouns, verbs, adjectives and adverbs into sets of synonyms (called *synsets* in their system; currently they have more than 100,000 of them). WordNet also uses other types of relations, such as antonymy, hyponymy and meronymy, which we are about to review in the following sections.

5.3.2 Antonymy

Antonymy is much more complicated than synonymy. Antonymy is part of a wider family of relations, that of **opposites**. Opposites are words that are similar in most respects, but differ in just one respect, which makes them contrast with each other. This is a tricky issue, because, as we mentioned before, words can have an infinite number of features; so choosing which of the feature(s) of two items stand in opposition to each other can be complicated. **Antonyms** are a more specific version of this opposition, and establish a 'binary' relation between two words, which in this way become associated by a clear contrast in their meaning. Probably that is the reason why antonymy does not apply equally to all types of words; it functions especially well with adjectives, which are somehow simpler than other words, since they tend to describe *one* specific attribute or aspect of an item. Paradis and Willners (2007) found antonymic relations in 59% of adjectives, 19% in nouns, 13% in verbs and 9% in the rest. Thus, it is adjective meaning that is mainly organized by means of antonymic oppositions; adjectives are the antonyms *par excellence*. Nouns, on the other hand, are typically more complex, and thus it is not so easy to find the antonymic pair of all nouns. We do find cases, of course (e.g., *victory–defeat, advantage–disadvantage, pessimism–optimism*), but in many cases, it is not so easy. For example, what would be the antonyms of *ostrich, window* or *book*?

Antonymic links have a very important role in structuring the lexicon; they tend to elicit higher priming effects than synonyms, for example. Acquisition studies have also shown that antonymy is also one of the first lexical-semantic relations acquired by children, and some authors consider antonymic links a reflection of our 'universal dichotomizing tendency' (Lyons, 1977).

Antonyms present the same problem we found in polysemy: it is not clear whether the relation is stored in memory (perhaps at a more formal, purely lexical level) or the opposition arises contextually from specific instances of discourse use, at a conceptual level. As we saw at the beginning of this chapter with our *owl* vs. *lark* example, it is sometimes context that makes us construe two meanings as representing two sides of a given dimension of meaning, but that is not always the case. Luckily both options, fixed/stored vs. dynamically/contextually construed antonymy can be attended by introducing the notion of *canonicity*.

Canonical antonyms are those antonymic pairs whose association has become maximally conventional and entrenched; they are therefore stored in that dual configuration in our minds. In word association tests, one member of the pair automatically elicits the other, and they prime each other strongly. Some examples of canonical antonyms would be *slow–fast, light–dark, weak–strong, small–large, narrow–wide* or *bad–good*.

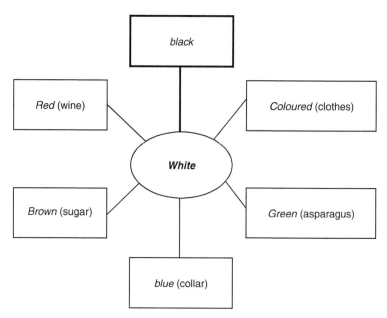

Figure 5.5 Different Colour Antonyms of *White*

Non-canonical antonyms are words that are construed as opposed to each other in a context-dependent way. So for example, the canonical antonym of *white* is *black*. But if we are talking about wine, *white* contrasts with *red*; if we are talking about types of asparagus, *white* contrasts with *green*; if we are talking about sugar, *white* contrasts with *brown* and if we are classifying clothes for the washing machine, *white* would contrast with *coloured*; the alternative to *white collar* is *blue collar* (Figure 5.5). More cases could be added to this list: e.g., the *white* vs. *yolk* contrast, when talking about eggs; or just think about the possible antonyms in cases like *white Christmas, white lie* or *white hair*.

This can explain why in one experiment (Paradis *et al.*, 2009), the word *calm* elicited up to twenty-nine different antonymic pairs from fifty participants. This dynamic establishment of antonymic opposition is sometimes 'triggered' by a number of grammatical constructions: when you use the construction [Both X and Y] you are inviting the hearer to construe X and Y in a contrasting way; the same would go for [Either X or Y], [Neither X nor Y], [Whether X or Y], etc. (For more options, see Jones, 2002.)

Beyond this entrenched-vs.-dynamic distinction, antonyms can also be classified using other criteria. For example, depending on the type of opposition that they establish, the following categories are often mentioned:

(A) **Gradable antonyms.** The most natural class; in this type of antonymy, we find adjectives that point to a scale that can have many different intermediate values; thus, these antonyms allow the use of comparative morphemes like -er, or -est. For example, *hot–cold* (e.g., *this is hotter/colder than that*). They are not absolute measures, but relative to a norm or scale. To put it another way, how big is *big*? *A big mouse* is smaller than *a small elephant*, and *a small galaxy* is bigger than *a big planet*. So, both *big* and *small* must be interpreted as 'of bigger/smaller size than the normal size of X'.

Another aspect of gradable antonyms is that one term of the pair is more 'neutral' than the other one; that is, one of them is **unmarked**, while the other is **marked**. For example, look at these two sentences in (3):

(3)   a. *How old is your sister?*
     b. *How young is your sister?*

In one case (3a), you are not implying anything special with your question; it is a neutral one; this indicates that *old* is the unmarked term. In (3b), however, the speaker is implying that the sister is young, which tells us that this member of the pair is the marked one. The same happens with questions such as *how far/near is it?* Or *how tall/short are you?* In both cases, the first member is the unmarked one and the second the marked one.

(B) **Ungradable antonyms**. Also known as *complementaries* (Cruse, 1986), these function differently: they do not allow variations along a scale. They are antonyms like *dead–alive, odd–even* or *married–single*. They do not take comparatives (you normally do not say *she is less married than me*), or any other word that implies some gradation: ?*I am fairly married*, ?*He is rather single*, etc.

Also while you can say that something is *neither hot nor cold*, or *neither far nor near* (being gradable antonyms), you cannot easily say that someone is *neither married nor single*; a number cannot be *neither odd nor even*. Also, very big (gradable) sounds better than very dead (ungradable); the opposite happens with completely (completely full/?fat).

(C) **Converses**. Also known as **reciprocals**, these are relational terms such as *husband–wife, buy–sell* and *above–below*. These antonyms signal a relationship between two entities, and depending which side you want to highlight, you get one or the other. So the examples in (4a) and (4b) and in (5a) and (5b) point to the same type of relationship or the same type of event, but only from one of the perspectives of the two participants:

(4)   a. *Bill is Hilary's husband*
     b. *Hilary is Bill's wife*

(5)   a. *Tom sold his car to Jerry*
     b. *Jerry bought a car from Tom*

The presence of nouns and verbs in these antonyms is higher than in the previous two cases. To these three types, a fourth one can be added which is often also mentioned:

(D) **Reversives** (also known as **reverses**). They are words that describe a process of change between two states: they describe one direction or the other, e.g., *dress–undress, create–destroy, assemble–dismantle* or *tie–untie*.

In the case of non-canonical antonyms, establishing the type of antonymy can be a complicated business. The classification we have offered is not evenly distributed across the different types of words. The first two types (gradable vs. ungradable) are more naturally applied to adjectives, though not always: probably verbs like *love–hate* or nouns like *friend–enemy* could be seen as gradable antonyms, for example (we have phrases like '*best friend*', for example, that indicate gradation). The verbs *live–die* could also be seen as ungradable. Converse antonyms can be nouns, as shown above, or prepositions (e.g., *above–below*), while reversives seem more appropriate for verbs. There are nonetheless more sub-groups than we could mention, formed by smaller sub-sets of words: to give just one example, in the case of reversives, another sub-group can be easily formed with **motion antonyms** (e.g., *advance–retreat, ascend–descend, enter–exit, rise–fall, come–go, push–pull*). As normally happens, there is no single, universal way to classify language phenomena; it all depends on what you want to do with the classification (that is, what type of generalization you are aiming to capture).

5.3.3 Hyponymy and Hyperonymy: Basic-Level Categories

Yet another similarity-based relation is that of **hyponymy** (and its counterpart, **hyperonymy**). They are the prototypical *taxonomic* relations. The notion of taxonomy is related to one of our most important cognitive abilities: abstraction. Humans are able to conceptualize an entity or a situation at very different *levels of specificity*. An illustration of this observation can be found in the following examples:

(6) a. *Something happened.*
  b. *An animal did something to someone.*
  c. *A dog bit a man.*
  d. *My little Pekingese bit the mailman on the leg.*
  e. *My little, but ferocious, Pekingese, Fred, bit the frightened mailman on his right leg with his incredibly sharp teeth.*

Sentence (6a) describes the situation with about as much abstraction as possible: it simply states that there has been an event of some kind. Sentence

(6b) adds some information, but is still quite vague as to the specifics of what actually happened. Examples (6c) and (6d) describe the event with increasingly more detail about the participants and the event itself. Finally, sentence (6e) is the one that provides the most detailed description of the event. All of them, however, could be used for exactly the same event.

It is interesting to note that this capacity for abstraction at the sentence level also has a parallel in the lexical level. Consider the expressions listed in (7):

(7)   *Entity > organism > animal > mammal > dog > hound > beagle > Snoopy.*

In this taxonomic hierarchy, the degree of specificity becomes progressively greater as one reads from left to right. In this way, *entity* subsumes all the other items in (7), while *organism* englobes only *animal, mammal, dog,* etc. (that is, *entity* subsumes *organism* but *organism* does not include *entity*).

Directly related to these taxonomic hierarchies are the so-called **basic-level categories**. Based on evidence from her categorization studies, Rosch (e.g., Rosch and Mervis, 1975; Rosch *et al.*, 1976) argued that there is a level of abstraction that is special, because it is the level of conceptual organization at which we tend to operate with the most cognitive efficiency. Think about the three versions of the same warning in (8):

(8)   a. *Careful with that animal!*
       b. *Careful with that dog!*
       c. *Careful with that golden retriever!*

It is the middle one, (8b), that conveys the right level of information most effectively. Example (8a) is too general; it does not prepare you as accurately for a specific defensive action; other superordinate versions have the same problem (e.g. *careful with that mammal/entity/thing*). On the other hand, (8c) is a bit too specific; it does not add any useful information that is not already conveyed by (8b), besides being longer than (8b).

All the possible variations in specificity can be subsumed into three levels: **superordinate level, basic level** and **subordinate level**. Let us briefly review each in turn. **Superordinate** categories, such as VEHICLE or FURNITURE, group together members that are diverse, bearing little similarity to each other; it is thus harder to find a concrete attribute list common to all its members. The category ANIMAL, for example, includes elephants, mice, starfishes, whales and dragonflies, all very different from each other. This is a rather abstract level, which does not provide a specific gestalt for all its members. On the other hand, we have finer-grained knowledge about a **subordinate** category like HOUND or SPORTS CAR than we do about its basic-level counterpart. However, this comes at the price of being less efficient: people recognize subordinate categories less quickly than basic-level concepts. In English, it is very common to find subordinate categories expressed with compound words: *rocking chair, mountain bike* or *sports car* are examples of this.

The intermediate or **basic level**, finally, is the level at which we possess the greatest wealth of knowledge; most of the 'distinctive' features are found here. Naming a list of differences between a dog and a cow is easier than, for example, between a golden retriever and a German shepherd. This is the highest level of abstraction at which we can generate detailed lists of attributes. Apart from this difference in the storage of attributes, basic-level categories are also special for other reasons:

- Basic-level categories are acquired by children before the rest (cf. Mervis, 1987); they are also more frequently used by adults.
- Basic-level categories constitute the highest level of a given taxonomic hierarchy at which we can interact with physical referents using the same motor programs. For example, consider a taxonomic hierarchy such as:

(9) *(Piece of) furniture > table > coffee table.*

We have certain motor programs for a basic-level object (that is, we know how to interact motorically with it), such as a table or a chair, as well as for a subordinate object, such as a coffee table or rocking chair, but at the superordinate level we simply do not possess any specific motor program for all the objects that can be subsumed under *(piece of) furniture* (e.g., *bed, shelf, dresser, mirror, lamp*, etc.).

- Basic-level categories are the highest taxonomic level at which a single mental image could be associated with a concept category in its entirety. We can easily produce a generic mental image of a basic-level category, such as TREE, but we cannot do the same for its immediate superordinate, PLANT, as such an image would have to be of A TYPE OF PLANT. The same can be seen when comparing FURNITURE to TABLE, FRUIT to WATERMELON or VEHICLE to BICYCLE. This situation turns out to be even more pronounced at even higher superordinate levels, where it is very difficult to arrive at any particular image at all (for instance, what kind of image does one associate with *organism* or *entity*?).
- Also, in general, basic-level categories tend to have shorter names than words belonging to other categories. Thus, *chair* is shorter than both *furniture* or *rocking chair*.

Table 5.2 *Summary Table of the Characteristics of Basic-Level Categories*

- Their names are shorter
- Children learn them first
- They have a common gestalt
- We have a motor program for them
- Most of our knowledge is stored at this level
- They are identified faster than the other levels

The 'vertical' organization of categories has been given a specific term in semantic studies. We say that a word is a **hyponym** of another if it is a more specific term. That is, *dog* is a hyponym of *animal*. Its (less frequent) counterpart makes reference to the same relation but from the other point of view: **hyperonym** (and so, *animal* would be the hypernym of *dog*). You can think as hyponymy pointing upwards (from less to more general) and hyperonymy as pointing downwards (from more general to less general). So, what traditionally is known as hyponymy is just a manifestation of our ability to categorize at differing levels of abstraction (Figure 5.6).

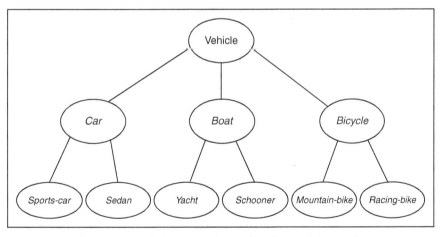

Figure 5.6 Lexical Taxonomies and Basic-Level Categories

5.3.4 Meronymy

Another semantic relation that is related to these relations we have been talking about in this section is that of **meronymy** (or **partonymy**). This distinction concerns the structure of things. We say that word X is a meronym of word Y if X is a part of Y. For example, *screen, keyboard* and *mouse* are meronyms of *computer*. Meronyms are one of the many possible part–whole relations. Cruse (1986) is one of the texts to look at if you want to know more about the different classifications you can make. In artificial intelligence and computational linguistic models, this relation is sometimes called HAS-A or PART-OF (while hyponymy would be IS-A). Another classic example of partonymy is body partonymy; clearly, our knowledge of the world often depends on this type of information. Doctors, for example, need to have a very clear idea of body partonymy (which bones are part of our wrist, for example); technicians need to know the partonymic structure of the objects they are working with (be it a computer, a car, a house, or a plane).

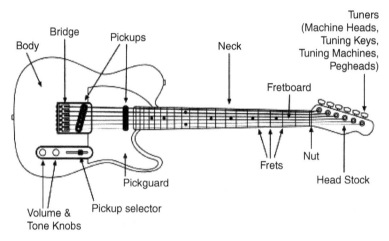

Figure 5.7 Different Meronyms of *Electric Guitar*

5.4 Association among Words

5.4.1 Collocations, Colligation, Semantic Preference and Semantic Prosody

As we have mentioned, two words can be related not just because their meaning is similar (as in synonymy or hyponymy) or opposite (as in antonymy), but because there is an association that arises from use (as we mentioned at the beginning, we are saving our discussion on thematic relations for Chapter 8). This is not discussed much in courses on semantics, though, because 'collocational' relationships are still not very well understood and lie half way between syntax and semantics (as a matter of fact, many authors would ascribe them more readily to syntax, which is probably the right thing to do in cases of 'pure' collocations). But we should be interested in these issues because of the intriguing idea, postulated by authors such as Sinclair (1996) or Stubbs (2001), that the real units of meaning to be found in language are not the isolated words, but rather certain combinations of words, extended units that go beyond the single, individual lexeme. This, as with many other cases we have seen throughout the book, is not a new idea: Gottlob Frege (who we saw as the logician who introduced the distinction between reference and sense in Chapter 4) already warned that 'a word has a meaning only in the context of a sentence, not in separation' (Frege, 1884: p. x).

In this view, meaning is normally 'spread out' over a number of different word-forms, typically found together in discourse and over which a number of common semantic features are distributed. This has been articulated in corpus linguistics by postulating a chain of four nested notions, in which the final two are especially important for semantics: **collocation, colligation, semantic preference** and **semantic prosody**. Let us start with a quick overview of collocations.

The most popular definition of **collocation** describes the phenomenon as *'the tendency of two (or more words) to appear together'*. This is a rather vague way to define a concept (a 'tendency'), but in all truth that is precisely what collocations are. That does not mean, however, that they are not real, or that their effects have no grammatical consequence. For example, you can say *turn off your thirst*, and people would normally understand you, but the most usual way is *quench your thirst*. We *grill meat* and *toast bread* but we do not toast meat. We say *fast food* and *quick meal*, not *quick food* or *fast meal*. As we saw, even very close synonyms normally have different collocational ranges. *Strong* and *powerful* are very similar in meaning, and can be interchanged in some contexts, but not in all, as we see in example (10):

(10) a. *strong/*powerful opinion*
      b. **strong/powerful tycoon*

The **collocational range** of a word is definitely an important fact that we store with words. Besides knowing the meaning of a word, we also know the contexts in which this word is normally used. Some words can collocate with almost anything (and we say they have a very wide collocational range). For example, the word *the* can collocate with any noun, etc. Some others have a very limited (or narrow) range. If we hear the sentence *he shrugged his ...*, we can guess that the next word is most probably going to be *shoulders* since there is nothing else you can shrug. Other examples of words with very narrow collocational ranges in English could be *blithering* and *excruciating*. Apart from their usefulness in distinguishing between near-synonyms, collocations are not very central in semantic research.

The next link in the chain is **colligation**. This term, introduced by the linguist Firth in the late 1950s, makes reference to the fact that some words show a certain preference (or avoidance) for certain grammatical categories. In a way, it could be defined as 'grammatical collocation'. Colligation is sometimes defined as the co-occurrence tendencies among word classes.

One interesting example is offered by Sinclair (1996): the phrase '*true feelings*' tends to colligate with a possessive adjective (e.g., *my/her/their true feelings*).

More interesting for our interests is the third link in the chain, **semantic preference**, which responds to a very commonsensical notion. Clearly, words are not combined at random: the meaning of a given word will make its combination with some 'compatible' words more probable than with others. This is what semantic preference attempts to capture. Hunston and Francis (2000: 137) state it in this way: 'A word may be said to have a particular semantic preference if it can be shown to co-occur typically with other words that belong to a particular semantic set'. An often-cited example is the case of the verb *break out*, which is usually combined with meanings such as diseases or conflicting situations: *war, disease* or *crisis*. A word such as *large* tends to appear together with words belonging to the area of 'quantities and sizes' (Stubbs, 2001).

An even more specialized notion is that of **semantic prosody**. This notion makes reference to the type of connotation that items combining with a given word share. The term has received beautiful, slightly poetic definitions in the literature; for example, Louw (1993: 157) defines it as 'a consistent aura of meaning with which a form is imbued by its collocates'; Partington (1998: 68) as 'the spreading of connotational coloring beyond single word boundaries'. That is, semantic prosody is linked to the probability that a word combines with others of a certain type, not just from a semantic field, but of a semantic connotation. This applies to words that seem to have neutral connotations, but nevertheless combine with words that *do* have a very clear positive or negative connotation. Such would be the case of the word *cause*, which does not have any special connotation (and can thus be said to be neutral), but nevertheless is most normally combined with negative nouns such as *harm, alarm, problems, trouble, distress, concerns, suffering* or *pain* (Stubbs, 1995). The study showed that 78% of the nouns combined with *cause* had negative connotations; 19% had neutral connotations and only 3% were positive. Normally, this type of information can only be detected using computational methods, by analysing the combinations of a word in a large corpus. Sometimes, this affects words that are quite close in meaning; *largely* combines with negative words, while *broadly* with positive ones. Many words can be categorized according to their semantic prosody: verbs with positive semantic prosody would be *accomplish, achieve, desire, congratulate, enjoy* and *respect*, while verbs with negative semantic prosody would be *commit, suffer, avoid, alleviate, complain, prevent, tolerate* or *minimize*; this also applies to adjectives: *impressive* collocates with positive nouns (*achievement, talent, research*) and *rife* with negative ones (*crime, misery, disease*);

adverbs with positive semantic prosody would be *perfectly, luckily* or *fortunately* while adverbs with negative semantic prosody would be *completely, utterly* or *totally*.

A recent development is the technology known as **sentiment analysis**. This is a computational tool that takes texts (from the Internet or the social media) and tries to extract from them the subjective feeling that users have about some object or event. For example, it will take all the comments that people write on Twitter or Facebook about a movie and will try to derive from them how the movie has been received by the public. Obviously, companies are quite interested in knowing how users feel about their products; this tool attempts to extract this information by using the connotations and semantic prosodies of the texts, trying to categorize the texts into favourable or unfavourable (or, as workers in this field call them, of positive, negative or neutral sentiment).

Table 5.3 *Definitions of Collocation, Colligation, Semantic Preference and Semantic Prosody*

- Collocation: co-occurrence relationship between a word and other individual words
- Colligation: co-occurrence relationship between a word or a word class and grammatical categories
- Semantic preference: relationship between a word and a semantic set of collocates
- Semantic prosody: connotative or affective meanings of a word with its typical collocates

---

5.4.2 How Combining Words Changes their Meaning

One of the problems of associating two words is that combining a word with another can greatly affect its meaning. For example, the meaning of *red* (that is, the hue it refers to) is different if we are talking about *red wine, red hair* or a *red lipstick*. In each case, we are invoking different shades of red; the shades invoked in each example are closer to purple (in the case of red wine) and orange (in red hair) than to red proper. Not to mention the political meaning of *red* that makes it equivalent to left-wing or its presence in idioms like *to be in the red* (which means to have no money), or *red tape* (official rules that seem unnecessary and delay results), *red herring*, etc.

There is even the case of words that have no meaning by themselves, and that can only appear as part of fixed, idiomatic expressions. Such is the case in English of *spick-and-span* (also written as *spic-and-span*). There is no such word as *spick* in English, but in combination with *and span*, the whole expression has a meaning ('spotlessly clean and neat'). On the other hand, sometimes there are word combinations in which one member of the pair does not add any factual information, but is just added for emphatic or stylistic purposes (cf. *to come full circle*, or *I completely forgot*), not to mention common redundant phrases such as *armed gunman, unexpected surprise* or *false pretense*.

5.4.3 The Many Problems of Combining Word Meanings

A slightly different but closely related problem is the following one: we have stated that very often words or expressions are ambiguous. But whenever we combine two words, the situation is even more dramatic. Think about the meaning of *red pencil*. Is the meaning of this expression clear and unambiguous? Well, we could be talking about a pencil that writes red (but has a blue cover), or a pencil that writes blue but has a red cover. In *red car*, we do not expect all the parts of the car to be red (engine, wheels, windshield and glasses, etc.), but only the external parts. Cases in which the variations are manifold are again very easy to find. The ways in which two words in a compound modify each other depend to a great extent on context, as the example in (11), mentioned in Aitchison (2012) and Sproat (1992), show:

(11)   a. *headache pill – fertility pill*
       b. *slug powder – talcum powder – face powder*
       c. *dog house – tree house – fire house*.

Roughly, a *headache pill* is supposed to get rid of your headache but a *fertility pill* does the opposite (aids fertility). *Slug powder* is powder to kill slugs; *talcum powder* is not powder to kill talcum, but powder made of talcum; and *face powder* is not powder to kill faces or made out of faces but powder to put on your face. Finally, *dog house* is a house for the dog to live in, a *tree house* is a house built on a tree (and not a house for the tree to live in), and a *fire house* is where the people that fight fires are located (and not a house for fire to live in or a house built on a fire). And it is easy to come up with many other examples like these; just think of *jail house, glass house, doll's house* or *beach house*. In each of them the relationship between both items is different.

The truth of the matter is that knowing what will happen when we combine the meaning of word A with the meaning of word B is very problematic: in language two and two are not always four. Meaning is only **weakly compositional**: quite often, the meaning of the whole cannot be fully recovered from the meaning of the parts. Remember the example we mentioned in the first chapter: in *blue eye*, we are referring to the iris; in *red eye*, we are referring to the white of the eye, the sclera – unless we are talking about photographs, in which case the red part is the pupil. Or we are talking about vampires or demons, in which case the red part is the iris. This could be seen as examples of 'emergent' meaning: meaning that is not explicitly mentioned in either of the individual members of the word combination. It is very easy to come up with more examples: in the embodiment literature, they have explained some of these cases as due to 'simulation' effects (remember Chapter 3): *lawn* elicits features like *green*, but *rolled-up lawn* elicits *roots* and dirt (because in the second case, those parts show up when you visually 'simulate' the phrase); for the same reasons, *watermelon* elicits green, but *half-watermelon* elicits *red* and *seeds*. The prototypical exemplars activated by each member of the combination can also be shifted: if you ask people to name a typical pet, they will answer *dog, cat* or *bird*; if you ask them to name a prototypical fish, they will say *trout, salmon* or *herring*. But if you ask them to name a *pet fish*, the answer will probably be a *goldfish*.

To conclude, think about the possible meanings of the expression *pumpkin bus*, which appeared as an example in Fillmore (1984). What could be the meaning of this expression? These are some possibilities (Figure 5.8):

   i.   An orange-coloured bus, like a pumpkin
  ii.   A bus in the shape of a pumpkin, like in the story of Cinderella
 iii.   A bus with pictures of pumpkins on its sides
  iv.   A bus that is carrying a load of pumpkins on its top
   v.   A bus that has driven over a bunch of pumpkins
  vi.   A bus that takes you to the pumpkin harvest field (vs. the tomato bus or the apple bus)
 vii.   A bus that takes you on a tourist trip to a pumpkin farm
viii.   The bus that takes a football team called 'The Pumpkins' to their field
  ix.   A bus that is normally driven by a guy called Fred Pumpkin
   x.   A 'campaign bus', serving as vehicle and centre of operations of the political candidate George Pumpkin

It seems clear that the number of cases in which this phrase could be used is limitless. This is a great thing for language users (since it makes language a wonderfully flexible tool) and a problematic thing for language analysts, who are hard-pressed to come up with a precise explanation of the scope and limits of such flexibility and adaptability. As we have mentioned, the final answer will have to go beyond the meanings of the words themselves, and include the knowledge and information that the participants in the communicative act bring to the task. We will talk a bit about these issues in Chapter 9.

Figure 5.8 Different Meanings of 'Pumpkin Bus'

5.5 **Chapter Summary**

In this chapter, we have taken a look at the different meaning relations. We have established a distinction between semantic relations, which link words that share some common meaning core, and associative relations, which are established between words that co-occur in discourse. We have also briefly introduced thematic relations, in which words that are part of a common scene establish an association between them (as in *hammer* and *nail*). We have reviewed the essential notion of polysemy (when a word has several distinct but related senses) as well as homonymy (two different words with the same form, each of them with meanings that do not have any relationship). Sometimes words extend their meanings in a systematic way, following a rule or pattern: this is the case of regular polysemy, which contrasts with irregular polysemy, in which the new meanings of a word are achieved by contextual adaptations.

In the second part of the chapter we examined similarity-based (i.e., semantic) relationships, starting with synonymy. We have seen how total synonymy is non-existent or very rare, given the many constraints that total synonyms should comply with; the most usual case is that of near-synonyms or partial synonyms. Antonymy is a more complex notion than synonymy, and probably even more basic in language. We have distinguished canonical antonyms (stored as conventional pairs) from non-canonical antonymy, in which it is the context that puts two given items in opposition. We have also distinguished several types of antonyms, namely, gradable and ungradable antonyms, converses and reversives; other types of antonymy (such as motion antonymy) have also been mentioned. The notion of basic-level categories, with their related superordinate and subordinate categories, was introduced in order to speak of taxonomic relations, especially hyponymy and hyperonymy. The last relationship in this block was meronymy, which relates a part to a whole.

The final section of the chapter was devoted to associative relations; we covered the corpus linguistic notions of collocation, colligation, semantic preference and semantic prosody. The last two are especially interesting for semantics, semantic preference being the tendency of the collocates of a word to belong to a given semantic set, and semantic prosody being more related to connotative meaning associations. We have even very briefly introduced the new computational tool of sentiment analysis, which tries to extract the impression of users about a product or an event from the polarity of the texts where they write about them. Finally, we discussed the complications that arise when we put two words together: the meanings of the individual words can be greatly altered, and then, the final meaning that is arrived at by combining the meanings of two words is especially difficult to predict accurately.

Exercises

Exercise 5.1   Are the meanings of the following list of words polysemous or homonymous?

expire	*old*	*horn*	*seal (animal vs. stamp)*
gay	*rock*	*bark (dog vs. tree)*	*file (archive vs. line vs. tool)*
light	*letter*	*step*	*row (of objects vs. boat activity)*

foot (of person vs. of page vs. measurement)

Exercise 5.2   Look for the meanings of these words in the dictionary; are the meanings polysemous or homonymous? If they are polysemous, how are they related?
table   ring   head   school   hand

Exercise 5.3   Read the following list of sentences; how many different senses of *over* would you establish?

    a. *The plane flew over the hill*
    b. *The lamp hangs over the table*
    c. *He lives over the hill*
    d. *The game is over*
    e. *To repair this will cost over 1,000 euros*
    f. *I heard them talking about it over the phone*
    g. *This was fun; let's do it all over again.*
    h. *I'm still getting over my divorce*
    i. *Kindness has a strange power over me*
    j. *There have been dramatic climate changes over the last few decades*
    k. *You must be over 18 to buy alcohol legally in most countries*
    l. *I prefer coffee over tea*

Exercise 5.4   As we mentioned in Chapter 1, derivational morphemes can be very polysemous; how many senses of -er can you find in the following list of words?

teacher	*baker*	*brewer*	*skyscraper*
toaster	*hairdryer*	*mixer*	*keeper*
eye-opener	*page-turner*	*doubledecker*	*stepper*
upper (pill)	*stroller*	*diner*	*New Yorker*
no-brainer	*cliffhanger*	*slipper*	*grasshopper*
weeper (movie)	*reader* (collection of readings)		

Exercise 5.5   Think of the following pairs of words; are they total or partial synonyms? In the case of partial synonyms, can you find what the differences are in meaning or in use?

    donkey/ass   shout/yell   near/close   sofa/couch   new/novel
    wealthy/rich wrong/incorrect mad/insane huge/enormous sick/ill

Exercise 5.6   Think of the following pairs of words; what type of antonyms are they?

arrive–depart	*bring–take*	*brother–sister*	*doctor–patient*
enter–exit	*fast–slow*	*fat–skinny*	*foolish–wise*
full–empty	*happy–sad*	*hard–soft*	*hired–fired*
identical–different	*lengthen–shorten*	*pack–unpack*	*parent–child*
pass–fail	*predator–prey*	*raise–lower*	*rise–fall*
servant–master	*single–married*	*teach–learn*	*tie–untie*

Exercise 5.7 Organize the following set in terms of hyponymy links (i.e., draw a taxonomic tree):

bird, insect, collie, animal, cocker, mammal, chihuahua, stork, dog, rabbit, fly, ant, bull-dog, eagle

Exercise 5.8 Organize the following list using meronymy links:
piston, engine, door, car, wheel, window, lock, valve, spark-plug

Exercise 5.9 Write a list of 'probable' collocations of these words:
_ harassment   _ treason   university _   drug _

Exercise 5.10 Think of four nouns and write them down twice in two columns. Now look for every possible combination. For how many of these combinations can you find some interpretation?

Exercise 5.11 Think of the meaning of the word *good* when it is combined with the following words: *teacher, student, gun, boy, baby, door, key, reason, dollar-bill, socialist, book, brick, sunset, time, person, month, name, look, chance, faith, afternoon*. What is the meaning of *good* then? What about the meaning of *dry* when it is combined with *season, mouth, martini, eye, sound, humour, cow* or *book?*

Key Terms Introduced in this Chapter
word association strength
priming
semantic relations
associative relations
thematic relations
polysemy
homonymy
regular and irregular polysemy
synonymy
total vs. near/partial synonyms
opposites
antonymy
canonical vs. non-canonical antonyms
types of antonyms (gradable, ungradable, converses, reversives, motion antonyms)
marked and unmarked
hyponymy
hyperonymy

basic-level categories
superordinate categorics
subordinate categories
meronymy/partonymy
collocation
collocational range
colligation
semantic preference
semantic prosody
sentiment analysis
weak compositionality

Further reading

Lyons (1977) and Cruse (1986) are two classic treatments of semantic relationships from a structuralist point of view. Murphy (2003) is a solid and up-to-date discussion of all the characteristics, problems and possible solutions in the study of semantic relations. Estes *et al.* (2011) is a good review of the concept of thematic relations and their many applications to language cognitive processing.

The conceptual approach to antonymy has been especially developed by Carita Paradis and colleagues (e.g., Paradis *et al.*, 2009). Ungerer and Schmid (2006) has a lengthy and clear discussion on the notions of superordinates, subordinates and basic-level categories and hyponymy and hyperonymy. A classic paper for the study of collocations is Sinclair (1996); the notions of semantic preference and semantic prosody can be seen in their slightly different views in Hunston and Francis (2000), Louw (1993), Partington (1998) and Stubbs (2001).

CHAPTER 6

Acquisition of Meaning and Cross-Linguistic Meaning

In this chapter ...

In this chapter, we look at how children acquire the meaning of words; after explaining the difficulties that children face when trying to learn the meaning of an unknown word, we review the ways in which the problem of word learning can be solved. We take into account the knowledge that children bring to the task (their knowledge and expectations about the structure of the world), their abilities to infer the communicative intention of the speaker and certain facilitative strategies which help acquire word meanings more efficiently once language acquisition has started (especially the role of syntax in constraining the possible meanings of words). We will also look at the relationships between cognitive development and language acquisition, to see how they influence each other. In the second part of the chapter we focus once more on the relationship between meaning and thought, trying to ascertain whether speaking a different language may have an impact on our cognitive processes. We shall see how this idea, which has been rejected outright for a long time, enjoys today a different status, even if the issue is not resolved yet.

6.1 Acquisition of Word Meaning

> Two and three year old children have poor motor control and bad manners; they are unreflective artists and inept dance partners. However, they're strikingly good at learning the meaning of words (Bloom, 2000: 1).

How do children acquire the meaning of words? This was one of the first questions about meaning that we included in our first chapter. This topic is important for many reasons: for example, a close examination of how children learn linguistic signs may help us achieve a more adequate idea of the true nature of language and meaning. One of the aspects that have attracted more attention is which cognitive capacities children must possess in order to acquire language. A second, closely related question is whether these capacities stem from innate, language-related mechanisms that children bring to the task, or whether meaning can be acquired using mechanisms which are used in other areas of cognition, different from language. In this sense, while there is considerable disagreement regarding the role of innate knowledge in other facets of language like syntax or morphology, the vast majority of scholars seem to agree that there are no innate constraints on word learning, and that most of the mechanisms that children use to arrive at the meaning of words are not domain-specific, that is, they are not special to this type of acquisition. The specific links between sounds and meanings have to be established on the basis of experience: babies have to learn that cats are called *cats* or that eating is called *eating* using the same mechanisms they use to learn other types of knowledge.

Another agreed-upon fact is that children are remarkably efficient word learners, as the quotation at the beginning of this section aptly indicates. Children start to use their first words by 12 months, and in the following years, they keep on learning new words at an increasing speed; by age 6, their vocabulary may exceed 10,000 words. This means that children learn between seven to nine words per day: just imagine having to learn that many phone numbers! Some scholars speak of a process called 'fast mapping': the ability to learn the meaning of a word from a single occasion, which is carried out with just 'minimal cues'. Many experiments have tested these processes; in one of them (Markson and Bloom, 1997), children were playing a game with several new objects. At one point, the experimenter introduced a new word just in passing ('Let's use the *koba* to measure this . . . we can put the *koba* away now'). The word was not mentioned again during the experiment, but a month later, children remembered correctly the name of the object. They also compared the memory of children for this new word and for an equivalent fact ('let's use *the thing that my uncle gave me*'). After a month, they remembered equally well which object the experimenter was referring to. This was taken as a proof that our memory for words is not special: our memory for facts works at the same level. Incidentally, adults did as well as 3-year-olds on this task; this is something to be highlighted, since children are better at learning phonology, morphology or syntax than adults. This could thus point at the possibility that there is a difference between word learning and other areas of language.

6.2 Gavagai: the Problem of Word Learning

Learning the correct meaning of a word is not as straightforward as it may seem at first, though; it is not equivalent to learning just any other fact. The philosopher **W. V. O. Quine** showed the deep complexity of the problem of meaning acquisition by proposing the following thought experiment. Imagine a linguist who is trying to learn a foreign language. This linguist is talking to a native speaker of the language, and in the middle of the conversation a rabbit suddenly scurries by, and the native shouts: '*Gavagai!*'. What should the linguist think that '*gavagai*' means? Well, our first option would be to think that it means 'rabbit', but thinking a bit harder, an almost unlimited number of alternative meanings can be found for this new word. It could refer to rabbits, but it could also refer to that concrete rabbit, which happens to be the pet of the native speaker; or perhaps it means just 'animal' or 'noise'. Or perhaps, 'I'm hungry' or 'Look! Dinner! Let's go hunting!' Then, other bizarre but equally possible (at least, logically) alternatives could be thought of: this word could refer to only the outer part of the rabbit, or to the way the rabbit runs, or perhaps it refers only to 'fast-moving rabbits'. It could also name the colour of the rabbit, or could be an expression of surprise or annoyance ('Hey! Another rabbit!'); it could be the word one uses in that culture when you want to shoo rabbits away. It could even be unrelated to the rabbit event, and be an expression meaning something like 'I'm tired of trying to teach you language; let's call it a day'. The linguist could probably leave out some of these possibilities by further questioning the native speaker, but some others are not so easy to dismiss without knowing the language in depth. It would seem that guessing the correct meaning of a new word, even one heard in a real-world context, is not such a trivial task after all.

6.3 How the Problem is Solved

We know that children *do* solve these problems of reference and generalization, since, after all, they finally learn the correct meaning of words. There have been different proposals on exactly how they do this. Over the years, many different constraints, biases and abilities have been proposed that may guide children when guessing the meaning of a word. Most of them appeal to general capacities used in non-linguistic realms. For example, scholars often mention the conceptual knowledge that children may have about the world; in some cases, this may take the form of innate constraints guiding their attention to some specific aspects of the world (e.g., a certain preferential attraction to 'whole objects', which influences their initial hypotheses). Another factor that is mentioned is their knowledge of social situations, which provides expectations about what will happen next. Most crucially, children also have abilities that allow them to infer the (communicative) intentions of others; this is a factor that allows the reconciliation of the cognitive and the social aspects of language. Nowadays, the importance of social interaction in the language acquisition process is hardly disputed. Finally, there are certain strategies that are used once language has taken off; e.g., children can use their (partial) linguistic knowledge to help them learn the meaning of words a bit faster. Let us try to see how some of these abilities and constraints interact and in which order.

6.3.1 Initial Preconditions

To begin with, there are certain **preconditions**: children must possess certain abilities before they actually start acquiring language. For example, they have to be able to identify what a word is; that is, they must have some speech segmentation skills. In natural speech, words are fused together and it is not easy to distinguish how many words there are in an utterance. Children solve this problem using their **statistical learning abilities** (Lany and Saffran, 2013). These abilities are crucial not only for segmenting speech into the relevant units (i.e., isolating words from speech), but for many other (linguistic and non-linguistic) tasks such as identifying the correct repertoire of phonemes in their languages and their most typical combinations (*phonotactics*), or to keep track of word co-occurrences (which form the basis of grammatical rules). Children are statistically sensitive to many other sequential regularities; for example, they are able to learn the order of the different sub-components of events (which are the basis of complex structures such as schemas or scripts).

As we mentioned before, scholars mention some **biases** in how we attend to the world (Markman, 1991). One of the most often invoked is the **whole object bias**: objects are very salient in real life (since, for example, they are quite easy to identify), and this could explain why our first guess when establishing the meaning of a word is that it corresponds to a whole object, and not to a part of it, or to the material it is made of. This explains why it is easier to learn *table* than *wood*. It also explains why *water* should be easier to learn than *wood*: normally, we find wood as material for concrete objects. In those cases the object itself becomes a distractor that attracts our attention (which is not the case of *water*: it is not so easy to think of objects *made* of water). Murray and Trevarthen (1985) argued that children also possess some type of innate 'protoknowledge' of **dialogic interactions** with adults. They confronted 2-month-old infants with a TV-screen where they could see their mother interacting with them in real-time, or, alternatively, a TV-screen where they saw a recording of their mother interacting with them on a previous occasion. In this second case, infants quickly became aware of the lack of contingency between their mothers reactions and theirs (and thus became restless much sooner).

Finally, the notion of embodiment also seems to play a role in explaining how children acquire some meanings. For example, there is research that shows that babies cannot recognize causation before the age of 6 months. Apparently, it is only when they have acquired the ability to experiment physically with the world, grabbing and dropping things, that they are able to form the abstract notion of causation. An experiment by Rakison and Krogh (2012) showed this to be the case: 4½-month-olds were able to recognize causative events after wearing Velcro 'sticky' mittens, which allowed them to 'grab' objects and move them around.

6.3.2 Joint Attention

Word learning starts in earnest between 10 and 12 months of age, so some special ability must emerge by that time that allows children to learn words precisely at that developmental stage. One of the main proposals is that children suddenly acquire attention-sharing abilities (Tomasello, 2003). For example, they learn to follow the gaze of others and identify what they are looking at; they can identify what you are pointing at and also learn to point at the things that they want you to pay attention to. In this way, they are able to select the elements in a scene that are important for the interaction with adults. In other words, they acquire the ability to establish **joint attentional frames**; they become aware of when their attention and the adult's are simultaneously focused on the same thing. This joint attentional frame sets up an initial '**common ground**' between adult and child that is absolutely basic in the establishment of meaning: only elements within the **joint attentional frame** will be considered relevant for the communicative event: other items outside this space will not be attended to.

Baldwin (1991) showed in an experiment how 18-month-old children use the direction of gaze to establish the meaning of a new word. In this study, children learned the label for an object when the relevant word was uttered while both the child and the experimenter were attending to the object, or alternatively, when only the experimenter was looking at the object but the child was subsequently able to trace the gaze of the experimenter. When the word was uttered while the attention of both of them was on something else, the label was not learned. Eye-gaze is used in other cases in language comprehension: Ibbotson *et al.* (2013) have shown how 3-year-olds (and adults!) use the active–passive alternation in a way that is consistent with the eye-gaze of the speaker (Ibbotson *et al.* 2013). There are other multimodal clues that can also contribute to the establishment of reference, such as body posture, gesture, facial expression or intonation (we will see some of these in the next section). Many scholars have suggested that the problems that autistic children have with joint attention is in all probability one of the reasons for their language learning problems.

6.3.3 Intention Reading

Once a joint attentional frame has been established and adult and child are both paying attention to the same things, children can invoke their knowledge of social activities and their intention-reading skills to successfully guess the communicative intention of their interlocutor. From a very young age, children and adults engage in repeated routines that follow roughly the same sequence of actions (and as we mentioned in the previous paragraph, children are very good at learning sequences of items): the bath routine, the diaper change routine, the eating routine, going out to the park, visiting grandparents, as well as all sorts of games. They all form structured interactive schemes that have some sort of repetitive structure. They provide the child with rich expectations about what will happen next; knowing these routines entails knowing about the expected goals, purposes and outcomes. Children thus learn these routines and participate with adults in these activities, paying attention to the same aspects. It is within this initial 'common ground', formed by these joint attentional frames embedded in structured social interactions, that they are first able to infer the specific communicative intentions of the adults. Children are probably guided by some 'relevance assumption' (Sperber and Wilson, 1995): they should assume that the vocal noise that the adult is producing is somehow related and 'relevant' to the situation at hand (we will discuss Relevance theory in some more detail in Chapter 9).

The ability of children to infer the intentions of others is considered to be the most important mechanism in establishing word meaning. It is based on the recognition that the other people are sentient beings, with goals, desires and beliefs similar to theirs; this ability receives the name of **theory of mind**. As we have seen, children use their theory of mind capacities to infer the communicative intention of other people when they are learning words: they will assume that a word refers to a given object if and only if there is evidence that the speaker intended to refer to that object; as we mentioned earlier, they are very good at finding out the speaker's intention, from quite different multimodal cues.

For example, one study tested babies in a context in which they were given one object to play with, while a different object was put into a bucket that was in front of the experimenter. When the baby was looking at the object in front of her, the experimenter looked at the object in the bucket and said a new word ('It's a *modi!*'). 18-month-olds looked at the experimenter and redirected their attention to what the experimenter was looking at, in this case, at the object in the bucket. And when later shown the two objects and asked to 'find the modi', children assumed that the word referred to the object the experimenter was looking at when she said the word – not the object that the child herself was looking at. There are lots of examples of these sophisticated intention-reading abilities: an experimenter is playing with a child and her mother with two different unnamed objects. After a short while, the mother leaves the room for a moment and while she is away, a third object is introduced. When she comes back and says 'Hey, look! A modi!', the child automatically assigns this new word to the new object (because her mother would not show surprise with the two other objects they had been playing with). 24-month-olds pick up intentions even quicker: in another study, an adult announced her intention to find an object – 'Let's find the toma!' – and then picked up and non-verbally rejected (by frowning) two other objects before picking up a third object and smiling. Despite the temporal gap, children inferred that this third object was what *toma* referred to. In another study, an adult used a novel verb to declare her intention to perform an action (e.g., 'I am going to *blork!*'), proceeded to do an action 'accidentally' (saying *Whoops!*) and then performed another action, with satisfaction (saying *There!* with a pleased expression). Children connected the verb with the action the speaker seemed satisfied with, not the accidental one.

Finally, it should be noted that it is not enough to identify the intention of the speaker, but his/her intention *when using a word*. Chen and Waxman (2013) tried to have 14-month-olds imitate a novel action (turning a light off with the head): only when a relevant word was used ('I'm going to *blick* the light') did children imitate the behaviour; other prompts ('Look at this!'; 'Look at what I'm doing') did not prompt the desired imitative behaviour. Their conclusion was that 'infants gain insight into the intentions of others by considering not only what we do, but also what we say' (Chen and Waxman, 2013: 1).

6.3.4 Emergence of the Linguistic Sign

Once the child has identified the main goal of a word, which is to call her attention to a given object or event, she can use it herself by reversing its structure: she can produce a word that will in turn manipulate the attention of the addressee and make him or her attend to the object or event of interest to the child. Once this operation is in place, a linguistic sign can be said to have been established. The linguistic sign is thus triadic: its complete use involves a speaker, a listener and an external entity (Figure 6.1).

Figure 6.1 The Bi-Directional Triadic Linguistic Sign: Speaker, Hearer and External Entity

Thus, in this view, language becomes symbolic once the child recognizes that a word is taken to mean something like *[I intend that [you share attention with me to [X]]]*. Words are then devices to direct and share someone's attention based on our Theory of Mind abilities (see Figure 6.1). The use of symbols is thus a social activity, involving an agent who wishes to communicate something to someone, and a receiver who recognizes that intention to communicate. All that we have said so far explains why the Gavagai problem is not really a useful way of thinking about the problem of word learning: in a communicative event, speaker and hearer are participating in a specific joint activity, and there are social expectations that guide the interpretations of what is said.

More strategies can be added to these; in Figure 6.2, we see how a child can compare two joint-attentional frames in order to find the cross-situational commonalities which associate a given word to a given referent.

Figure 6.2 Cross-Situational Regularities in Two Joint Attentional Frames (adapted from Ibbotson, 2013)

6.3.5 Catalysts

Once children have started learning language, there are certain strategies that can be used to accelerate the process, hence our term 'catalysts'. At first, children follow the strategy known as **lexical contrast**: once they have associated a given meaning with a specific word, their initial guess is that any other word must have (at least a slightly) different meaning (since that meaning, is, so to speak, 'taken'). Again, there are two possible explanations for this strategy. The first one is that this is a specifically *linguistic* strategy, which says that words cannot be complete synonyms (we talked about the difficulty of finding perfect synonyms in Chapter 5). Alternatively, this could be a *pragmatic* strategy based on children's understanding of the communicative intentions of the speaker, i.e., on their theory of mind. The idea is that, if a child is shown two objects, one of which she knows the name of, say, a cup, and another one which is unknown, and she is asked 'Give me the *dax*', she will assign this new word to the unknown object. If she is using her theory of mind abilities, she will tend to think that if the speaker has chosen not to use the word that both have in common (*cup*) and has decided to use a new one, it's because he/she intends to focus on the new object (in other words, 'If he wanted me to select the cup, he would have used the word that both of us know, *cup*'). In this second interpretation of the strategy of lexical contrast, children do not have any initial assumptions about words themselves, but are guided instead by what they believe to be the 'cooperative' rules that guide communication (we will have more to say about cooperation in the final chapter of this book, Chapter 9). This strategy can also be helpful for them to find the right level of generalization of a word. Children are known to struggle with these issues: sometimes they underextend words (using the word *doggie* only for their neighbour's dog) and sometimes they overextend them (applying the label *doggie* to all four-legged animals). Lexical contrast can be helpful in this regard; if on a given occasion we call a specific dog *poodle*, instead of *dog*, this word must have a different meaning.

Children also use their **conceptual knowledge of the world**. For example, when they are told that a given word corresponds to an animal, they will extend its meaning to other objects with the same *shape*; if they are told that it corresponds to a rock, they will extend it to other objects with the same *texture* or *colour*, even if they are a different shape (Keil, 1994); if they are told that the word corresponds to a man-made object, they will use *function* as the basis for extension (Gentner, 1978; Diesendruck *et al.*, 2003). In this way, children use their ontological knowledge about the world to select the attribute (shape, function, colour, texture, type of motion . . .) that should be selected as a basis for extending the meaning of a word to other possible members of the category.

Another strategy that is extremely helpful to increase the learning rate of word meanings is **syntactic bootstrapping**: the way the syntactic environment that a new word appears in constrains the hypothesis space. If you look at the examples in the first column of Table 6.1, you will see that the expected meanings are highly constrained by the syntactic environment in which they appear. Of course, the meaning of the rest of the words also helps: if someone tells you that when they

Table 6.1 *Different Examples of Syntactic Bootstrapping*

Syntactic Context	Expected Meaning
There's a glorp there	Individual member of a category
There're two glorps there	Several members of a category
Here! Have some glorp!	Substance, non-individuated stuff
Hey, look! Glorp has arrived!	One specific individual
I left the toy glorp the table	Spatial relationship
There's a glorp present waiting for you	Attribute of an object
Shush! Grandma is glorping!	Action that involves just one participant
Susan is glorping Helen	Action that involves two participants
Valerie glorped her suggestions to me	An event of sending or communicating

went to a party and they '*ate a lot of* borps', you might not know what borps are, but you know that it refers to some type of food. Thus, normally we find syntactic bootstrapping in combination with selectional restrictions and simulation of scenes.

There are still many questions that have to be answered with more precision, such as the different acquisition processes that may be in place for different types of words (concrete or abstract concepts; states, events, properties or relations). For example, the **whole object bias** can help explain the acquisition of certain words, most obviously object names, but its usefulness in explaining how we acquire words for actions or states (i.e., verbs) is not so clear. Actions and processes have many facets, and each of them can be the clue to their categorization: the manner of motion (as in *float*), the instrument used (e.g., *hammer*), the result (*to clean*), the action itself (*to wave*), whether the cause is included (*to kill*) or not (*to die*), etc. This rather thorny issue is sometimes called the 'packaging problem'.

A more complete and detailed picture of how we combine our different conceptual abilities (our categorization skills, our statistical learning capacities, our understanding of social situations and our theory-of-mind abilities) needs to be spelled out. But the idea that is emerging is that the combination of all these capacities will allow us to describe language meaning in a more complete way, taking into account both its cognitive and its social side.

6.4 Cognitive vs. Linguistic Development

One issue that has also created some controversy concerns the order which cognitive development and linguistic acquisition follow. Do children first develop concepts and once they have them in place, they learn a name for them (that is, learning to speak is learning labels for the things you already have in your mind) or is language somehow responsible for the formation of some concepts? The first option is quite commonsensical: we first establish the concept of 'chair' and then learn its correct name. Scholars such as Elizabeth Spelke argue that children are born with innate knowledge about certain specific domains (e.g., space, number or physics) and they draw on this knowledge in their word learning process. But the second option, that language guides conceptual development, is also possible, and in fact, there are many studies showing how word learning influences the conceptual organization of children. Again, this makes sense: as we saw in the previous chapter, words can be considered as 'invitations to form categories'

(Waxman and Markow, 1995), that is, a suggestion that we should focus on certain features of the members of the category, and disregard others (Waxman, 2004). The case of superordinates (which we covered in the last chapter) is specially relevant here: in order to form the category ANIMAL, FRUIT or FURNITURE, you have to skip over the many differences existing among the members of the category and focus only on the things they have in common. In those cases, it is probably the presence of a given word that makes children attend to certain features and disregard others and thus organize the world into the relevant conceptual categories. The agreement so far is that both processes go in tandem: in some cases, cognitive development takes the lead, with language following it, and sometimes it is language that guides the creation of the relevant cognitive categories. Cognition and language develop in close interaction in a cyclical fashion.

6.5 Linguistic Relativism: the Sapir-Whorf Hypothesis

In the previous chapter we saw how our conceptual system takes the different objects of the world and puts them together into groups called 'categories'. As we have just commented, quite often the formation of categories is guided by language; in many cases, it is the existence of a given word which makes us pay attention to the similarities existing among members of its category and the differences with items which lie outside its category (our recurrent idea of 'words as invitations to form categories'). Therefore, to the extent that the categories that we perceive and identify are a reflection of *linguistic* categories, it would follow that our languages make us see reality in a specific way. Our conceptual world is thus somehow shaped by the categories embedded in language, which, by making us perceive certain similarities and differences in the world while hiding others, may facilitate or hinder different mental processes. This is what the **Linguistic Relativity Hypothesis** (LRH) holds: that different languages with different categories will make us see the world in different ways and thus will have an influence on our reasoning. The LRH is also known as the **Sapir-Whorf hypothesis** due to its original proponents (though its roots can be traced back to the nineteenth century, in the writings of Wilhelm von Humboldt). These two scholars described language as a 'net' through which we perceive the world; words are the different 'holes' in the net, which segment the world in different ways. There is even the extreme possibility that some languages could provide thoughts that are not 'thinkable' in other languages. In the dystopian novel *1984* by George Orwell, a totalitarian government attempts to create 'Newspeak', a language which allows them to manipulate people's thinking by providing only the words conforming to the ruling party's ideals, thus making subversive thinking impossible.

The LRH has provoked many a controversy since it was first proposed at the beginning of the twentieth century. The famous quotation in which Whorf proposes the basic idea is this one:

> We cut nature up, organize it into concepts, and ascribe significances as we do, largely because we are parties to an agreement to organize it in this way – an agreement that holds throughout our speech community and is codified in the patterns of our language' (Whorf, 1940; in Carroll, 1956, pp. 213–14).

And not to leave Sapir out:

> Human beings ... are very much at the mercy of the particular language which has become the medium of expression for their society ... The fact of the matter is that the 'real world' is to a large extent unconsciously built upon the language habits of the group (Sapir, 1929; in Mandelbaum, 1958, p. 162).

Nowadays, scholars tend to distinguish two versions of this argument, depending on their strength:

- *Linguistic determinism*: language determines what we see and conceive, and therefore it is impossible to escape the mode of thought imposed by our language;
- *Linguistic relativism*: different languages favour different ways of seeing the world, though these ways are compatible and complementary: they just emphasize different features. Each language has to pay attention to the meanings that are grammatically coded in it.

These two options are sometimes known as the 'strong' and 'weak' version of the LRH. There are many examples that show how different languages focus on different aspects of reality:

- In Turkish you can't say *it rained last night*. There are two types of past, one for things you have seen personally and another for hearsay or inference (each type would have different grammatical marks) and you have to opt for one of them; you cannot just be neutral in this regard.
- In Navaho, you must pay attention to the shape of things (whether they are round, or long, etc.).
- In English, you must pay attention to whether somebody is alive or not. For example, if we compare the sentence *Cole Porter has written many songs* with the sentence *Taylor Swift has written many songs*, the second

sounds better, just because Taylor Swift is still alive and active, while Cole Porter is not.

- In Chinese the word *uncle* has to include information about whether he is a maternal or paternal uncle, or whether the relation is by blood or by marriage.
- In Spanish, you can't say *I went to the movies with a friend*; there are two options for *friend*, 'amigo' (male friend) and 'amiga' (female friend) and you must choose one of them; you can't ignore gender.
- In Russian, verbs must also include information about the gender of the subject, and also whether the event has been completed or is still in progress.
- In many IndoEuropean languages, you have to pay attention to the social relationship between speaker and hearer, and accordingly use a formal form of the second person pronoun, or an informal one (German *du–Sie*, French *tu–vous*, Italian, *tu–Lei*, Spanish *tú–Usted*); for all these examples, English can use *you*.

We can see, then, how the different grammatical systems of the different languages force us to pay attention to different aspects of the world. Different vocabularies correspond to different distinctions: speakers of different languages end up classifying the world differently, and it is this differential attention to world aspects that could in turn affect how they perceive the world, remember it or reason about it.

6.6 Initial Evidence against the LRH

Initial arguments in favour of the LRH did not resist close scrutiny or experimental verification. Perhaps the most (in)famous case is that of words for snow in Eskimo languages. Allegedly, there are lots of words for snow in these languages (snow recently fallen, hard, soft, in dust, etc.), which would make Eskimo speakers perceive different objects (different types of snow), where speakers of other languages would perceive just one (e.g., English or Spanish). However, some critics pointed out the existence of many different words for snow in Eskimo was actually a myth, and claimed that there are not so many words in Eskimo after all (though the debate still goes on, see Krupnik and Müller-Wille, 2010). And furthermore, there are lots of words for snow in English (e.g. *snow, sleet, slush, hail, hardpack, ice, icicle, pack, powder, snowflake*, etc.). Some scholars objected that the existence of many words in a given domain should not necessarily imply that thought in that given domain is affected.

The second argument in favour of the LRH involved words for colours. Colour categories do not exist out there in nature; what we find are just variations in the wavelength of light reflected on objects. Colour is therefore more of a continuum than a list of distinct categories. Now, each language divides that continuum into discrete sections in different ways. There are languages that establish only two distinctions, like Dani, a Papuan language, which only has two words for colours (roughly, dark and light), and languages such as English, which has around eleven basic chromatic terms. The categories established are also different: Russian or Italian have two different words for blue (*siniy* and *goluboy* and *blu* and *azzurro*, respectively, corresponding to dark blue and light blue) while Navaho or Welsh have only one word for green and blue; Ossetian has one word for light blue and green which also includes grey, and a separate word for a different type of green ('grass' green). All these variations found in the different languages of the world could make us think that, to a certain extent, colours are an example of 'reality' created by language.

However, this idea had to be abandoned in light of the experimental evidence gathered. If the LRH were correct, speakers of languages with different colour words should see and categorize coloured objects differently. However, several psycholinguistic experiments showed this was not the case: linguistic systems have no effect on colour perception or categorization. Also, the wild variations in the number of colour words are more principled than was thought at first. Berlin and Kay studied over ninety languages and found many regularities across them, thereby successfully disproving the idea that each language 'randomly' divides the colour spectrum. It seems that if a language has two words for colours, those two words will correspond (approximately) to black and white. When a language has three words for colours, they are black, white and red; languages with four words for colours add either green or yellow, and those with five words, green *and* yellow. It seems that just by looking at the number of words for colours, we can have a very approximate idea of which words they will be. The order of the first twelve colour categories is found in Table 6.2:

Table 6.2 *Order of Colour Categories in Languages*

white > black	red >	green > yellow	blue >	brown >	pink > orange	purple grey

The origin of these regularities can be found in the neurophysiology of the human perceptual system: there are three 'colour foci' which have direct neural codification, that is, we have specialized visual cells, physiologically identifiable, in an area of the brain called the lateral geniculate nucleus, which become active for each of these hues. The rest of the colours can be arrived at from combinations of the activations of these cells, together with other visual cells that are sensitive to the black and white distinction. In conclusion, it became clear that what guides colour perception is not language, but the human perceptual apparatus.

6.7 The Return of the LRH

For a long time, attempts to find Whorfian effects in language (i.e., cases in which language affects cognitive processing) were unsuccessful, and it was found that separating language from cognitive effects is a trickier business than it might at first seem. This situation may also have been due to the initial assumption that these effects would not be found. For a long time, the main opponents of the LRH have been generativists (cf. Pinker in *The Language Instinct*), who propose a universalist view of language deemed incompatible with linguistic relativism, and so the theory was rejected outright. However, there has recently been a renewed interest in the LRH, due to the growing empirical evidence that seems to point towards some linguistic effects on thought. Scholars such as John Lucy, Lera Boroditsky or Stephen Levinson are all firm supporters of the thesis that languages influence thought. These are some of the domains that have been investigated.

6.7.1 Colour

As we saw in the previous section, the colour spectrum can be segmented in different ways; for example, the English colour word *blue* corresponds in Russian to two different colours: *siniy* (dark blue) and *goluboy* (light blue). Winawer *et al.* (2007) conducted a number of experiments comparing the perception of different shades of blue by English and Russian speakers. In the experiment, subjects saw three blue-coloured squares forming a triangle; their task was to indicate which of the two bottom squares matched the colour of the top one. Researchers manipulated the colours of the squares so that there was a smooth transition between them, going from dark to light blue. For English speakers, all squares fell into the category *blue*; for Russian speakers, the first half were *siniy* and the rest were *goluboy*. Results showed that English speakers carried out the task at an equal speed throughout the selected colour spectrum; however, Russian speakers responded quicker when the two colours corresponded to two different labels in their language; that is, there was a categorical perception effect (just in the middle, between the frontiers of *siniy* and *goluboy*) that can only be explained by language differences.

Drivonikou *et al.* (2007) carried out a similar experiment; in their case, they showed their participants a circle formed by twelve coloured squares: eleven of them were exactly the same colour, and one was slightly different. Subjects had to say whether the different coloured square appeared on the right or on the left hand side. Again, subjects were quicker at distinguishing colours belonging to two different categories (eleven blue squares and one green one) than when they belonged to the same category (eleven blue squares and one slightly different blue square), even when the chromatic distance was the same. This experiment also showed some surprising results: the Whorfian effects appeared only on one side of their visual field, namely, the right visual field. This field is processed by the left-hemisphere, where most linguistic processing is carried out. This is what made these scholars say that only half of our brain is Whorfian (see also Regier and Kay, 2009).

Finally, another experiment by Tan *et al.* (2008) had people signal when two coloured squares were the same or different while they had an fMRI of their brains. There were two conditions: one in which they had to carry out the task with squares belonging to focal colours that had an easily accessible lexical label (e.g., red, blue and green), and another condition that involved colours which, although chromatically just as different, could not be mapped easily to a clear lexical label. When participants carried out the first task, for the easily named colours, the brain area responsible for word-finding became active (though they were not asked to name the colours, but only to press one button if they were the same and another if they were different). This means that perceiving a colour may involve the automatic activation of its name, something that obviously opens the door to Whorfian effects in this and other tasks.

6.7.2 Space

Languages of the world display great variability in how they structure space. To describe spatial locations, most languages (e.g., English) rely on *relative* spatial terms: they define the position of objects relative to one another or to the speaker (e.g., *right, left*). However, there are also *absolute reference* languages, which locate objects with respect to cardinal points (e.g., north, south). Levinson (1996) performed several experiments with speakers of two dialects of Tamil, rural and urban, which belong to these two different systems (absolute and relative, respectively). His results found different behaviour in different speakers in non-linguistic tasks.

For example, after looking at Table A (see Figure 6.3), subjects had to find the most 'similar' object in Table B, for which they had to make a 180-degree turn. What they chose depended on the language they spoke: speakers of the relative reference language chose the object which had the same position relative to themselves, the box in front of them (Box A in Figure 6.3); speakers of the absolute dialect chose the object which had the same absolute orienta-tion, say, on the north side of the table (Box B in Figure 6.3). The same results were found when transferring the solution to a maze from one table to the other. There were additional effects; for example, speakers of absolute lan-guages were found to be more aware of their orientation with respect to the cardinal points, a fact that has been confirmed in other experiments (e.g., Boroditsky and Gaby, 2010).

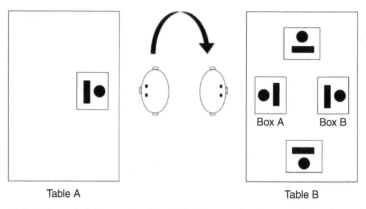

Table A   Table B

Figure 6.3 Using a Relative vs. an Absolute Frame of Reference in Levinson (1996)

6.7.3 Motion

According to psycholinguist Dan Slobin, when we talk about motion, the language we speak affects which elements of the motion scene we attend to. He had participants describe a story with twenty-four pictures with no words. He found that English children paid more attention to elements like the 'manner' of motion, and were more specific about the 'paths' that participants followed than speakers of languages such as Spanish or French. He showed how this is due to the linguistic characteristics of English and Spanish: English tends to conflate manner in motion verbs (so they express motion *and* manner at the same time: *walk, climb, slide, tip-toe, crawl*, etc.); Spanish tends to conflate direction/path in motion verbs: *subir* (go up), *bajar* (go down), *entrar* (go in), *salir* (go out) or *cruzar* (go across). Since English speakers have more verbs expressing manner, it is more natural for them to use one of these verbs, which makes them more attentive to manner information. These results have been replicated in dozens of languages: the results are pretty consistent and at least two types of languages can be identified (manner-conflating and path-conflating) which guide attention to different parts of a motion scene. It should be noted, though, that Slobin's Thinking for Speaking theory is only weakly Whorfian; he says that we attend differently to different elements of the motion scene only when we are about to describe it verbally.

Some experiments have explored a 'beyond Thinking for Speaking' effect: an effect of language on some non-linguistic task. One of these is described in Kersten *et al.* (2010), who had English and Spanish subjects look at a number of animated computer-generated animals. These animals had different shapes and colours, and could move around the screen following different paths, and with different manners of motion. When asked to sort the novel creatures into different categories using their manner of motion, English speakers were more efficient than Spanish speakers; when the sorting was based on path of motion, no difference of performance was found. This shows again how which type of language you speak can have an influence on a non-linguistic task.

6.7.4 Gender

Boroditsky and her colleagues studied the effect of grammatical gender on the way we think about inanimate objects (Boroditsky *et al.*, 2003). She compared Spanish and German, two languages with grammatical gender (which is different from biological gender; forks and frying pans have gender in both languages). The tests were conducted with German and Spanish L1 speakers but in a second language, English, which has no grammatical gender. She tested the effects of grammatical gender on:

(i) *Memory for objects*: she assigned proper names to a number of inanimate objects, e.g., an apple would be called 'Patrick', and participants had to memorize these names. Participants tended to remember better the cases in which the proper name coincided with the gender of the word in their native language (though the test was conducted in English). So German people remembered the name given to an apple better when it was masculine, e.g., Patrick (German *apfel* has masculine gender) and Spanish speakers when the name was feminine, e.g. Patricia (Spanish *manzana* has feminine gender).

(ii) *Object descriptions*: When given two photographs of words with different gender in Spanish and German (e.g., *bridge* and *key*), participants were asked to describe them using adjectives. The gender of the word in their native language again influenced the participants' choice of adjectives. Thus, German speakers described keys (which are masculine in German) as *hard, heavy, metal, serrated* and *useful*, while Spanish speakers, for whom keys are feminine in their native language, as *golden, intricate, little, lovely, shiny* and *tiny*. Also, German speakers described bridges (feminine in German) as *beautiful, elegant, fragile,*

159

pretty and *slender* and Spanish speakers (for which bridges are masculine) as *big, dangerous, long, strong* and *towering*. Further tests also discovered that grammatical gender had an effect on the way people remember things as well as in their judgment of picture similarities.

6.7.5 Tense

Boroditsky *et al.* (2002) tested whether the fact that Indonesian verbs have no tense could affect the classification of events or memory of events by Indonesian speakers as compared to English (which is a language that has tense). To clarify: you can express when something has happened in Indonesian; however, it is not grammatically compulsory to include this information along with a verb. For example, take a look at Figure 6.4, which shows three pictures of one person performing the same action at different temporal points:

Figure 6.4 Three Pictures of the Same Action at Three Moments in Time

In English, to describe these scenes, you would have to say, respectively *John is about to kick the ball, John is kicking the ball* and *John has just kicked the ball* (or some variant: in any case, you would have to include some sort of temporal description). In Indonesian, you could say '*John kick ball*' in the three cases (you could add, if you wanted, more precise temporal specifications, using lexical means, e.g., John kick ball before, John kick ball now, John kick ball after, but this is optional, not compulsory).

The idea of Boroditsky *et al.* (2002) was that if language has any influence on memory tasks, English speakers should be able to remember more correctly which version of a given event they had seen. And, sure enough, this was the case: English speakers were able to discriminate later which of the pictures they had seen better than Indonesian speakers, thus demonstrating the effect that having 'tense' in your language has on remembering certain things. Curiously, when Indonesian-English bilinguals were given the task, they performed differently depending on whether the experiment was conducted in English or in Indonesian, following the pattern of monolinguals.

Another test consisted of finding pairings between pictures. For example:

SAME TENSE. DIFFERENT ACTOR

DIFFERENT TENSE. SAME ACTOR

Figure 6.5 Finding the More Similar Picture in Indonesian and English Speakers

Both groups of subjects were given an initial picture (the one on the left in Figure 6.5) and were asked to find a similar picture. English people tended to choose as more similar the second picture in the top row (same tense, different actor); Indonesian speakers tended to view as more similar the second picture in the bottom row (different tense, same actor). So again, we find that a linguistic factor (whether your language has tense or not) affects cognitive processing (in this case, memory and categorization).

Finally, a more recent study by the economist Chen (2013) examined over seventy-five languages and classified them as *Strong Future Time* languages (in the case of those that must express tense grammatically, like English, Greek or Spanish and the other Romance languages) or *Weak Future Time* languages (in which the expression of tense is optional, like Indonesian or Chinese). After cancelling out all the parameters he could think of (such as level of education, level of income, religion, geographical area, etc.), he found that speaking one of these two types of language was the key factor that predicted how much those populations saved, and how much they prepared for the future (Weak Future language saved more and prepared better for the future). The idea is that languages that impose a grammatical marking on the future differentiate it more markedly from the present: this grammatical difference puts some type of 'psychological distance' between the future and the present times, which means that your actions in the present and its consequences in the future are distant and less directly related. On the other hand, for those languages that do not impose this distinction, the future and the present are perceived as much more similar and thus more interconnected (since they are the same thing). This is actually a much stronger (and thus probably more controversial) claim than others discussed in this section.

6.7.6 Time

Time is an abstract domain that is very often conceptualized in terms of other more simple domains (this is what **Conceptual Metaphor** is about, which we will examine in more detail in Chapter 7). In both English and Spanish (as in many other languages), time can be conceptualized with the help of the domain of space: we think of time in spatial terms, and thus speak of *long* days, a *short* time, or Monday *coming* before Tuesday. But besides space, there is also the possibility of speaking of time as quantity, and in fact, in languages such as Greek or Spanish, the most frequent metaphor involves quantity, and it is more normal to say *much time* (*mucho tiempo*) than *long time*.

To explore the effects of this TIME AS LENGTH vs. TIME AS QUANTITY difference, Casasanto and Boroditsky (2008) conducted an experiment in which English and Greek subjects watched lines growing on a computer screen. Lines could grow to different lengths and at different speeds; after each line had stopped growing, it disappeared from the screen, and participants had to reproduce with clicks of the mouse the length that the line had grown or the time that the line had been growing. The idea was that the perception of the time that lines had been growing would be affected by length in the case of English speakers, who use the *long/short time* metaphor. And this was indeed the case: when, in the same amount of time, one line had grown longer than another one (because it had been growing more quickly), English subjects tended to overestimate the time, because in English, it is difficult to conceive of time without thinking of distance (unconsciously making the transfer *long line = long time*, and *short line = short time*). Greek speakers, who do not have the TIME-AS-LENGTH metaphor, were not affected by the length of the lines in their time estimations. These researchers also performed a version of the task in which participants watched a basin being filled with dots at different speeds and again, they had to reproduce with clicks of the mouse the amount of time that the basin had been filling up. This time, Greek speakers were misled by the quantity effect: they overestimated the time the basin had been growing when it was fuller, and underestimated the time when it was less full. These effects were reverted when English subjects were taught to 'speak like the Greek', training them with made-up sentences that somehow imitated the Greek patterns, and that made them think of time in terms of quantity.

6.7.7 Agency

A number of studies have found language-based differences in the eye-witness memory of intentional or unintentional actions (e.g., English vs. Japanese speakers, Fausey *et al.*, 2010; or English vs. Spanish speakers, Fausey and Boroditsky, 2011). For example, Fausey and Boroditsky (2011) had English and Spanish speakers look at a number of videos that depicted intentional and accidental actions. Participants would see a video in which an actor purposefully spilled a glass of water, or another one in which the actor spilled the water accidentally. Now, the description of intentional actions is quite similar in both languages: both make use of 'agentive' language (e.g., *The guy broke the glass*). However, they differ in how they depict unintentional events. Spanish has a number of constructions that allow hiding the presence of the agent quite easily; thus, it is perfectly natural (much more so than in English) to say something like *se rompió el vaso* (approx. *the glass broke*). The experiment then had both groups of speakers look at a number of videos and later asked them about the actor involved in the action. English speakers remembered equally well actors of intentional and unintentional actions, but Spanish speakers could remember the actor of the unintentional actions less accurately.

Filipović (2013) is another study that compared the witness memory of speakers of different languages. Her study also compared the expression of causal intentionality in English and Spanish. Thus, while in English a sentence such as *she dropped the keys* is ambiguous with respect to intentionality (since it can have both an intentional and an accidental reading), in Spanish the difference in the expression of intentional vs. non-intentional actions is quite clear, since non-intentional actions are expressed with a different construction (*se le cayeron las llaves*; approx. 'the keys dropped to her'). In her experiments, she showed how this language-guided habit of distinguishing intentional from non-intentional readings favourably affected the witness memory of Spanish speakers as compared to English speakers when describing intentional actions. The lack of pressure of English speakers to express the causation component in a linguistically explicit way made them pay less attention to it and accordingly weakened their memory of it.

6.8 Within-Speaker Relativity Effects: the Case of Bilinguals and L2 Speakers

If speaking a different language affects mental processing in different tasks, what happens when the same person switches from one language to another? In other words, what happens with bilinguals? How are we affected when we switch from a first to a second language? The case of bilinguals has already been briefly examined here: in the Indonesian experiment with tense, bilingual Indonesians who took the test in Indonesian behaved as monolingual Indonesians did; however, when they took the test in English, they behaved like English speakers (and thus, their memory for the correct pictures was enhanced). This has been found in many experiments: depending on the language you use during the experiment, you will function like other speakers of that language.

Relativity effects have also been examined in the case of second language speakers. For example, Costa *et al.* (2014) found that when people are using a foreign language and they are faced with a moral dilemma, they are able to take less emotional and more rational decisions than when they are using their native language. These researchers presented participants from the United States, Korea, France, Spain and Israel with the following scenario: a trolley is about to kill five people and the only way to stop it and save them is to push a fat man off a bridge in front of the trolley. The more rational (or less emotional) decision would accept the sacrifice of one person in order to save five. Across all language groups, the number of participants who selected the 'utilitarian' decision increased when they were using a foreign language; they were less willing to sacrifice the man when they were using their native language. Researchers attributed this to the psychological distance imposed by the use of a foreign language: emotional effects are especially strong in your native language.

This has also been demonstrated in a different area: swearing in a second language is not half as effective as in your native language (Harris *et al.*, 2003). One study measured the skin conductance of participants in an experiment and discovered that their emotional response when swearing was much greater in their L1 than in their L2. That is probably the reason why when you hit your finger with a hammer, you tend to use your mother tongue to swear, no matter how proficient you are in a second language. Nonetheless, the lack of emotional response in a second language was found to be inversely correlated with language proficiency: as the proficiency level increased, the responses became more emotional and the choices tended towards the one that subjects made in their first language.

6.9 Within-Language Relativity Effects: the Case of 'Framing'

From everything we have said so far, it is clear that using a specific linguistic choice always imposes a given perspective on an object or an event. Our linguistic choices will shape the way we conceptualize a given situation, what is highlighted and what is kept in the background. The conscious use of language in order to present the perspective of the world most favourable to the speaker's goals has been studied for a long time (since Classic Rhetoricians). Nowadays, this sometimes receives the name of 'framing'. In a way, this type of effect could be considered an 'internal-language' relativity effect. For example, when talking about sensitive topics such as abortion, followers of a particular option may call themselves 'pro-life' (thus highlighting the role of the fetus) while those of a different option call themselves 'pro-choice' (thus highlighting women's right to choose).

Fausey and Boroditsky (2010) conducted a number of experiments that confirmed the all-important role of linguistic framing in the attribution of blame and financial liability. For example, participants read a story about an individual ('Mrs Smith'), who accidentally became involved in a restaurant fire. There were two versions of the story, which were identical except for the verbal frame used in the description of the accidental event: one used a transitive (and thus, agentive) frame: e.g., *Mrs Smith flopped the napkin on the centerpiece candle*. The other version used an intransitive (and thus, non-agentive) verbal frame: e.g., *Her napkin flopped on the centerpiece candle*. Participants who had been given the transitive version tended to

165

attribute more blame to Mrs Smith and also thought that she should be required to pay more money to the restaurant for damages. In another experiment in the series, participants watched a video: the well-known controversial incident which took place during the 2004 US Super Bowl finals, in which Justin Timberlake ripped the costume of Janet Jackson, exposing her bare breast. While they were watching the video, participants were provided with a verbal description that contained an agentive version of the incident (*he ripped the costume*) or a non-agentive one (*the costume ripped*). Though all participants watched the same video, participants who heard the transitive version tended to attribute more blame to Justin Timberlake and less to chance than those given the intransitive version. They also tended to think that the financial responsibility of Timberlake was higher. This experiment shows how the way in which we construe an event, and specifically, the attribution of blame, can be greatly influenced by the linguistic choices we make in its description, even in the case of eyewitnesses.

Linguistic framing can be established by a number of different mechanisms, from lexical choices, to grammatical choices or the use of different metaphors (we will look at examples of framing-by-metaphor in Chapter 7). In the lexical realm, there are mechanisms such as **euphemisms**. Euphemisms diminish the strong emotional connotations of the swear words they replace, and this has been demonstrated in galvanic skin-response experiments (e.g., Bowers and Pleydell-Pearce, 2011). Closely related to the notion of euphemism is the (ever-increasing) use of 'politically correct language'. The idea behind politically correct language is that we can use language to get rid of undesirable connotations, and in this way, try to shape how people think about issues such as race or gender; the existence of politically correct language shows that the general public does have a sense of the influence of language on how we conceptualize certain issues. In this way, instead of *policemen* or *firemen*, now we have *police officers* and *fire fighters*. On a more negative note, the 'establishment' also manipulates language in this way to decrease the negative impact of certain notions, which has made critics of this type of language consider it as a modern version of Orwell's Newspeak. Thus, when workers hear that managers are thinking about '*resizing the company*', they should get nervous, because that means that people will be fired. Ways to avoid saying the harsh phrase '*sacking people*' proliferate: *right-sizing, deselectment, deployment, destaffing, head-adjustment*, etc. Compare the connotations of '*you are fired*' with those of '*We have no option but to let you go*' or '*We are going to apply our labour force adjustment plan*' vs. '*We are going to fire people*'.

6.10 **Does Language Influence Thought?**

After all these recent experiments, it is quite clear that the Linguistic Relativity Hypothesis is in the spotlight again, and this time is being examined with methodological tools that are sounder, more sophisticated and more rigorous. Its effects are being investigated in first language users (as we have mainly seen here), and there are also quite interesting results in second language acquisition (see Bylund and Athanasopoulos, 2014, for a review). Overall, the results seem to reveal some Whorfian effects in language, though sceptics tend to disagree about the importance of these effects, which, while accepted by the academic community, are sometimes regarded as merely 'mild' effects of language on thought. The debate is still going on; for example, some authors claim that when you block access to language (in a carefully designed laboratory task), these non-linguistic effects disappear, a point which is then dismissed by some other authors with the argument that in real life, we just do not go around with access to language blocked, which undermines the relevance of such findings. At any case, the mere possibility that people who speak differently also think differently is interesting enough to warrant more research in the coming years.

6.11 **Chapter Summary**

In this chapter we have examined the ways in which children learn the meaning of words. We have reviewed the abilities that they bring to the task, especially their statistical-association abilities and their conceptual knowledge of the world, and have examined how the establishment of joint-attentional frames in highly structured social environments facilitates the identification of the communicative intention of the speaker. These intention-reading abilities are considered to be the most important factor in establishing language. Once language is in place, children can use strategies such as lexical contrast or syntactic bootstrapping to facilitate the further acquisition of words. We have also seen how cognitive development and language acquisition go hand in hand and mutually influence each other. In the second part of the chapter we examined the Linguistic Relativity Hypothesis, which proposes that different languages may facilitate or hinder certain cognitive processes in different tasks. We considered empirical results showing relativity effects in the domains of colour perception, space, motion, gender, agency, tense and time.

Exercises

Exercise 6.1 We have seen how syntactic information can be used to guess the meaning of words (syntactic bootstrapping). Now, selectional information and knowledge about social situations and expectancies can be just as helpful. Try to guess the selected words in each example. Why don't we have a 'gavagai' problem in these cases?

    a. *(Mother to teenager who goes on her own to her grandmother's)*
       Don't forget to *glorp* me as soon as you get there!

    b. What a waste of time! That movie was the biggest *glorp* I've ever seen!

    c. Are you serious? Did that really happen? I cannot *glorp* it; did she really tell you that?

    d. Take a jacket! It's really *glorp* out there today!

    e. *(Teacher to rowdy children in a classroom)*
       If you don't stop *glorping*, I'll have you sent to the principal!

    f. Johnny! *Glorp* to your room immediately! That's no way to behave!

    g. Please, madam, can I *glorp* another piece of cake? It's really delicious!

    h. I can't find my keys! I thought I'd left them *glorp* the table.

Exercise 6.2 Words like 'wanderlust', 'karoshi' or 'déjà vu' have no direct translation into English. Can you find a word in a language that you know that has no direct translation into English? What do you think that tells you about their cultures?

Exercise 6.3 Can you find options with more neutral connotations?
hunger   *death*   *jail*   *difficult*   *rape*
have sex   *genocide*   *abortion*   *pornographic*   *movies*

Exercise 6.4 Another group of words tries to get rid of gendered language, especially for jobs and occupations. Try to find the neutral version of this list of words:

    fireman   *policeman*   *stewardess*   *waitress*   *mailman*
    barmaid   *housemaid*   *foreman*   *spokesman*   *chairman*

Can you add more words to this list?

Key Terms Introduced in this Chapter

word acquisition
fast mapping
whole object bias
statistical learning abilities
joint-attentional frames
intention-reading abilities
theory of mind
triadic vision of the linguistic sign
lexical contrast
syntactic bootstrapping
linguistic relativity hypothesis
Sapir-Whorf Hypothesis
linguistic determinism
linguistic relativism
framing

Further reading

Bloom (2000) *How children learn the meaning of words* is one of the most popular books on language acquisition; most of the ideas in the chapter, though, have been taken from Tomasello's book *Constructing a language* (Tomasello, 2003), which is an articulate defence of the socio-pragmatic approach to language; the main ideas can also be found in Tomasello (2000). Elizabeth Spelke is the firmest supporter for innate knowledge systems in children (Spelke and Kinzler, 2007). Lany and Saffran (2013) is a thorough revision of the multiple applications of statistical learning abilities to different aspects of language, from phonotactics to word-co-ocurrences. As for the linguistic relativity hypothesis, a review can be found in Boroditsky (2011). For a radically dissenting view, see Pinker (1994), and a slightly mollified version in Pinker (2007). Filipović and Ibarretxe-Antuñano (2015) is a recent review of the wide literature on relativistic effects on motion. Aneta Pavlenko has written extensively on the topic of bilingualism and its effects on cognition (Pavlenko, 2002, 2005, 2011).

CHAPTER 7

Figurative Meaning

In this chapter . . .

In this chapter, we go beyond the literal meaning of words and examine figurative meaning. The cases in which language cannot be understood literally are incredibly abundant, and figurative mechanisms such as hyperbole, understatement, irony or tautology, to name a few, are extremely common. We will focus on two figurative mechanisms that have attracted a great deal of attention in the last decades: metaphor and metonymy. This chapter will introduce the main ideas behind Conceptual Metaphor Theory, which provides a tentative (though plausible) explanation for the extension of embodiment to abstract domains. We will take a look at the different types of metaphor, their behaviour and their possible origins. We will also review empirical work that has examined their conceptual nature. In the second part of the chapter, we will take a look at the important notion of conceptual metonymy, which is often explained along-side metaphor and is just as essential in any explanation of how meaning is constructed and communicated.

Metaphor and metonymy have proved very useful as commonsense explanatory mechanisms for many central topics in semantics. For example, they are among the main mechanisms that extend the meanings of words in a principled way; this chapter will look at their role in the establishment of regular polysemy patterns. The chapter closes with a critical evaluation of the theory.

7.1 Introduction: Literal vs. Figurative Language

Whenever we invoke notions such as 'figurative language', 'metaphor', 'metonymy' and the like, the first thing that comes to mind is literary language. Typical examples of metaphor are phrases like *your eyes are stars* or *your teeth are pearls*, a type of language that is associated with poetry, song lyrics or literature in general, and does not correspond to the way people normally speak. There is a very clear separation between what constitutes 'normal' (or literal) language and what is 'figurative' language. If somebody told you that *your teeth are pearls*, you would have to reject the initial, completely impossible literal interpretation, and would have to go on trying to construct another meaning, this time a non-literal, figurative one (probably something like 'your teeth are white and shiny').

For a long time, this was the way most people thought figurative language worked. However, in recent times this view has been challenged. To start with, everyday language is packed with expressions that cannot be taken literally:

- What would you think if a friend uttered the sentence *I'm dying for a beer*? Most probably, you would not take it literally (otherwise, you would have to take him/her to a doctor). Instead, you would understand that this is just a **hyperbolic** use of language, which merely puts a bit more emphasis on the person's desire to have a beer. The same can be applied to expressions like *Nobody understands me* (which would be literally true only if you tried to communicate in Swahili in a typical English city, for example), or others such as these: *I've told you a million times, He was boring me to death/tears, This guy cracks me up*, etc.
- Sometimes, we also say things such as *A promise is a promise*, or *Boys will be boys*, which are **tautological** and should make no sense, since you are just repeating the same thing twice. Still, people have no problem understanding these very common expressions and use them all the time (and there are many tautologies in colloquial English: *If we're late, we're late, We'll get there when we get there, A win is a win, The law is the law, A bet is a bet*, etc.).

- Sometimes we also use expressions such as *not bad* to mean *good*, *not unlike* to mean *like*, or *You are not wrong* to mean *You're right*; these are examples of **litotes** or **understatement.**

- We are also often 'ironic': an approximate definition of **irony** could be something like 'use of words that mean the opposite of their literal meaning'. Thus, if you arrive at the beach after a long trip and prepare everything for a picnic and suddenly it starts raining, a statement such as *Oh, great! Now it starts raining!* will normally be understood as the opposite of what you are actually saying: you do not think it is great; rather, the opposite is true.

- If you're angry at someone and say *You like being a fool, don't you?* you are not really asking that question: you are being **sarcastic**, which corresponds to an aggressive use of irony.

- If you hear that someone has *kicked the bucket*, you understand that the person is dead (and you expect no kicking and no bucket to be involved literally); that is what happens in most **idiomatic** uses of language. There is a huge number of idiomatic expressions that cannot be understood literally (e.g., there is no leg and there is no pulling in *pulling someone's leg*; nothing flies when something *flies in the face of* X; and there is no driving and no nuts in *it drives me nuts*).

- The same can be said about **proverbs**: the sentence *To kill two birds with one stone* involves no birds and no stones; instead it is interpreted metaphorically as solving two different problems with one single action.

- Even such common sentences as *Can you open the door?* cannot be understood literally: in this example, we ask somebody about his/her ability to do something in order to convey an order or petition in a more polite way. This is a special case of **indirect speech acts**; we can also express an order by making a statement, in order to avoid the harshness of an imperative: *Officers will wear evening dress* (we will deal with this topic in Chapter 9).

- A similar mechanism is found in **rhetorical questions**: when somebody asks you *Why don't you try the other key?*, you understand that they are not really asking you about your reasons not to try the other key, but actually suggesting that you use it.

It is thus clear that language is not understood 'literally' on countless occasions, and that figurative uses of language (Table 7.1) are extremely common and natural (leaving aside the fact that a strict distinction between literal and figurative language is much harder to establish than it seems at first). In any case, it has been successfully demonstrated that in most cases of figurative language, people process language just as quickly and with the same amount of effort as in more 'literal' cases (Gibbs, 1994; Glucksberg, 1998).

Table 7.1 *Some Examples of Figurative Language*

Understatement	*The house needs a touch of paint*
Hyperbole	*Nobody understands me*
Oxymoron	*True lies*
Idioms	*Let the cat out of the bag*
Irony	*And now it starts raining: great.*
Sarcasm	*You like to be a fool, don't you?*
Tautology	*Boys will be boys*
Proverbs	*Birds of a feather flock together*
Indirect speech acts	*Can you open the window?*

Finally, when you talk about a *big day*, the *big boss* or a *big decision*, you are not talking literally about size (e.g., you are not talking about a twenty-five-hour day or a very tall boss). Rather, you are talking about the relative importance of these items: if something is important, we say it is *big* (or sometimes *gigantic, enormous* or *monumental*), and if it is unimportant, we use *small*. These expressions, and many others, are usually offered as examples of **conceptual metaphors** (Lakoff and Johnson, 1980, 1999). These types of expressions are special because they have been the main focus of a concrete theory: Conceptual Metaphor Theory (CMT). CMT has been highly influential both in the field of language studies and in cognitive science at large. In linguistics, it has been able to explain a large number of grammatical and linguistic phenomena that could not be easily explained before (as we shall see when we review the role of metaphor in explaining regular polysemy patterns later on). At the same time, it is one of the main existing proposals in cognitive science aiming to solve the problem of the embodiment of abstract thought (as we saw in Chapter 3). In the following sections, we will look at the main tenets of this theory, some of its applications and some of the more common criticisms aimed at it.

7.2 What is a Conceptual Metaphor?

The first thing to say about conceptual metaphor is that it is *not* a linguistic phenomenon: rather, it is a *cognitive* phenomenon in which one semantic area or domain is represented conceptually with the help of another one. In this way, domains that are somehow more difficult to conceptualize because they are vague, lack inner structure or are only accessible through introspection (the paradigmatic case being abstract domains), are structured and understood with the help of another domain, typically more concrete and easier to conceptualize; in the paradigmatic case, a sensorimotor domain. The domain from which we take the information is called the SOURCE DOMAIN and the domain that is structured with this information is the TARGET DOMAIN; the usual convention is to write both domains with small caps and name their connection with the form TARGET DOMAIN IS SOURCE DOMAIN.

Take for example the case of AFFECTION; this is a domain that can be said to be abstract since we cannot perceive it visually, hear it, smell it or touch it with our fingers. In this case, we can use a domain that can be experienced directly through our senses, such as the domain of TEMPERATURE, as an aid for our mental work with the domain of AFFECTION. The result is the AFFECTION IS WARMTH metaphor, which motivates expressions such as *a warm welcome* or *a cold reception*. In this way, we can use the domain of temperature to structure the domain of affection and thereby talk and reason about it more easily. IMPORTANCE is another vague and subjective notion; in order to structure this domain and deal with it more easily, we can import information from the domain of PHYSICAL SIZE, in such a way that important things are conceptualized as big, and unimportant things as small. This gives rise to the IMPORTANT IS BIG metaphor, responsible for the linguistic expressions *big day/boss/decision*, mentioned above, among many other expressions, such as *It's a small issue* (or as Neil Armstrong famously said as he stepped onto the moon: *This is one small step for a man, one giant leap for mankind*). This is the basic idea behind conceptual metaphors: they allow us to reason more effectively about abstract domains which would otherwise be more complicated to deal with.

Most target domains can be structured by different source domains; in the same way that our conceptualization of an object can be altered when we classify it in different categories (remember our 'apple' example in Section 4.4.1 of Chapter 4), each metaphoric mapping will highlight certain parts of the target domain and conceal others. For example, we can conceptualize LOVE as a JOURNEY, but also as MADNESS, as A WAR, as MAGIC or as a PATIENT: each of these metaphors will allow us to see the target domain in a different way, alternatively highlighting its irrationality, its competitiveness, etc. In the same way, conceptualizing ANGER as a DANGEROUS ANIMAL emphasizes the violent and irrational aspects of the emotion, as a NATURAL FORCE the experiencer's inability to control the emotion, as AN ILLNESS, the harmful effects for the experiencer, as FIRE, the intensity of the emotion, and so on. It is easy then to see why metaphor has always been considered an important rhetorical device: it is a very effective 'framing' mechanism, as we mentioned in Section 6.9. Lakoff (1992) analysed the type of metaphors used in the public discourse of the American Government, showing how they had been carefully chosen with the purpose of justifying the first Gulf War. Also, Thibodeau and Boroditsky (2011) carried out an experiment that showed how activating the CRIME IS A BEAST or the CRIME IS A VIRUS metaphor in a text made people opt for more punitive or more social solutions to the problem of crime.

7.2.1 Metaphorical Expression vs. Conceptual Metaphor

As we have mentioned, the great difference with previous approaches to metaphor is that here, metaphor is not seen as something linguistic, but as mental. There is thus a distinction between **conceptual metaphor** and **metaphorical expression**. What we call a conceptual metaphor is the connection, established between two domains, which transfers information from one to the other. It is this mental schema or gestalt of both domains connected by a number of projections which globally receives the name of conceptual metaphor. Since we conceptualize one domain in terms of another, this will have a very definite influence on how we communicate information about it. In the cases in which communication is linguistic, we produce a number of different 'metaphorical expressions', all based on the same metaphor. For example, TIME is another abstract domain, which cannot be seen or touched. We therefore typically use other domains in order to conceptualize it. One of them is the domain of MONEY, a more tangible and concrete domain. Since we conceptualize TIME in terms of MONEY, we tend to speak about time (when we are using this metaphor, at least) with expressions that we normally use to talk about money, as can be seen in (1):

(1)   a. *I've invested a lot of time in this project*
   b. *How do you spend your time these days?*
   c. *This will save you time*
   d. *You're losing your time*
   e. *I have no time to waste*
   f. *Can you give me a couple of minutes of your time?*
   g. *We are running out of time*
   h. *Can I steal two minutes of your time?*
   i. *Can you spare some time for me now?*

All these expressions do not correspond to different metaphors; they would be different 'metaphorical expressions' of only one conceptual metaphor, TIME IS MONEY. Of course, conceptualizing one domain in terms of another will have an effect not only on how we talk about it, but on other modes of expression, such as gestures or images and even on cultural conventions and objects.

7.3 Types of Metaphor

As could be expected, not all metaphors are of the same type. CMT has proposed a number of distinctions throughout its thirty-odd years of existence. Some of these distinctions can be seen as overlapping; as happens in other realms of theorizing, the problem with the different classifications is that each focuses on one specific criterion, and the result is that there is no single classification that is correct. Here, we review two of the most popular classifications.

7.3.1 Structure of the Domains

One way to classify metaphors depends on whether the domains involved have a lower or higher degree of inner structure. These are the usual distinctions:

(A) IMAGE-METAPHORS

This is the simplest type of metaphor: the external appearance of an object is connected to the form of another object. One example would be ITALY IS A BOOT, in which the shape of a boot is mapped onto the shape of Italy in a map. Another famous example is the case of the computer mouse; its creator, Douglas Engelbart, and his assistant, Bill English, decided that their invention, a grey object which had a cable that connected it to the computer, was visually similar to a mouse, and decided to give it that name. Different sub-parts of the images that are being compared can be connected in these metaphors (e.g., we can talk about Brindisi being located at the heel of Italy's boot; the cable of the computer mouse corresponds to the tail of the real mouse), but there are no complex inferences besides these partial connections. Another popular example comes from modern computers, which exploit this sort of image metaphor. So, we are used to looking at our computer screen and calling it a 'desk' (the desktop) where we keep 'files' in 'folders' and delete them by moving them to the 'trash can'. Image metaphors can also give rise to polysemic links, such as 'the *teeth* of a comb', 'the *leg* of the table', the '*arrow*' we find in maps and drawings, or 'the *rings* of Saturn'. Another example is the English word *pomegranate*, which comes from Spanish *granada*; the reason the bomb was named in this way (*grenade*) was due to its resemblance to the fruit (see Figure 7.1).

(B) SPATIAL METAPHORS

Sometimes, the source domain corresponds to a very simple, spatial domain, such as VERTICALITY (*up/down*) or PROXIMITY (*near/far*) and the target

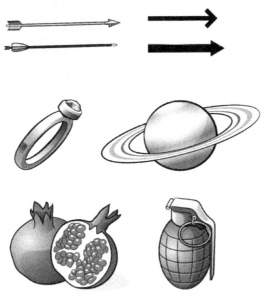

Figure 7.1 Some Image-Metaphors in Polysemic Extensions

domain corresponds to a scalar concept, again with two poles, such as HAPPINESS (*happy/sad*) or QUANTITY (*more/less*). In these cases, we talk about **spatial** or **orientational metaphors**. For example, in the metaphor MORE IS UP, the domain of verticality helps to structure the domain of quantity. This explains the examples in (2):

(2) a. *Prices are going up*
    b. *A high percentage of Americans go to the movies every week*
    c. *Prices have risen a lot lately*
    d. *Prices are soaring*
    e. *The unemployment rate is very high*
    f. *Interest rates have come down*
    g. *Prices have continued to fall on Wall Street*
    h. *My income is very low*

In 2(a), for example, prices are not moving physically in space to a higher position; it is the metaphor that tells us that an increase in verticality corresponds to an increase in quantity (the same analysis could be applied to 2(b–e). In the examples 2(f) and 2(g), a downwards movement corresponds to a decrease in quantity. A large number of metaphors have to do with spatial orientation; a partial list can be seen in Table 7.2:

Table 7.2 *Some Orientational Metaphors (Lakoff and Johnson, 1980)*

HAPPY IS UP	SAD IS DOWN	*I'm feeling up. My spirits rose. You're in high spirits. I'm feeling down. My spirits sank.*
HEALTH IS UP	LACK OF HEALTH IS DOWN	*He's at the peak of his health. He's in top shape. He fell ill. He came down with the flu. His health is declining.*
CONTROL IS UP	LACK OF CONTROL IS DOWN	*I have everything under control. She had a great influence over him. Under the rule of Stalin, people were scared.*
GOOD IS UP	BAD IS DOWN	*Things are looking up. We hit a peak last year, but it's been downhill ever since. Things are at an all-time low. He does high-quality work.*
VIRTUE IS UP	DEPRAVITY IS DOWN	*He is high minded. She has high standards. She is an upstanding citizen. That was a low trick. I wouldn't stoop to that.*
SIMILARITY IS CLOSE	DIFFERENCE IS FAR	*Their political views are close. Your opinion and mine cannot be farther apart.*

(C) CONCEPTUAL METAPHORS

Finally, there are 'conceptual' or 'structural' metaphors, in which two different and complex domains, that is, domains that have an internal structure made of several interacting elements, are put into contact. A very typical case is LOVE IS A JOURNEY, which is behind metaphorical expressions such as those in (3):

(3) a. *Our relationship has hit a dead-end street*
     b. *This relationship is not going anywhere*
     c. *From now on, we'll have to go separate ways*
     d. *Their marriage is on the rocks*
     e. *After all that we've been through*
     f. *He wanted to go too fast*
     g. *Look how far we've come*

Both the domain of journeys and the domain of love have their own complex structure: the domain of JOURNEYS has elements such as the travellers, the vehicle that carries them, the origin and destination of the journey, its route and the obstacles that can be found during the trip. In the same way, the domain of LOVE has as components the lovers, the moment they first met or the moment they started the relationship, their vital goals as a couple, the problems that their relationship goes through. All this internal structure from both domains can put into correspondence, with the result that we conceptualize LOVE IS A JOURNEY (see Figure 7.2).

Figure 7.2 LOVE IS A JOURNEY

Sometimes, we can also transfer inferences based on the functioning of the source domain, which are analogically extended to the functioning of the target domain. In this way, we can use our knowledge about the way one source domain works and apply it to the target domain. For example, to understand a sentence such as *she wasn't really in love but she felt that this was her last train*, you have to know that normally trains keep a schedule, and take you from one place to another at given points in a day, so that if you miss the last train of the day, you may not get home. Therefore, applied to the domain of relationships, the sentence means that the person we are speaking about felt that this was her last chance for a romantic relationship.

This type of metaphor is pervasive across languages and a huge amount of academic work has looked at many conceptual metaphors in many different languages. In English, some of the most often cited are ARGUMENTS ARE WARS, LOVE IS WAR, LIFE IS A JOURNEY, ANGER IS A HOT FLUID IN A CONTAINER, EMOTION IS A FORCE, THEORIES ARE BUILDINGS, IDEAS ARE FOOD, and a long etcetera (a compilation of conceptual metaphors can easily be found on the internet by searching for 'Master Metaphor List'). All of them offer a new way of conceptualizing the target domain that brings about a new perspective. Thus, these metaphors make us see old matters in a new light; we will see the practical uses of this in Section 7.6.

7.3.2 Complexity Criteria

Grady (1997) introduced the distinction between 'primary' and 'complex' metaphors: complex metaphors are those formed by simpler metaphors, while primary metaphors function as 'atomic' elements that can be combined to form complex metaphors. What then is a primary metaphor? A primary metaphor (also called 'correlational') is one that arises from the correlations found between two domains in our early experience of the world (an idea closely related to the notion of embodiment, which we reviewed in Chapter 3). Lakoff and Johnson (1999) claim that we acquire hundreds of these primary metaphors during our earliest years. For example, the metaphor MORE IS UP is a primary metaphor; first, because it cannot be decomposed into simpler metaphors, and then, because this metaphor emerges from a correlation between two domains that we experience bodily. For example, when we fill a bottle with water, there is a direct correlation between the quantity of water and the height of the level of the water within the bottle. The same happens when we pile books on top of each other: the more books, the higher the pile. It is this correlation between quantity and height that creates the metaphor in our mind.

Another example is the AFFECTION IS WARMTH metaphor. In real life, the expression of affection is usually correlated with an increased thermal sensation from body contact: when a mother cuddles her baby, the baby feels both affection and warmth at the same time; we experience the same when we hug a friend. This experiential correlation between both aspects creates the conceptual metaphor AFFECTION IS WARMTH that motivates expressions such as *warm welcome* or *cold reception*. Something similar could be said for the relationship between INTIMACY and CLOSENESS, found in linguistic examples such as *close friend* (Figure 7.3). There are many primary or correlational metaphors: some of them are listed in Table 7.3:

Table 7.3 *Some Primary Metaphors*

• AFFECTION IS WARMTH	• LINEAR SCALES ARE PATHS
• IMPORTANT IS BIG	• ORGANIZATION IS PHYSICAL
• HAPPY IS UP	STRUCTURE
• INTIMACY IS CLOSENESS	• HELP IS SUPPORT
• BAD IS STINKY	• TIME IS MOTION
• DIFFICULTIES ARE BURDENS	• RELATIONSHIPS ARE ENCLOSURES
• MORE IS UP	• CONTROL IS UP
• CATEGORIES ARE CONTAINERS	• KNOWING IS SEEING
• SIMILARITY IS CLOSENESS	• UNDERSTANDING IS GRASPING
	• SEEING IS TOUCHING

Figure 7.3 A Close Friend?

On the other hand, metaphors such as ANGER IS A HOT FLUID IN A CONTAINER, responsible for expressions such as *you are making my blood boil, he was fuming,* or *she flipped her lid,* would be made of a combination of simpler metaphors, like EMOTIONS ARE SUBSTANCES, OUR BODY IS A CONTAINER and INTENSITY IS HEAT. Another example is the LOVE IS A JOURNEY metaphor, which would be a conflation of different simpler metaphors, such as PURPOSES ARE DESTINATIONS, DIFFICULTIES ARE IMPEDIMENTS, A RELATIONSHIP IS A CONTAINER or INTIMACY IS PHYSICAL CLOSENESS.

7.4 Empirical Evidence for the Existence of Metaphorical Projections

CMT emerged from a very specific phenomenon: the presence of a large number of linguistic expressions that use vocabulary from a particular domain to speak about another. For example, it was observed that there were many expressions using words from the domain of money (e.g., *invest money, spend money, waste money, save money, loan money*) that are also used to speak about time (*invest time, spend time, waste time, save time, loan time*). Similar patterns could be detected in groups of sentences concerning other topics, which could be consistently arranged according to a source and a target domain. In this way, conceptual metaphors were postulated as mental patterns that were able to organize a large amount of textual material. Therefore, it was the presence of a large quantity of linguistic expressions that pointed to the existence of a conceptual organization pattern behind all of them. The existence of conceptual metaphors allowed us to go beyond specific words, and connect a great number of words belonging to a particular domain.

The assumption of a conceptual organization of this type facilitated coherent explanations for many linguistic issues, such as models of polysemic extensions of many different linguistic elements (from morphemes to lexical items to grammatical constructions), or patterns of diachronic evolution in the meaning of these elements (and sometimes, their function). But, crucially, the model also proved instrumental in the extension of the notion of embodiment to abstract domains, which could only be applied to concrete concepts.

As we saw in Chapter 3, this is in fact one of the main problems of embodied accounts of cognition: if meaning is the re-enactment of the sensorimotor activation derived from our experience with a given entity, we can use this explanation naturally with objects with which we have embodied and sensorimotor interactions, i.e., concrete objects. But abstract concepts, by definition, cannot be seen, heard, touched, smelled or physically manipulated: such is the case of justice, importance, love or intelligence. How are these concepts represented then? One of the proposals comes from CMT: abstract concepts achieve indirect embodied grounding by means of their structuring from more specific sensorimotor domains. Thus, though we cannot touch or see directly importance, we can conceptualize it more adequately and facilitate its mental processing by connecting it to the sensorimotor domain of PHYSICAL SIZE. Theoretically, then, this metaphoric mechanism fills an important gap in embodied accounts of cognition.

However, there is an often-quoted problem in this explanation: the problem of circularity. As we shall see in the final section about criticisms of CMT, there is a certain scepticism in some fields of cognitive science about the psychological existence of these metaphorical patterns. The main reason is the method used to propose these mental metaphors: linguistic evidence. Many critics object to the use of language as the only evidence to postulate mental structures. There is a circular argument that can be constructed as follows: (1) a large number of linguistic expressions can be found that take vocabulary from one domain to describe a different domain; (2) these expressions can be grouped according to projection patterns between a source domain and a target domain, and organized into a list of conceptual metaphors; (3) these conceptual metaphors are assumed to exist at a mental level, and to be behind the existence of many of these linguistic expressions; (4) we know that these conceptual metaphors really exist mentally because ... (1) a large number of linguistic expressions can be found that take a domain vocabulary from one domain to describe another domain. That is, language is both the starting point and the evidence for the existence of these proposed patterns (Figure 7.4).

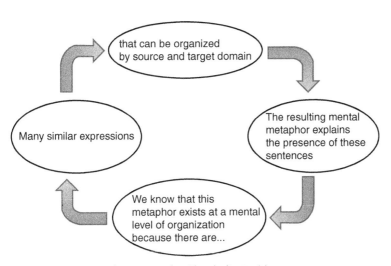

Figure 7.4 The Circularity Problem

The solution to escape from this vicious circle is to look outside language: non-linguistic expressions (e.g., drawings, objects), gesture studies, or psycholinguistic studies. In this section we will review a number of psycholinguistic studies that look for the non-linguistic consequences you should find if metaphors really exist as patterns of organization in our conceptual system. For example, if you really represent target domain concepts by projections from a source domain, then variations in the conditions with which we meet the elements of the source domain should affect how we represent the target domain. To give a concrete example, if there is a connection between the domain of verticality and domain of happiness, manipulating the verticality of the stimuli in experimental situations should affect how we process these stimuli effectively. What follows are some of the cross-domain connections that have been discussed in the literature.

- TIME IS SPACE. This is quite probably the most thoroughly researched metaphor so far. In Chapter 6 we discussed the experiments by

Casasanto and Boroditsky (2008); in one of the experiments, English speakers had to calculate the amount of time that a line was growing on the screen. Consistent with the English metaphor of TIME AS LENGTH (*long/short time*), the estimation of time by English speakers was influenced by the length of the growing line: the spatial source domain was automatically activated and caused interferences in the processing of time, as predicted by CMT. As mentioned, this experiment demonstrated the connection between space and time at a conceptual level, not a merely linguistic one, since participants did not have to utter a single word: they just saw lines growing on a screen and then calculated time with two clicks of the mouse.

- MORAL IS BRIGHT/UP/CLEAN–IMMORAL IS DARK/DOWN/DIRTY. Morality is a highly abstract domain, so people frequently use metaphorical projections from a more concrete domain to structure it. Meier *et al.* (2007) found a connection between the domain of VERTICALITY and the domain of MORALITY: words related to moral values were recognized more quickly if they appeared at the top of the screen, and immoral words were recognized faster when presented at the bottom of the screen. Similarly, Sherman and Clore (2009) also found a connection between dark and bright colours and morality using a Stroop test: subjects had to name the colour of the letters of a given word. They were quicker at naming the colour 'black' in words like *greed* and the colour 'white' in words like *honesty* than the other way round. Finally, Zhong and Liljenquist (2006) found that participants who were allowed to clean their hands judged a moral action less severely than those who had not been subjected to cleansing manipulation. All of these cases showed how manipulating the source domain (the brightness of the colour of a word, its height or the cleanliness of the participants) affected its associated target domain, i.e., MORALITY.

- IMPORTANCE IS WEIGHT. Jostman *et al.* (2009) asked their subjects to provide judgments of importance while they were holding a heavy or a light clipboard. For example, subjects would be asked how important it was for them to have their voice heard in a decision-making procedure (one that involved them). Those who held heavy clipboards tended to give more importance to this question than those who held light clipboards.

- GOOD/HAPPY IS UP. Meier and Robinson (2004) asked their subjects to classify words that could appear at the top or the bottom of the screen. Subjects classified words as having positive connotations faster when they appeared at the top than when they appeared at the bottom of the screen; the opposite was found for words with negative connotations. Casasanto and Dijkstra (2010) implemented the concepts of up and down with motion by having participants move a marble from a lower shelf to a higher one or the other way round. While they were moving marbles up or down, they were asked about positive or negative memories in their lives; participants took longer to respond when the movement they had to do was contrary to the valence of the memory they had to tell (i.e., they took longer starting to speak when they had to remember a sad story in their lives while moving marbles up than moving them down; the opposite pattern was found when they had to remember a positive memory).

- POWER/CONTROL IS UP. Schubert (2005) studied the connection between the power relationships established between two entities (a rather abstract type of connection) and the more concrete dimension of verticality. He showed participants words like *master* or *servant* and they had to classify them as belonging to a powerful or a powerless group. Participants carried out this task faster when the members of the powerful group were shown at the top of the screen than when they appeared at the bottom. He manipulated his stimuli in order to disentangle positive and negative valence from power, by presenting positive and negative powerful entities; even powerful entities with a negative connotation (e.g., *dictator*) showed an advantage of vertical position. Valenzuela and Soriano (2009) conducted a study with Spanish subjects where they asked them to choose which word pairs were semantically related. Some of the semantically related pairs were word pairs involved in a controlling relationship, such as *captain–soldier, warden–prisoner*. Both words were shown at the same time, vertically aligned; subjects recognized a semantic relationship more quickly when the position was canonical (with the powerful member on top and the powerless one below) than in the opposition orientation.
- SIMILARITY IS PROXIMITY. Casasanto (2008) had subjects rate the similarity of two abstract concepts (e.g., *justice* and *truth*, or *love* and *serenity*) on a scale of 1 to 5. Subjects saw the two words horizontally aligned but with three different degrees of separation: close, mid-distance or far apart. Subjects tended to judge these abstract concepts as more similar when they were shown in closer positions than when they saw them further away from each other. Similar results were obtained by Boot and Pecher (2010) and Winter and Matlock (2013).
- AFFECTION IS WARMTH. Williams and Bargh (2008) had subjects experience a cold or hot sensation by making them hold a cup of hot tea or a glass with a cold drink; subjects were not told this was related to the experiment. After this preparation, subjects were asked to rate a series of photographs of people. Subjects who had experienced heat tended to rate the photographs with characteristics associated with affection;

185

subjects who had experienced cold rated the same set of pictures with characteristics more associated with lack of empathy.

7.5 Where do Metaphors Come From?

So far, we have painted a rather sketchy picture of the origin of metaphors; we have actually only mentioned the case of experiential correlations in some primary metaphors. But what about the rest? Is this the only way in which these metaphorical connections are established? The three possibilities that have been proposed in the literature are (1) embodied experience; (2) our cultural systems; and (3) language itself.

As we saw in the case of primary metaphors, embodied experience can supply correlations between aspects of our interaction with the world that can be connected. This would be the case of AFFECTION and WARMTH, or QUANTITY and VERTICALITY as we saw in Section 7.3.2. In real life, there is a correlation between important things and their size: a big dog should be given more importance than a small dog, because it is more dangerous; the bigger an obstacle in our way is, the more important it becomes (imagine trying to cross a small river or a big one). Thus, this is a possible location for the establishment of metaphors. There are, nonetheless, limits to this strategy. As a child, your parents are important to you, and they are also bigger, but if your father is taller than your mother, he is not necessarily more important to you than she is.

Another basic notion from our embodied experience that serves as a sort of 'bridge' linking source and target domain is that of **image-schema** (Johnson, 1987). Image-schemas are very abstract and basic structures that are derived from our interaction with the world. They are, so to speak, 'skeletal' schemas that capture the underlying common structure of a number of different actions and scenes. For example, the **source–path–goal** schema abstracts away from detailed experiences such as walking from one point to another, throwing a ball to a friend or feeding a child with a spoon. All these experiences share a certain common structure: in all of them there is something that moves from a specific point (the origin or Source), follows a given Path, and reaches a final point of destination or Goal. Another example is the case of the **Container** image-schema, which corresponds to a very basic structure with an Interior, an Exterior, a Boundary and an Entity that moves in or out of it. This structure is abstracted from experiences such as going in and out of houses, of rooms, getting out of your car, putting things in your pocket or into your body and a long string of similar experiences.

Now, these embodied structures (they are embodied because we need a body to experience them) can be extended to non-physical domains. The extension from the pure physical to the abstract can be seen to proceed in small steps. For example, there is a clear connection between change of location and change of state. Going in or out of certain containers, for example, can radically change our physical state: while you are within a cave, you experience darkness and are protected from the rain and the wind; if you leave the shade of a tree, you experience an increase in heat; when you jump into a swimming pool, entering the water space radically changes your physical perceptions. Going from these to other less tangible changes of state is not such a big step; thus, you come *out* of a trance, or go *into* a depression. The same can be seen with other image-schemas; consider the relation between the source–path–goal image schema and argumentation. In logical argumentation, you *start from* some premises and try to *arrive at* a conclusion, and do so taking a number of different 'logical' *steps*. This explains why the expression *jump to a conclusion* is used in English: if instead of arriving at your destination (the conclusion) proceeding step by step, you *jump*, then you skip a couple of steps which would be necessary in the logical argumentation. We see how using reasoning from an embodied source domains helps us reason with a target domain: if somebody is explaining something to you and you say *You lost me there*, your interlocutor knows that you did not understand his argument and you are no longer 'following' him/her along the logical path. There are many other expressions such as *come to the point, by the way* or *so far*, which make sense in the particular context thanks to the application of this basic schema. This can be applied to many cases: we can now explain easily how we can go from *I gave John the parcel* to *I gave John the solution*. Other image-schemas that have been mentioned in the literature are shown in Figure 7.5.

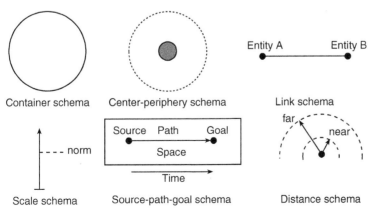

Figure 7.5 Some Image-Schemas

Cultural conventions are another force that need to be taken into account; some connections are established on the basis of a 'perceived' similarity between source and target domain that can only be found in certain cultures. For example, the metaphor *He is a pig* makes sense in a culture that, as Western culture does, considers pigs to be dirty. Another very specific example of the influence of culture on metaphor involves the TIME IS SPACE metaphor again. Many languages spatialize time using the sagittal axis (that is, a front-back axis). English is one of these languages, as can be seen in sentences like *you have a brilliant future* in front of *you* or *we have left the bad memories* behind *us*. Now, languages like Mandarin, which have the cultural practice of writing vertically (top-down) can also structure time using the vertical axis: for them, the 'past' or 'next' month can be expressed as the 'up' or 'down' month. Incidentally, the lateral axis is also used in the spatialization of time in English, even if it has no explicit linguistic manifestation (actually, there is no language on Earth that uses 'left' and 'right' to indicate past or future). However, it has been experimentally shown that English speakers locate the past on their left and the future on their right. The flow of time within this lateral axis depends on culture: for cultures whose writing system goes from left to right (English, for example), the past is located on the left, and the future is on the right; for cultures that write from right to left (like Hebrews or Arabs), the opposite is true: past is on the right and future on the left. The importance of culture in metaphor research has grown exponentially in recent times, in consonance with what some authors have termed the 'cultural turn' in cognitive science.

Last but not least, another possibility is that language itself guides our conceptualization of certain domains. As we have mentioned several times in this book, language can inform our conceptual structure, and sometimes words can be indications of what type of categories we should establish (cf. Chapters 4 and 5). Having a number of linguistic expressions that connect two domains could thus be an invitation for the conceptualizer to organize a given domain in terms of another, as suggested by the linguistic expressions. There is in fact experimental evidence that this process is at work in some cases; Gentner (2001) presented a number of experiments which showed how experience with a special type of linguistic metaphor made participants establish a number of cross-domain mappings that were not present before. In one of the experiments by Casasanto and Boroditsky (2008) reviewed in this chapter and in Chapter 6, English speakers were trained to use 'Greek-like metaphors', that is, metaphors that invited them to construe TIME AS QUANTITY, instead of their more usual TIME AS LENGTH. After just twenty minutes of training, the behaviour of English speakers became much closer to that of Greek speakers. In another experiment, with vertical metaphors of time, English participants trained to speak about time with vertical metaphors (with 100 made-up sentences such as *Bush was president above Obama*), showed a tendency to organize time vertically in non-linguistic tasks, in a way similar to Mandarin speakers (Boroditsky, 2000).

These facts contradict one of the assumptions we described in this chapter. We said at the beginning that CMT proposes roughly that 'we speak with these metaphors because we think with these metaphors'. Now we see that the opposite may also be true (that is, we may think in a specific way because we use certain linguistic metaphors) in a cycle whose starting point is difficult to see. The truth of the matter is that disentangling the different aspects of metaphors (embodied experience, culture or language) can be an incredibly complicated task.

7.6 What is Conceptual Metonymy?

Another mechanism that is usually discussed alongside conceptual metaphor is **conceptual metonymy**. Metonymies are just as ubiquitous as metaphors, if not more; many of the expressions we use in our colloquial language are based on metonymies. They are so normal and frequent that it is sometimes hard to think of them as 'figurative' language. Consider the following examples in (4):

(4) a. *I'm parked outside* b. *Buses are on strike*
     c. *The sax has the flu* d. *I went to fill my car with gasoline*
     e. *You've broken/stolen my heart* f. *The kettle is boiling*
     g. *Boris is a heavy drinker* h. *I see new faces today*

In (4a), it is a car that is parked outside, not the speaker; in (4b) and (4c) we are referring to persons, not to objects; in (4d) the whole car is not filled with gasoline, but just the tank; in (4e) we are referring to the emotion of love; in (4f) it is water that boils, not the kettle; in (4g) we use the verb 'to drink' in the more specific sense of 'drink alcohol'; in (4h) we use 'face' for 'person'.

As in the case of metaphor, more traditional studies tend to treat metonymy as a purely linguistic or literary device, in which one word is used in place of another. More recent studies, though, ascribe metonymy to the realm of cognition, just like metaphor. Basically, what happens in this view of metonymy is that one conceptual entity (termed the **vehicle** or **reference point**) provides mental access to another (named the **target**). This is possible, among other things, because both entities enjoy a certain **conceptual contiguity** within the same domain. We see this at work in example (5):

(5)   *The ham sandwich just left without paying*

Sandwiches do not walk (not even ham sandwiches), so the sentence cannot be understood literally (as in Figure 7.6). What the sentence does is to mention the food in order to refer to the customer who has ordered it. The two elements involved have a very close association in the restaurant scene (which contains other elements such as waiters, menus, tables or chairs), and that is why referring to customers by the thing that they have ordered makes sense, at least for waiters. In this way we use the food as a vehicle that grants access to the target – in this case, the customer. As a matter of fact, here we have one distinguishing factor between metaphor and metonymy: while in metaphor there are two distinct domains involved (e.g., FOOD and IDEAS), in metonymy, you only invoke one single domain, since both vehicle and target belong to the same domain.

Why do we do this? Why should we mention one thing in order to access another, instead of saying directly what we are referring to? In the same way that we saw that metaphor had a very clear function (facilitating mental processing of the target domain), metonymy must exist for a reason. Which is that, normally, the vehicle is more 'cognitively salient' than the target; it is easier to access for a number of reasons. For example, concrete entities are easier to identify than abstract ones: that is why we often use *heart* to mean 'feelings' or 'love', *brain* to mean 'intelligence', or *hand* to mean 'help'.

Figure 7.6 Literal Interpretation of *The Ham Sandwich Left Without Paying*

We also prefer things that have a good gestalt (i.e., a recognizable shape) over things that have a bad gestalt (as for example in *I'm going to fill the car with gasoline*, where *car* is the whole, a highly imageable gestalt, while the target, the *gas tank*, is not so easily accessible). Other preferences normally listed are human over non-human (cf. *I am parked outside*), bounded over unbounded (cf. *We ate chicken*), or specific over generic entities.

Depending on the relationship between vehicle and target, metonymies are sometimes classified as (a) PART-FOR-WHOLE (when the vehicle is a part of a whole, and naming it activates the whole), as in *The White House has declared Ebola to be a top national-security concern*; (b) WHOLE-FOR-PART, as in *Obama was the first Afroamerican president of America* (where *America* is the vehicle, a whole continent, and *United States of America*, a country part of that whole, is the target); and (c) PART-FOR-PART (as in our example, *the ham sandwich just left without paying*, where one part of the domain, the food, activates another part, the customer). Metonymies can sometimes be classified at a lower level, looking at a more specific relationship between vehicle and target (e.g., PRODUCER FOR PRODUCT, PLACE FOR EVENT, etc.). We will review some of these specific metonymies in our next section, when we talk about the applications of metonymy to polysemy extension.

Metonymy is quite useful to explain many linguistic phenomena, from polysemy extension to word-formation or diachronic evolution. Metonymic thought also helps us explain many of the inferences we are able to draw from speech. Think of expressions such as *Saying 'I do'* or *Walking down the aisle*: they immediately activate a more complex scene, the 'marriage scenario'. In the case of complex events made up of a number of separate actions, we can name one of them and activate the whole event, in a PART-FOR-WHOLE metonymy. We will cover more examples like this in Chapter 9.

Finally, as in the case of metaphor, since metonymy is a conceptual phenomenon, it is found in realms outside language; actually, the indexes we presented in Chapter 1 (Section 1.5) could be considered as cases of conceptual metonymy. For example, when you see a sign showing a plate with a knife and a fork, you know it means restaurant; those elements act as vehicle to the target concept, in a PART-FOR-WHOLE relationship; the same could be said about smoke being an index of fire (PART-FOR-WHOLE).

7.7 Applications of Conceptual Metaphor and Metonymy Theory

As we mentioned before, metaphor and metonymy are quite useful mechanisms for explaining many linguistic phenomena, providing a coherent account of aspects that would seem incongruous from other points of view. In what follows, we examine their role in mechanisms of regular and irregular polysemy, which we mentioned briefly in our previous chapter.

7.7.1 Regular Polysemy: Metaphor

There are many polysemic patterns of extension; many of them involve metaphoric processes. In some cases, these metaphoric projections are applied in specific areas that are seen to generate polysemic extensions across many different languages. One of these cases, which applies to English but is found in many other languages as well, is the metaphorical extension of perception verbs (Sweetser, 1990; Ibarretxe-Antuñano, 1999, 2008). There is a very systematic pattern of connections between the physical sense of verbs of perception and a number of polysemic extensions related to internal sensations and cognitive activities. More specifically, Sweetser (1990) proposes the following connections between the physical senses and its polysemic meanings (Table 7.4):

Table 7.4 *Verbs of Perception and Metaphorical Sense Extensions*

1. VISION	→	KNOWLEDGE
2. HEARING	→	HEED → OBEY
3. TASTE	→	LIKES/DISLIKES
4. TOUCH	→	FEELINGS
5. SMELL	→	FEELINGS OF DISLIKE

Thus, (1) words related to seeing in English are often used with the extended meaning of 'understanding'; that is the meaning of the verb *to see* in *I see what you mean*. This would be an example therefore of the UNDERSTANDING IS SEEING metaphor.

(2) The domain of hearing is quite often extended to mean 'paying attention' or 'heeding' (like in *he was deaf to my pleas*) or even 'obedience' (e.g., *you should listen to your doctor's advice*). This type of mapping, in which a cognitive act such as obeying, or heeding (or even knowing) is linked to hearing, is found in many different languages, including Spanish, French, German, Italian, Romanian, Hebrew and Greek, among others.

(3) Words related to taste are used to indicate your subjective opinion about something (*I found your proposal unpalatable; he has very good taste in music*); again this is a pattern found in many different languages in Europe, for example.

(4) The verb *to touch* is connected to feelings; when we say that *that movie is very touching*, we mean it made us feel emotional.

Finally, (5) when people say things like *that business doesn't smell good* or *smells fishy* (or *a movie stinks*), the sense of smell is connected to feelings of dislike.

What we find in all these cases is that a verb of perception is linked to some sort of 'mental' activity; thus, they could all be grouped in a very general metaphor, which sometimes receives the name THINKING IS PERCEIVING (another name it receives is the MIND AS BODY metaphor). Sweetser (1990) has used this metaphor to explain mechanisms of diachronic evolution in English. It has been documented in many languages (cf. Ibarretxe-Antuñano, 2008, for a discussion of overlaps among English, Basque and Spanish) and thus is a good example of a seemingly universal strategy for regular polysemy extension found across languages.

7.7.2 Regular Polysemy: Metonymy

Probably, the 'purest' case of regular polysemy is the one connected to metonymy. As we saw, the connection between vehicle and target in metonymy is one of contiguity; the ANIMAL FOR FOOD pattern that we discussed in Chapter 5 when talking about regular polysemy would be a great example of metonymic connection. The following are some metonymic connections found in English that are patterns to create polysemic extensions (Table 7.5):

Table 7.5 *A Partial List of Types of Metonymies*

PRODUCER FOR PRODUCT	*I'll have a Heineken*
	He bought a Ford
AUTHOR FOR WORKS	*I don't like Freud*
	She bought a Picasso
OBJECT USED FOR USER	*The sax has the flu today*
	The buses are on strike
CONTROLLER FOR CONTROLLED	*Obama threatens with attacking Iraq again*
	Napoleon lost at Waterloo
INSTITUTION FOR PEOPLE	*Apple has spent a lot of money on its new image*
	The European Bank has lowered interest rates
PLACE FOR THE INSTITUTION	*Hollywood loves disaster movies and biopics*
	Wall Street is euphoric
PLACE FOR THE EVENT	*Chernobyl showed us the dangers of atomic power*
	Only a third of Vietnam veterans are still alive
CONTAINER FOR PHYSICAL CONTENT	*He drank four bottles of beer*
	I want a glass of water
CONTAINER FOR REPRESENTATIONAL CONTENT	*That book is very funny (vs. 'that book is yellow')*
	The CD is quite long (vs. 'the CD is round')

Srinivasan and Rabagliati (2015) surveyed patterns of polysemy extension that recur across many languages; they examined twenty-seven patterns of polysemy found in English (some of them are the ones we mentioned
before in our list of metonymies, plus other metonymies such as ANIMAL FOR
MEAT – *I tried ostrich last week*; ANIMAL FOR FUR – *she likes to wear mink*,
MATERIAL FOR ARTIFACT – *he filled the glass with water*, etc.) and checked
for their existence in fourteen other different languages. Almost 90 per cent
of these metonymically based polysemic extensions were found in their
language pool. This clearly indicates that metonymy is a very robust
mechanism for creating polysemic extensions across languages. These
authors link these data to the innate mechanisms of children's mental
processing.

7.8 Some Criticisms and a Conclusion

There is no denying that despite its inherent interest, CMT is a controversial
theory. Some of its assumptions have been questioned from different areas
of cognitive science. These are some of the most frequent criticisms:

(1) The first one is related to the assumption that linguistic patterns can be
    taken as a direct reflection of conceptual representations (e.g., Murphy,
    1996, 1997). This criticism was addressed in Section 7.4 above; there,
    we reviewed a great body of experimental work that has uncovered
    many cases in which there is automatic activation of a source domain
    when processing the target domain, even in non-linguistic tasks. This
    means that at least some conceptual metaphors are psychologically real.
    This does not mean, though, that *all* metaphors proposed by CMT are
    psychologically real; in fact, the only metaphors that have been tested
    tend to be correlational (more than what we have called complex or
    structural). But after several decades of experimental work, it can no
    longer be said that CMT is supported only by linguistic metaphors.

(2) Another criticism concerns some basic distinctions that have been
    identified as highly relevant in other approaches to metaphor and
    which are not sufficiently taken into account by this theory; for exam-
    ple, the distinction between novel or entrenched metaphoric patterns.
    In Gentner's theory, for example, this is an absolutely basic distinction,
    since each of these types of metaphor (novel and conventional) behaves
    in a radically different way. She calls this the 'Career of Metaphor':
    metaphors start in a creative way, with new mappings being dynami-
    cally established between two domains, and, gradually as a result of use
    and conventionalization, they are entrenched and are finally stored as
    alternative senses of the source term (Bowdle and Gentner, 2005).

Other scholars (e.g., Givón, 2005) also propose gradations that go from literal utterances, on to (contextually bound) metaphorical extensions, to full metaphoric meanings, to idiomatic units (when the metaphor becomes entrenched) and finally dead metaphor (when the original meaning is no longer active).

(3) An overarching criticism of CMT is that it is more a model of representation than a model of processing. This means that there are plenty of details that still need to be filled out before we can arrive at a more complete description of how these representations are actually used in understanding and thought. We find an illustration of this in the problem of context: it is currently not clear how context affects or modulates the use of metaphors. Currently, CMT conceives metaphors as stored mapping patterns, which are recovered automatically for their use with a given target domain. However, this does not explain when or how we choose between different possible source domains for a target domain (cf. GOOD IS UP/NEAR/WHITE/RIGHT or LOVE IS A JOURNEY/WAR/MAGIC/MADNESS). How do we decide which domain needs to be structured and which domain will supply the relevant information? Obviously, this cannot be purely a personal decision; some type of bias must be found in the system (i.e., in our linguistic system or in our shared conceptual system). The interaction between context and metaphor is thus insufficiently explained; other theories (see for example, Cacciari and Glucksberg, 1994; Fauconnier and Turner, 2002; or Givón, 2005) opt for more dynamic and contextual explanations, giving more space to the possibility of on-line contextual adaptation. This would be more in line with everything we have seen at work so far in many semantic issues throughout this book (e.g., reference, polysemy or antonymy, to name some of them); context is always a powerful force that has an influence on linguistic choices and on cognition at every level.

There are of course more problems that we could come up with; for example, the role of experience has quite possibly been overemphasized in the theory, while the role of language in the creation of these cross-domain projections has been less explored. Some of the theory's initial claims towards cognitive universality have had to be toned down in the light of research conducted with non-English cultures. Also, it is still not clear at all which parts of a source domain are going to be used to structure a target domain. The theory acknowledges that metaphorical structuring is always partial (both domains do not end up being the same one), but specifying beforehand which parts of a domain are going to be useful in the structuring of the second one is quite hard. One proposal argues that metaphors preserve the 'cognitive topology' of the source domain (meaning its 'image-schematic' structure) in a way which is coherent with the inherent structure of the target domain; Lakoff calls this the 'invariance hypothesis'. But the issue of which is the structure of the target domain by itself, however, remains unsolved (as pointed out by Murphy, 1996). Similar things could be said about conceptual metonymy: for example, the notion of 'conceptual contiguity' which is said to exist between reference point and target is not enough to predict why some metonymies work and other do not (e.g., why we can say 'I had a beer' to mean a glass or bottle of beer, but we cannot say 'the beer cracked' to mean 'the bottle/glass of beer cracked').

However, in spite of all these issues, CMT still merits a thorough discussion, for many reasons. On the one hand, a substantial part of its assumptions have been sufficiently verified by solid experimental work: people do think metaphorically in a significant number of domains. Source domains are automatically activated when we are processing a great number of target domains, a phenomenon that has been seen to happen in both linguistic and non-linguistic tasks, which supports the idea that conceptual metaphors are psychologically real. CMT is still a plausible explanation for the extension of embodiment to abstract domains, even though research addressing this specific issue is still missing. And last but not least, CMT is still useful to explain many linguistic phenomena; it has been fruitfully applied to first and second language acquisition studies, and to specific problems in translation; it has been able to provide coherent explanations in discourse studies; and it seems to be basic in central problems in semantics such as the extension of senses in polysemy or the diachronic evolution of meaning.

Conceptual Metaphor Theory addresses a crucial problem in semantic studies that, whatever the ultimate explanation is, is undeniably important and worthy of research. It has also managed to attract the common attention of many different scholars from different disciplines across cognitive science: linguists, cognitive, developmental and social psychologists, neuroscientists, philosophers and artificial intelligence scholars have been contributing to the debate, and their interaction can only enrich our knowledge of how meaning is created, structured and communicated.

7.9 Chapter Summary

In this chapter, we have moved beyond the literal meaning of words and have taken a look at figurative meaning. Though there are many figurative mechanisms (examples of language that cannot be understood literally, such as hyperbole, understatement, tautologies, etc.), we have focused our attention on the notions of conceptual metaphor and conceptual metonymy. In this chapter we have introduced the main ideas behind Conceptual Metaphor Theory, presenting conceptual metaphor as a cognitive mechanism by which we represent a semantic area in terms of a different one. Conceptual metaphor is useful at two levels: on the one hand, it provides a tentative (but plausible) explanation for the extension of embodiment to abstract domains; on the other, it provides a useful mechanism for explaining very central topics in semantics, such as the extension of senses in polysemy. We have reviewed two ways of classifying metaphors: one that depends on the inner structure of the domains involved (with image-metaphors, orientational metaphors and structural metaphors) and another one that depends on their internal composition, where we have introduced the notion of primary metaphor. After reviewing some empirical works that have examined their psychological reality, we have briefly considered their origin (embodied experience, culture or language). We have also looked at the related notion of conceptual metonymy, and have seen both notions at work as mechanisms in regular polysemy, in which the meanings of words are systematically extended. In the last section of the chapter, we have listed some of the main criticisms directed at the theory and have concluded with a note about the importance and utility of CMT for semantic studies.

Exercises

Exercise 7.1   To which metaphor do these three groups of expressions belong?

GROUP 1
- *All this paper has are raw facts, half-baked ideas and warmed-over theories*
- *There are too many facts here for me to digest them all*
- *I just can't swallow that claim*
- *That's food for thought*
- *She devoured the book*
- *We should let that idea simmer on the back burner for a while*

GROUP 2
- *To be on top of the situation*
- *It's under control*
- *Lofty position*
- *To rise to the top*
- *The bottom of social hierarchy*

GROUP 3

- *Do you follow my argument?*
- *Now we've gone off in the wrong direction again*
- *That line of argumentation won't take us anywhere*
- *I'm lost*
- *You're going around in circles*
- *Let's get to the point*

Exercise 7.2   The following are groups of expressions about morality; how would you group them? How many metaphors do you think underlie them?

1. *Let him out, he's clean*
2. *He doesn't want to get his hands dirty*
3. *He is a deviant*
4. *He is as pure as the driven snow*
5. *He owes a debt to society*
6. *He'll get even with you for this*
7. *He's gone straight ever since the accident*
8. *His record is spotless*
9. *His reputation is besmirched*
10. *I owe you more than you'll ever know for what you've done for me*
11. *I think he's being straight with me*
12. *I'll make up for any harm I've done*
13. *I'll make you pay for what you did!*
14. *I'll pay you back for what you did to me*
15. *One mistake cost me years of suffering*
16. *She has strayed*
17. *She is of pure heart*
18. *The magazine got the dirt about him*
19. *You owe me an apology for your rudeness*
20. *You saved my life! How could I ever repay you?*
21. *He's a crooked businessman*
22. *You'll get what you deserve for that!*

Exercise 7.3   Try to come up with examples of the metaphors AN ARGUMENT IS WAR, AN ARGUMENT IS A BUILDING and AN ARGUMENT IS A JOURNEY. How do they make us conceptualize arguments differently?

Exercise 7.4   Look for texts that discuss immigration. What type of metaphors do they use? How are they used for rhetorical purposes?

Exercise 7.5   Try to find the most frequent metaphors to talk about the Internet.

Exercise 7.6   Look for expressions in English that express going in or out (using the prepositions *in* or *out*, or with a verb such as *enter, extract*, etc.). How many can you find that do not refer to physical containers? What type of abstract notions tend to be construed as containers?

Exercise 7.7   Think about these expressions. Can you see a metonymy in them? Can they be classified as PART-FOR-WHOLE, WHOLE-FOR-PART or PART-FOR-PART?

1. *A redskin*
2. *The whole theatre applauded him*
3. *She's taking the pill*
4. *I've got valuable china at home*
5. *The long straw starts*
6. *Pick up the gauntlet*
7. *To iron the shirt*
8. *He'll be behind bars for a long time*
9. *Pick up the phone!*
10. *He went on a cruise around England*
11. *Unlock the prisoners*
12. *The pen is mightier than the sword*
13. *I'm all ears*
14. *With John's departure, the group has no guitar now*

Exercise 7.8   Below you can find a dictionary list of the different senses of the word *ring*. What is the relationship between the different senses? Which of them are metonymic and which metaphoric?

RING
1. A circular object, form, line, or arrangement with a vacant circular centre.
2. A small circular band, generally made of precious metal and often set with jewels, worn on the finger.
3. A circular band used for carrying, holding, or containing something: *a napkin ring*.
4. A pair of circular metal bands suspended in the air for gymnastic exercises, on which balancing and swinging manoeuvres are performed while holding the bands as motionless as possible.

5. A circular movement or course, as in dancing.
6. An enclosed, usually circular area in which exhibitions, sports, or contests take place: *a circus ring*.
7. *Sports*
    a. A rectangular arena set off by stakes and ropes in which boxing or wrestling events are held.
    b. The sport of boxing.
8. *Games*
    a. An enclosed area in which bets are placed at a racetrack.
    b. Bookmakers considered as a group.
9. An exclusive group of people acting privately or illegally to advance their own interests: *a drug ring*.
10. A political contest; a race.
11. *Botany* An annual ring.
12. *Mathematics* The area between two concentric circles; annulus.
13. *Mathematics* A set of elements subject to the operations of addition and multiplication, in which the set is an abelian group under addition and associative under multiplication and in which the two operations are related by distributive laws.
14. Any of the turns constituting a spiral or helix.
15. *Chemistry* A group of atoms linked by bonds that may be represented graphically in circular or triangular form. Also called *closed chain*.

Exercise 7.9   Take a look at the following examples with the verb *see*. They are different polysemous senses of the basic meaning 'to perceive with your eyes'. Try to establish the groups of senses and think about its relationship with the basic one. Is it metaphorical or metonymic?

1. *I can't go to the cinema tomorrow; I have to go see my grandmother*
2. *I'll see you tomorrow at the conference at 11 o'clock*
3. *You should go see a doctor about this*
4. *I see that you are upset*
5. *I don't see the problem in this way*
6. *I see what you mean*
7. *It's hard to see this guy as the future president of Europe*
8. *Where do you see yourself in ten years' time?*
9. *Please, do not move, I'll see myself out*
10. *Don't worry about this issue; my secretary will see about it*
11. *I don't think John is seeing anyone at the moment; his divorce is too recent*

Key Terms Introduced in this Chapter

hyperbole

tautology

understatement or litotes

oxymoron

irony

sarcasm

idioms

proverbs

indirect speech acts

rhetorical questions

conceptual metaphor

source domain and target domain

metaphorical expression

image metaphor

spatial metaphor/orientational metaphor

structural/conceptual metaphor

primary metaphor

complex metaphor

image schema

source–path–goal image schema

container image-schema

conceptual metonymy

vehicle/reference point and target

conceptual contiguity

PART-FOR-WHOLE, WHOLE-FOR-PART and PART-FOR-PART metonymies

Further Reading

The main and original text about Conceptual Metaphor Theory is Lakoff and Johnson (1980); the second main reference is Lakoff and Johnson (1999). An excellent collection of essays covering many different aspects of the theory is Gibbs (2008). Two good compilations about empirical works on conceptual metaphor are Landau *et al.* (2010) and Meier *et al.* (2012). Metonymy is also analysed in Lakoff and Johnson (1980), but two classic studies which examine its assumptions are Kövecses and Radden (1998) and Peirsman and Geeraerts (2006), both of which describe the possible relationships between vehicle and target; Barcelona Sanchez (2000), Dirven and Pörings (2002), Panther and Radden (1999) and Panther and Thornburg (2003) are collections of papers on metonymy and metaphor. Glucksberg (2003) provides an alternative view.

CHAPTER 8

Sentential meaning

In this chapter . . .

We look at a different aspect of language understanding; we go beyond the level of words to talk about the meaning of sentences. For this task, we will focus on the information supplied by one specific grammatical category: the verb, the main element in the organization of the meaning of sentences. Verbs are 'predicates', relational items that must be combined with other free-standing items, the 'arguments', in order to complete their meaning. The combination of a verb and its arguments forms the backbone of the meaning of a sentence. Verbs specify how many arguments they need, the roles that those arguments play in the event or scene they describe, and also how those elements should be expressed linguistically. The semantic relations between an argument and a predicate can be classified into a number of different 'semantic roles', like agent, patient or instrument. Semantic roles are linked with grammatical functions to construct the whole meaning of a sentence. The union between a predicate and its arguments forms one special type of entity, called 'proposition', which some authors have described as 'complete units of meaning', and the most adequate level to capture the meaning of sentences. We review some of the assumptions and empirical evidence for the existence of propositions as representations of sentence meaning, as well as some criticisms aimed at propositional structures.

Then, we will examine some of the problems faced by semantic roles, such as the difficulty of agreeing on their number and their exact coverage, and the two possibilities for their definition: the more abstract, syntactically based approach to semantic roles and the more specific, semantic-based one. The final part of the chapter will explore this second option: the possibility of having very specific semantic roles, which capture information at the level of specific events. We will review empirical evidence showing that thematic event-based knowledge is activated incrementally in the understanding of sentences and we will see how all this could come together by examining the function of a concrete example, the commercial transaction frame. The chapter closes with a discussion of the challenges and the future directions of this field of semantics.

8.1 Events: Who did What to Whom

So far, we have concentrated mainly on lexical semantics. The meaning of words, though more or less variable depending on context, can be said to be stored in our long-term memory. In this sense, the basic meaning of the word *cat*, for example, is kept somewhere in our minds, along with its link to the sound pattern of the word (/kæt/). However, other types of meaning work in a different way. Probably, we would not want to say that we have the meaning of the sentence (1) stored somewhere in our brains:

(1)   *D'Artagnan attacked the musketeer with his shiny deadly sword*

To understand this sentence, we have to resort to a different strategy, since direct retrieval from memory is not possible. We have to find the way of combining the words in the sentence so that we can create a coherent 'scene'. In the case of sentence (1), we identify three entities, *D'Artagnan*, *the Musketeer* and D'Artagnan's *shiny deadly sword*. The way in which these three entities are to be combined is indicated by the verb *attack*. Thus, our knowledge of this verb tells us that D'Artagnan is the entity that starts and carries out the action of attacking, that the entity that is attacked is the musketeer and that the instrument that D'Artagnan uses to do the attacking is his shiny deadly sword (Figure 8.1)

In the conceptualization and description of events, we identify a number of entities and put them in some sort of relation, noting their interaction: an entity does something to another one, or perhaps just does something without affecting any other entity (roughly, the cases of transitive and

Figure 8.1 How Different Entities are Related by the Verb *Attack*

intransitive verbs, respectively). Sometimes, we can also make reference to an entity that is in a particular position or state, not 'doing' anything special. The linguistic element that organizes all this information is the verb. Verbs are the most important element in the organization of the sentence. They are the elements that 'glue' together semantic and syntactic information. Verbs tell us at least two things:

a. The activity that is going on and the entities associated with such activity (specifying their role in the scene described).
b. How to express this linguistically. The action/state being described is indicated by the lexical meaning of the verb itself; then, each of the roles that are associated with a verb will be linked with a given grammatical device (for example, with grammatical functions such as subject, object, indirect object, oblique, etc.) which will specify how to express it linguistically.

As we shall see, one of the key elements that help us relate semantics and syntax in verbs are **semantic roles**. But before entering their discussion, we need to introduce a further technical notion: the distinction between **predicates** and **arguments**.

8.2 Predicates and Arguments

Broadly speaking, we can distinguish between two types of linguistic expressions. On the one hand, there are words that denote *individuals*, things that are independent and can stand on their own. Thus, the reference of the word *London* can be understood regardless of any other consideration of time, person or circumstance. It can be used without being attributed to anything or anyone.

On the other hand, certain words make reference to *relations* between entities, and cannot be understood except by association with an individual. Consider the meaning of the preposition *on*. This word expresses a given spatial relationship between two entities; we talk about *the cat on the mat*. This word directs our attention to the spatial superiority of a given entity over another one; it further indicates that both entities touch each other. Unless we specify which are the two entities that are put into contact, the word *on* cannot be properly used or understood. A similar situation is found with other word categories, such as *adjectives* and, above all, *verbs* (some nouns would have to be added to this list, especially those derived from verbs). So, the adjective *solid* has to be used in relation with a noun, for example *a solid table*. Likewise, the meaning of the verb *dance* is dependent on an entity, the dancer, who performs an action, the special type of rhythmic motion that we call 'dancing'. It is difficult or even impossible to imagine the meaning of *dance* without any entity doing something.

These two types of words receive different names in the semantic literature: words that indicate relationships and are thus inherently dependent on other words are called **predicates**, and the independent individuals are called **arguments**. Predicates are associated with relations and properties; arguments are associated with the individual objects that complete the meaning of predicates. For example, in the expression *The boy is eating the pizza*, the nominal phrases *the boy* and *the pizza* are the **arguments**, and the event of 'eating' is the **predicate** (because 'eating' must be done by someone and of something). The linking of a predicate to its arguments is known as **predication**. By the way, this corresponds roughly to our two basic types of words, as we mentioned in Chapter 1: verbs (predicates) and nouns (arguments).

The distinction between predicate and argument has been described as absolutely basic, not only in language but also in cognition: some authors claim that it is an innate mechanism by which we structure the world, distinguishing actions and events and the elements involved in those events. In this sense, it has even been traced back to old primate vision systems. There is a currently widely accepted theory in visual processing called the 'dual-pathway hypothesis' (also known as 'two visual streams theory'). This theory specifies that visual information travels from our eyes to the visual areas of our brain following two different pathways: the first one, the 'ventral' pathway, is involved in the identification of objects (which is why it is known as the *what* system); the second one, the 'dorsal' pathway, is involved in the processing of spatial locations (and is thus known as the *where* system). The idea is that, as animals, we are interested in locating potentially interesting items in our environment quite quickly (*where* something is), and then in a next step, we must identify the category to which the items belong (*what* something is). Some authors (e.g., Givón, 2002;

Hurford, 2003; Landau and Jackendoff, 1993) affirm that these two mechanisms are in fact the precursors of the predicate–argument distinction that organizes linguistic information: the ventral/what system is the one that identifies arguments, and the second system, the dorsal/where pathway, is the origin of relational information (Figure 8.2).

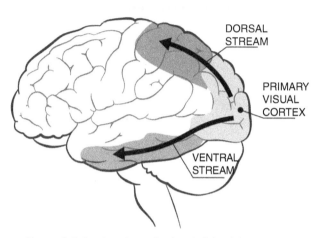

Figure 8.2 Dual Pathway in the Brain's Vision System

Each predicate 'needs' or 'selects' a different *number* of arguments. For example, intransitive verbs like *sleep* or *snore* need only one argument (the entity that performs the sleeping or the snoring). Transitive verbs select two arguments; for example, *eat, break* or *attack* make reference to events where at least two entities are involved: one entity that performs the eating/breaking/attacking and another entity that is eaten/broken or attacked. Some verbs select three arguments, like *put* (cf. *I put my keys on the table*) or *give* (*I gave my girlfriend a present*). There are even verbs that select (at least, semantically) no arguments: such is the case of *weather verbs* like *rain* or *snow* (cf. *it is raining again*). The technical term for the number of arguments that a verb takes is sometimes known as its **adicity**.

However, knowing the number of arguments that a predicate takes is not enough. The verbs *weigh* and *see* both take two arguments, but we have the intuition that the relationship with their arguments is very different. This can be easily seen in their syntactic behaviour: for example, we can say both *I saw the cat* and *The cat was seen by me*. However, while we can say *My suitcase weighs 20 kilos*, the passive alternation is clearly odd: *Twenty kilos are weighed by my suitcase*. What we need to know then is what type of relation there is between an argument and its predicate, that is, the different roles that an argument can play in relation to a given predicate. In other words, we need the notion of **semantic role**.

8.3 Semantic Roles

A **semantic role** is *the semantic relation that holds between an argument and its predicate* (which is a more specific and narrow definition than just 'the roles that entities play in events'). As could be expected, there are many terminological variants of this notion; almost all linguistic theories use some version of them to give their grammar some grounding on semantics; in fact, the structure formed by a verb and its slots also receives different names in different theories, such as 'subcategorization frame', 'argument structure' or 'thematic structure'. In our case, we have chosen the label 'semantic role', which is arguably the most neutral of all possibilities, trying to dissociate our discussion from any specific linguistic theory. In Table 8.1, we find some of the most common terminological variants of semantic roles:

Table 8.1 *Some Terminological Equivalents*

Semantic cases	Thematic relations	Theta (θ) roles	Participant roles	Thematic roles	Functional roles
Fillmore 1968	Gruber 1976	Chomsky 1981	Allan 1986	Dowty 1991	Cruse 2000

Semantic roles are thus the key elements in establishing the basic information in a sentence: the 'who did what to whom'. There are many types of possible relationships between an argument and its predicate, and accordingly, the list of semantic roles mentioned in the literature is very long. There is also a great variability in the length of this list: some authors mention only two of them, and some authors (e.g., in natural language processing) mention more than thirty-five. The most usual list contains normally between twelve and eighteen. This is the list we have selected:

(1) AGENT

The *agent* is the deliberate, active causer or instigator of any action. Normally, the agent is human, and therefore agency is connected with volition, will, intentionality, etc.

Bart pushed Lisa
Lisa was pushed by Bart

(2) INSTRUMENT

It is the means by which a predicate is carried out, the thing used by an agent or experiencer, usually in order to do something to a Patient (semantic role number 4) or to perceive a Content (semantic role number 6). Instruments exert no action of their own.

Voldemort attacked Harry with <u>a killing curse</u>
Hermione used <u>her wand</u> to fix Harry's glasses

As instruments are causally involved in the action, they can sometimes surface as subjects in English: *<u>This key</u> will open the door.*

(3) STIMULUS

This is whatever causes a psychological response in an Experiencer (semantic role number 5); this response can be either negative or positive.

<u>The situation</u> scared me
<u>Bernadette</u> really turns Howard on

(4) PATIENT

It is the argument that is changed or affected by an action instigated by an agent or simply the undergoer of a process.

The Rebel Alliance destroyed <u>the Death Star</u>
<u>The Death star</u> was destroyed by the Rebel Alliance
<u>The Death Star</u> exploded

(5) EXPERIENCER

This is the sentient being that perceives or conceives something, aware of the action or state described by the verb but does not control it.

<u>Homer</u> saw the boys
<u>Homer</u> likes beer
Homer accidentally frightened <u>Marge</u>

(6) CONTENT

This is an idea, a psychological state, mental representation or percept that is entertained or perceived (also called PERCEPT; Saeed, 1997: 143).

Woody heard <u>the bark of a dog</u>
Andy saw <u>the toys</u>

(7) BENEFICIARY

It is the element for or against whose benefit the action is performed (also called BENEFACTIVE).

I'll buy you a beer
He bought a beer for me

(8) THEME

It corresponds to the entity which is located somewhere or that changes place moving from one place to another.

The ring was in Frodo's pocket
Frodo threw the ring into Mount Doom

(9) SOURCE

This is roughly the starting point of a trajectory.

I come from Alabama with a banjo on my knee
Jojo left his home

(10) GOAL

This is roughly the endpoint of a trajectory.

The hobbits walked to Mordor
Sam returned home safely

(11) PATH

This is roughly the portion of a trajectory that lies between the source and the goal.

The ball rolled across the floor
Steve walks warily down the street

(12) LOCATION

This is used to designate where a situation takes place or where an object is located (also called LOCATIVE sometimes).

He was gambling in Las Vegas
The money was on the table
The boss was at his office

On this list of roles, not all of them stand at the same level. We could, for example, group them around common themes: the first three, AGENT, INSTRUMENT and STIMULUS, function as 'initiators' of actions, and that is why Frawley (1992) calls them 'logical actors'. On the other hand, PATIENT, EXPERIENCER, CONTENT and BENEFICIARY form a group of 'logical patients' (entities that somehow receive the action); the last group, THEME, SOURCE, PATH, GOAL and LOCATION all make reference to spatial concepts.

Another broad distinction can be established within semantic roles: **participant roles** vs. **non-participant roles**. Participant roles are those needed by the predication itself; they are the more 'central' type of participants and, roughly, answer the question 'who did what to whom?' Non-participant roles are optional roles that express the context of the predication, and usually answer questions such as why, where, when and how. Normally, participant roles are perceived as obligatory and nuclear, while non-participant roles are optional and less central to the meaning of the predication itself. Thus, in *Ken kissed Barbie with passion*, the 'kisser' and the 'kissed' are perceived as necessary: to have an event of 'kissing' you have to specify both entities. The other element, *with passion* is not as essential: you could omit this type of information and the result would not be perceived as incomplete.

These two types of roles are given different names in grammar; obligatory arguments are called **arguments**, while optional elements are called **adjuncts**. Theoretically, arguments are supplied by verbs (that is, they form part of the lexical entry of the word), while adjuncts are supplied by external sentential phrases. As we shall see below, this 'bottom-up' strategy has been slightly modified by certain approaches to grammar, the so-called 'constructional approaches', which allow grammatical constructions to supply with new arguments that augment those provided by the verb. The distinction between arguments and adjuncts, though basic and acknowledged as essential in both linguistic and psycholinguistic accounts, proves to be hard to establish in some cases. Many authors have suggested different tests to identify obligatory elements from optional ones. However, these linguistic tests have often been deemed unreliable (e.g., Koenig *et al.*, 2003). Most of the alternatives offered tend to suggest a less dychotomic and more graded treatment of the argument-adjunct distinction (e.g., Langacker, 1987; MacDonald *et al.*, 1994; Manning, 2003).

8.3.1 Jackendoff's Two-Tier Approach

Similar approaches have been proposed for the assignment of semantic roles. For example, Jackendoff (1972) suggested adding phrases like *deliberately, on purpose, in order to*, as a test for agenthood; in this respect, only those entities that can be combined with such phrases can be considered agents, as in (2):

(2)   a. *Gandalf opened the door (in order to enter)*
       b. *?The key opened the door (in order to enter)*

However, in the case of motion events, especially when we include human participants, there is a conflict: we can very often think of the participants in those scenes in two different terms. For example, consider the sentences in (3):

(3) a. *Iron Man flew to the top of the building*
     b. *Spiderman jumped off the skyscraper*

In (3a), *Iron Man* is both an AGENT, who performs the action, and at the same time, is the THEME, since it is the entity that is displaced. Something similar is seen in (3b) with *Spiderman*. This is solved by Jackendoff by positing two tiers of roles, one having to do with actions and the second with movement. This is what we found in examples in (4):

(4) a. *Clark kissed Lois*
        Theme   Goal   (spatial tier)
        Agent   Patient   (action tier)
     b. *Thor threw his hammer*
        Source Theme   (spatial tier)
        Agent   Patient   (action tier)
     c. *Dracula entered the room*
        Theme   Goal   (spatial tier)
        Agent   (action tier)
     d. *Mina received a letter*
        Goal   Theme   (spatial tier)
                          (action tier)

In cases like (4a), the most natural level of description is the action tier (agent/patient), and the spatial tier can feel a bit forced; however, in (4b) both tiers are perceived as equally appropriate. In (4c), only the spatial tier can be completely filled out (since from the point of view of the action, the room is not affected in any way by the action), while in (4d) the spatial tier is more useful; though we could perhaps try to fill the slots in the action tier with Beneficiary and Patient.

8.4 Propositions as Units of Meaning

The union of a predicate with its arguments (and its adjuncts) has a special status in many theories of meaning, especially in amodal or symbolic approaches to meaning. Such a union forms a **proposition**. Propositions have been regarded as *the semantic processing units of the mind* (Kintsch, 1988: 69). A proposition is the smallest unit of meaning that can be put in predicate-argument form; they are said to capture the abstract, deep and explicit meaning of sentences. Kintsch (1998) showed how propositions can summarize the ideas expressed in sentences, though a sentence is not the same thing as a proposition. A proposition is just the union between a predicate and its arguments, and different versions of the same sentence

211

can be captured by the same proposition. For example, sentences like *Mary bakes a cake, Mary is baking a cake, a cake is being baked by Mary, Mary's baking of a cake* or *the baking of a cake by Mary* would correspond to the same propositional content: (BAKE, MARY, CAKE). A sentence has as many propositions as predicates. So, while *the cat sleeps* corresponds to one proposition (SLEEP, CAT), the sentence *the quick cat captured the slow mouse* would contain three different propositions (since adjectives are also predicates): (QUICK, CAT), (SLOW, MOUSE) and (CAPTURE, CAT, MOUSE).

The information of a sentence that can be captured in this propositional form corresponds to its 'deep meaning' or 'gist'. There are studies that show that we tend to forget the specific form with which we heard something, and remember instead only the gist, the proposition corresponding to the underlying predicate-argument structure. So, if people hear *John gave Peter the ball*, they will not remember correctly whether they heard this sentence or the alternative one *John gave the ball to Peter*, since both of them have the same propositional structure (GIVE, JOHN, PETER, BALL), which is what they store in memory. Another source of evidence comes from online sentence understanding: sentences with fewer propositions are understood quicker than sentences with more propositions. For example, the sentence *the kitten climbed over the fence* has six words and one proposition (CLIMB, KITTEN, FENCE); the sentence *the truck Susan was driving crashed* also has six words but corresponds to two propositions: (DRIVE, SUSAN, TRUCK), (CRASH, TRUCK): people take less time to understand the first one, with the same number of words but fewer propositions.

There are nevertheless a number of criticisms of propositional representations. To start with, as part of a fully symbolic account, propositions are amodal, abstract and arbitrary representations of the meanings of language and thus fall prey to the same problems of symbolic accounts, including circularity and 'lack of grounding' (what we saw in Chapter 3 as the Symbol Grounding Problem). In fact, many of the embodied effects we reviewed in Chapter 3 were originally provided as examples of how propositional representations fall short of their duties in some cases. Take the examples we included in that chapter: *the ranger saw the eagle in the sky/nest*. In its propositional representations the word *eagle* is represented in the same way: roughly (SEE, RANGER, EAGLE, SKY) or (SEE, RANGER, EAGLE, NEST). There is nothing in these representations that informs us about the shape of the eagle (with wings stretched or not), but as we saw in Chapter 3, people recognize those shapes faster after hearing the appropriate version (Figure 8.3).

(SAW, RANGER, EAGLE, IN (EAGLE, SKY))   (SAW, RANGER, EAGLE, IN (EAGLE, NEST))

The ranger saw an eagle in the sky   *The ranger saw an eagle in the nest*

Figure 8.3 Representing the Meaning of *Eagle* Propositionally or Imagistically

We saw a similar thing happen with examples such as the orientation of a nail in *he hammered the nail into the floor* vs. *he hammered the nail into the wall*. Those effects cannot be so easily accommodated by propositional accounts (you could explain them, though much more indirectly). Zwaan (2000) is a revision of these effects that are not included in propositional representation. Barsalou (1999) claims that his Perceptual Symbol System, that uses embodied symbols, is in fact an 'embodied propositional system', since it can do all the things that a propositional system does (e.g., remember the gist of a sentence, etc.). Other criticisms include their biological implementation, which is far from clear at the moment, and then their insufficient coverage of expressions that cannot be assigned a truth-value, such as questions, commands or exclamations. The role of truth-value is normally applied to propositions, though it is not altogether clear whether the term **proposition** as used here is equivalent to the one used in predicate logic; authors such as Kintsch tend to keep both separate.

8.5 Linking: Semantic Role + Grammatical Function

The next question to be asked is how semantic roles are expressed linguistically. The most usual way to describe this is by associating them with a given grammatical function. Thus, in a verb such as *write*, the AGENT is normally linked with the grammatical function 'subject', which tells us how to express it linguistically: simplifying matters a great deal, in English, the subject is the Noun Phrase which comes before the verb. In most cases, Agents are Subjects (e.g., *John broke the vase*), Patients are Direct Objects (e.g., *John broke the vase*) and Instruments are Obliques (e.g., *John broke the vase with a hammer*), but this is not always the case. For example, the same grammatical function can be associated with different semantic roles. Such is the case of subject, as we see in Table 8.2:

213

Table 8.2 *One Grammatical Function (Subject)*
Linked to Several Semantic Roles

AGENT	*The <u>player</u> kicked the ball*
EXPERIENCER	*The <u>referee</u> saw the whole thing*
PATIENT	*The <u>man</u> suffered an injury*
THEME	*The <u>rocket</u> soared up in the sky*
INSTRUMENT	*The <u>key</u> opened the door easily*
STIMULUS	*<u>The noise</u> frightened the baby*

At the same time, the same semantic role can be associated with different grammatical functions. Such is the case of STIMULUS (Table 8.3):

Table 8.3 *One Semantic Role (Stimulus) Linked to*
Several Grammatical Functions

Direct Object	*Luke fears <u>the dark side of the Force</u>*
Subject	*<u>The dark side of the Force</u> frightens Luke*

The preferential linking between AGENT and Subject, on the one hand, and PATIENT and Object, on the other, is found in many of the world's languages, and has been related by some authors to perceptual advantages in the processing of agents and patients. For example, Verfaillie and Daems (1996) carried out an experiment in which the trajectories of different moving balls interacted on the computer screen; some of the balls affected others, pushing them and deviating them (i.e., they were playing 'agent' roles), while others were more 'patient-like', being affected by the behaviour of the other balls. Subjects identified 'agent-like' balls more quickly than 'patients', suggesting an interesting parallelism between the perceptual advantage of agents in visual perception and their privileged status as subjects in sentences (subjects tend to appear first in sentences and thus receive more attention linguistically than objects).

In any case, since the mapping between semantic roles and grammatical functions is not one-to-one, but many-to-many, the precise way in which the correct correspondences are chosen must be specified. This problem is addressed by a very active zone of linguistic research called **Linking Theory**. The first studies on this topic appeared in the sixties (e.g., Gruber, 1976; Fillmore, 1968); many theories since then have studied this issue and have tried to propose a definitive solution, which, judging by the amount of papers published on this topic every year, has not been found yet.

One popular way to predict how a given semantic role will surface syntactically is to use what has been called the SUBJECT HIERARCHY. Again, we have many different versions of this hierarchy (e.g., Fillmore, 1968; Jackendoff,

214

1972; Givón, 1984; Bresnan and Kanerva, 1989; Grimshaw, 1990; Dowty, 1991; Saeed, 2009), but all versions work in the same way. Let us examine a slightly modified version of Bresnan and Kanerva (1989), shown in (5):

(5)   The SUBJECT HIERARCHY:
       Agent > Recipient/Experiencer/Goal > Instrument > Theme/Patient > Location

What this hierarchy does is tell you which semantic role will be linked to subject; that grammatical function will be assigned to the semantic role closer to the left of this hierarchy. For example, let's suppose we have a verb, like *break*, which is used with an AGENT, a PATIENT and an INSTRUMENT. This hierarchy says that the 'normal' mapping will be of AGENT with SUBJECT, as in (6a). If this verb is used with an INSTRUMENT and a PATIENT, the semantic role that will be linked to subject is the INSTRUMENT, since it is located to the left of PATIENT in the hierarchy (6b); see how we cannot add a phrase specifying the agent, since if we wanted to mention the agent, it would have to occupy the subject position. And only when the verb is used only with a PATIENT can this semantic role be associated with the grammatical function subject (6c).

(6)   a. *John broke the window with a hammer*
       b. *The hammer broke the window (*by John)*
       c. *The window broke*

The use of this hierarchy does not fully satisfy everyone, though. On the one hand, it is difficult to come up with a definitive version that is accepted by all linguists, and all sort of variations on its functioning are being proposed. On the other hand, there are other more serious criticisms: some scholars think that this hierarchy does not take into account the fact that there are combinations of roles that are not possible: only a small group of all the possible combinations licensed by the hierarchy are actually found. For example, we do find configurations such as {AGENT, PATIENT}, {STIMULUS, EXPERIENCER} or {THEME, GOAL}, but other combinations are probably impossible (or at least, are unattested): {BENEFICIARY, GOAL}, {INSTRUMENT, GOAL}, {PATIENT, INSTRUMENT}, and a long etcetera.

For many authors, it makes little sense to conceive semantic roles as isolated elements, since they always show up in certain combinations. These combinations are very often related to different types of events. That is, some combinations of semantic roles have a special status, since they form the skeleton of basic scenes in human experience. For example, the combination {AGENT, PATIENT} is related to action events (somebody does something to someone else) and is the one found in most transitive verbs. The combination {STIMULUS, EXPERIENCER} (or its inverted counterpart) is normally used to describe psychological events (i.e., somebody experiences something); the combination {THEME, GOAL} corresponds to motion events, etc. This was actually the basis for the theory of Construction Grammar (Goldberg 1995, 2006). This theory, already mentioned in Chapter 1 when talking about how to express meaning in syntax, provides an alternative explanation to the inclusion of semantic roles in a sentence.

So far, we have assumed, as most linguistic theories, that the element that provides the semantic arguments to a sentence is the verb (the so called *lexicalist* hypothesis). However, as we saw in Chapter 1, in Construction Grammar, grammatical constructions by themselves can contribute semantic information. Thus, the verb *cook* is typically transitive, that is, it involves an AGENT and a PATIENT. However, we can see this verb in sentences that include other combinations of arguments, as in those in (7):

(7) a. *The chicken cooked all night* (intransitive inchoative)
     b. *Pat cooked the steaks* (transitive)
     c. *Pat cooked the steak well-done* (resultative)
     d. *Pat cooks* (deprofiled object)
     e. *Pat cooked Chris some dinner* (ditransitive)
     f. *Pat cooked her way into the Illinois State bake-off* (*way* construction)

A lexicalist theory would have to propose six different senses of the verb *to cook*, each with a different argument structure. Instead, in Construction Grammar, it is postulated that the number of arguments present in the sentence results from the integration of the argument structure of the verb and the argument structure of the grammatical construction itself. In this sense, instead of a purely bottom-up approach to argument structure we have a fusion of bottom-up (verb) and top-down (construction) processes.

For example, there is a *Ditransitive Construction* that contains 'slots' for three arguments: a Sender (the Subject), the Thing Sent (Object 1) and a Receiver (Object 2). This is the structure in a sentence such as *John gave his girlfriend a nice present*, which uses the verb *give*, which is a three-place predicate. But it can also be used with verbs that would not normally be thought of as three-place predicates, like those in (7):

(8) a. *John kicked his brother the ball*
     b. *John wrote his brother a note*
     c. *John baked his brother a pie*
     d. *John sang his girlfriend a song*
     e. *John crutched his brother the ball*

The first four verbs in (8), *kick*, *write*, *bake* and *sing* are listed in dictionaries with two different types of entries, intransitive and transitive, but neither of them is associated with a ditransitive sense. A version of example

(8e) was seen in Chapter 3 when we talked about affordances: it includes the invented verb *to crutch*, which in this constructional context acquires the meaning 'to transfer something to a receiver using a crutch'.

There are lots of examples that work like these ones from many other argument structure constructions. In *She sneezed the napkin off the table*, the intransitive verb *sneeze*, which in principle is not associated to the meaning 'to move something by sneezing', suddenly acquires such a meaning in this example and is found with two additional roles (a Theme/Patient, *the napkin*, and a Goal, *off the table*); this would be an example of the *Caused Motion Construction*. This construction helps to explain other 'unconventional' examples involving caused motion such as *They laughed the poor guy out of the room* or *Mary urged Bill into the house*. In these cases, again, we see how the verb *laugh* acquires the meaning 'to make somebody move by laughing at him/her' by its inclusion in the construction; something similar happens with the verb *urge*. Goldberg (1995, 2006) includes a detailed explanation of how both types of roles (those supplied by the verb and those supplied by the construction) are fused in the final constructional configuration. In Table 8.4, a list is shown with other argument structure constructions, which supply their own semantic roles and their associated meaning.

Table 8.4 *Some Argument Structure Constructions*

Construction	Basic scene	Form	Example
Intransitive motion construction	Something moves to a place	Subj-Agent Verb Obl-Goal	*He went to the door*
Transitive construction	Something acts on something	Subj-Agent Verb Obj-Patient	*He broke the vase*
Caused-motion construction	Someone causes something to move	Subj-Agent Verb Obj-Theme Obl-Goal	*He pushed the ball into the room*
Cause-receive construction	Someone causes someone to receive something	Subj-Agent Verb Obj1-Goal Obj2-Theme	*He gave her a flower*

8.6 Issues with Semantic Roles

Semantic roles are very useful to explain the linking between the semantic and the syntactic realms, and almost every single theory includes them in their explanations. However, they suffer from a number of problems. The most immediate one is that, even if every theory tends to assume that there is a finite list of them, no agreement can be reached about their total number.

For example, the list we presented in Section 8.3 is clearly insufficient, and could be easily expanded with further notions:

- REASON: Yoko Ono split the Beatles *out of spite*
- PURPOSE: I've come to your house *to tell you a big secret*
- TOPIC: Steven and Amy were discussing *their divorce*
- METHOD: I usually cook vegetables *by heating water*
- MANNER: He kissed the bride *in a passionate way*
- POSSESSOR: This house belongs *to John*
- COMITATIVE: I came to the party *with Helen*
- RESULT: He hammered the metal *flat*

Another problem is that the terminology used is sometimes quite different. For example, the list we have provided in this book is basically the same as the list found in Saeed (1997), but if you look at another similar semantics textbook, such as Kreidler (1998), you find something completely different (see Table 8.5).

Table 8.5 *A List of Semantic Roles by Kreidler (1998)*

Actor	The role of an argument that performs some action without affecting any other entity. *Sylvia left*
Affected	The role of an argument that undergoes a change due to some event or is affected by some other entity. *A window broke. Tom broke a window. Betty likes opera. Opera delights Betty*
Affecting	The role of an argument that, without any action, affects another entity. *Betty likes opera. Opera delights Betty*
Agent	The role of an argument that by its action affects some other entity. *Tom broke a window*
Associate	The role of an argument that tells the status or identity of another argument, the theme: *Roger is a student*
Effect	The role of an argument that comes into existence through the action of the predicate. *Tillie baked a pie*
Place	The role of an argument that names the location in which the action of the predicate occurs. *The fireman climbed a ladder*
Theme	The role of an argument that is the topic of a predicate that does not express action – a stative predicate. *Audrey is a computer expert*

If we compare this list with the list in Saeed (1997), there are important disagreements; the example in Kreidler's ACTOR would be called a THEME in Saeed (1997); Kreidler's AFFECTED spans over two semantic roles in Saeed (1997): PATIENT and EXPERIENCER; two of the roles he mentions (ASSOCIATE and EFFECT) are simply not mentioned in Saeed (1997); his notion of AGENT is more restricted than Saeed's; in fact, Saeed's AGENT would cover both the ACTOR and the AGENT in the list in Table 8.5. Finally, the THEME in this table is different from the THEME in Saeed, which contains no role that is similar to this one (a stative predicate). As we can see, a direct comparison of these two lists is not that simple; generally speaking, deciding what it is that a semantic role should encompass is not a trivial task. It also becomes evident that finding the right level of generality-specificity is an open question: do we need more general/abstract roles or more specific/concrete ones? Some authors think that AGENT is just a special type of a more general role, called ACTOR, which would correspond to any entity that performs or controls the situation expressed by the predicate. The subject of example (9) would be an ACTOR; it performs the action, but no volition is involved.

(9)   *The falling tree destroyed my bicycle*

There are also suggestions for conflating PATIENT and THEME under one broad semantic role; BENEFICIARY is often distinguished from RECIPIENT; as we have seen, Kreidler subsumes EXPERIENCER and PATIENT under the same category (AFFECTED). Some theories only make use of two very broad and basic roles (ACTOR and UNDERGOER; this is the case of Van Valin's *Role and Reference Grammar*), while others incorporate many more. In general, the more 'concrete' you need your semantic roles to be, the bigger your list of semantic roles will have to be. Table 8.6 presents a number of semantic roles lists from different theories, ending with the list used by the machine translation system METAL.

In general, two possible strategies can be identified: (a) defining these notions broadly; and (b) defining these notions more specifically. Each option has potential advantages and disadvantages. On the one hand, these notions can be defined broadly; in this way, you can keep a reduced number of them. This makes the whole system more manageable, and then you also gain generalizing power: if you define a role in a more inclusive way, when you describe its behaviour, it will affect a great number of cases. The problem in this case is a certain degree of vagueness in the definition of the roles, since many different cases will have to be grouped under the same label. On the other hand, these notions can be defined in a more specific way. In this manner, the labels will be more 'exact' and adaptable to specific cases; the internal coherence of each notion will be greater. However, this means that their number will grow strongly and therefore their generalizing power will be reduced, since each role covers 'less ground'.

Quite probably the decision on which level is more adequate depends on your particular interest or purpose. We have already seen that categories are always established for a reason: to enable the transfer of inferences from the behaviour of one member of the category to the rest of the members. That is, all categories are there because of the type of generalization they allow. This

Table 8.6 *Different Semantic Role Lists*

Van Valin (2004)	ACTOR	UNDERGOER		
Dik (1978)	AGENT	GOAL	DESTINATARY	BENEFICIARY
	INSTRUMENT	LOCATION	TIME	DIRECTION
	PROCESSED	FORCE	POSITIONER	SOURCE
	EXPERIMENTER	POSSESSOR		
Croft (1991)	AGENT	PATIENT	EXPERIENCER	STIMULUS
	COMITATIVE	INSTRUMENT	MANNER	MEANS
	BENEFICIARY	CAUSE	PASSIVE AGENT	RESULT
	PURPOSE			
Hirst (1987)	AGENT	DURATION	BENEFICIARY	QUANTITY
	PATIENT	INSTRUMENT	CO-AGENT	GOAL
	LOCUS	MANNER	TOPIC	PURPOSE
	TIME	METHOD	INTERCHANGE	DESTINATARY
	ORIGIN	PATH/TRAJECTORY		
METAL	*(Central)*			
	AGENT	INSTRUMENT	GOAL	BENEFICIARY
	DESTINATARY	REFLEXIVE	TOPIC	BODY-PART
	CONMUTATIVE (CO-AGENT)			
	(Peripheral)			
	COMPOSITION	EFFECT/RESULT	MATERIAL	MEASURE
	METHOD/ME	PURPOSE/REASON	SIMILARITY	CONTRARY
	IN-SPITE-OF	CONTEXT	EXCEPTION	MANNER
	POSSESSOR	PARTITIVE	RESPECTIVE/COMPARATIVE	
	(Locative)			
	LOCATION	PROXIMITY	SOURCE	GOAL CIRCUMFERENT
	TRAVERSED-AREA			
	(Temporal)			
	PUNCTUAL	DURATIVE		

is even more evident in the case of scientific or 'academic' categories: what the analyst tries to do is to group together elements that show a similar behaviour in some respect. That is why trying to find the 'ultimate' list of semantic roles makes little sense: if you are trying to describe some syntactic aspect of lexical elements, you will be interested in one type of list, probably, a shorter one allowing a wider type of generalization. That is, if you have a rule about the behaviour of a semantic role and your total number of semantic roles is just two, that rule will apply to a great number of cases; that is what we mean by 'generalizing' power. On the other hand, if you are more interested in semantic generalizations, you will need a longer list, with cases that capture semantic behaviour more effectively (and again, in that case, the generalizing power of those 'smaller' semantic roles will be reduced). Semantic roles can in fact be increasingly refined and defined at an increasingly more specific level, until the most specific type of role possible is found: one specific role for each verb. In this way, the verb *kiss*, instead of having an AGENT and a PATIENT, would have a KISSED and a KISSED, and so on. Some authors (e.g., Langacker, 1991) have mentioned that even the agents of very similar verbs are slightly different (e.g., the agent of *bite* is slightly different from the agent of *chew*). Lately, different groups of scholars, coming from different traditions, are exploring this specificity strategy, which we will review in the next section.

8.7 Thematic Knowledge and Frame-Specific Roles

One of the overarching controversies throughout the book is which amount of work in language comprehension is carried out by information linked specifically to words, and which is taken over by our general conceptual knowledge, modulated by context (as we saw in the case of polysemy or antonymy, for example). A popular version of sentence understanding establishes a clear division between linguistic knowledge, on the one hand (which is linked to the verb, and stored in the lexicon) and encyclopaedic knowledge or knowledge about the world, on the other. According to this view, this latter type of knowledge is indeed used in constructing the meaning of sentences and discourse, and its influence on several aspects of sentence parsing and understanding cannot be disregarded, but it should nevertheless be considered as a different source of information. These two sources of information should thus be kept separate not only because they have different origins, but also because they become active at different moments in processing.

In this view, there are two stages in the construction of sentence meaning. In a first stage, we activate the more 'lexically based' information, tied to the verb, that specifies argument structure (number of arguments) and role of the arguments (i.e., semantic roles). This syntactic and lexical information is 'informationally encapsulated' and takes precedence when constructing the meaning of the sentence. At this stage, we should also include the lexical information (supplied by verbs), specifying the requirements that an element must have in order to fill the semantic role in their argument structure: this is called 'selectional restriction' information. Selectional restrictions are thus semantic constraints that verbs impose on the semantic type of objects that can be inserted as its arguments.

Initially, selectional restrictions were regarded almost as 'syntactic markers', and were tied to very abstract and generic notions such as 'animacy', but soon had to be associated to more detailed information. For example: the sentence *he drank a piece of rock* is slightly odd because in our entry for *drink* we have information about what can be drunk. The event evoked by this verb contains at least two elements, the entity that does the drinking and the substance that is drunk; the agent must be animate, and the patient must correspond to a liquid substance. Analogously, the verb *to eat* selects edible patients. This is slightly tricky, though: following this path would suggest that there are as many selectional restrictions as verbs (for the verbs *inflate, debate, catch, lift*, etc, [+inflatable], [+debatable], [+catchable], [+liftable] and so on). Quite clearly, this is a slippery slope to world knowledge: take the case of the verb *to mail* (Myers and Bloomstein, 2005). This verb requires an agent who is animate, human and capable of volitional action; its patient requires an object that is 'mail-able'. In this case, we are fully immersed in world knowledge: what is mailable depends on the different postal systems (in terms of size and weight).

In this sense, there is some evidence now showing that within selectional restrictions, the distinction between lexical-grammatical constraints and conceptual event-based knowledge is, in fact, quite difficult to establish. In Chapter 2, as an example of the use of eye-tracking in semantic studies, we reviewed the study by Altmann and Kamide in which subjects were looking at a screen with four different objects. When they heard *the boy will eat . . .* their eyes started looking at the picture of a cake (something that did not happen when they heard *the boy will move . . .*), showing that the verb *eat* had activated the list of objects which could serve as patients, and thus allowed subjects to anticipate quite early on the next word they were going to hear. In another study by these same researchers, participants looked again at four pictures; two of those pictures were a motorbike and a carousel. When participants heard *the boy will ride the . . .* they started looking at the motorbike; when they heard *the girl will ride the . . .* they started looking at the carousel. This again reveals a deep knowledge of the world (if somehow stereotyped), with participants choosing as more likely a patient of *ride* a different object depending on who is doing the riding.

The second stage involves world knowledge, which, as you might remember, is mostly structured in the form of schemas. These schemas provide the base for what we called in Chapter 5 'thematic relations', which establish links among the participants that are found together in a given scene. For example, *lion* is associated with words such as *jungle, zoo,* or *cage; dog* would be associated with *bone* or *cat, hammer* with *nail, chalk* with *blackboard* and so on. These relations can be spatial, temporal or causal, and can include relations between agents, patients, instruments or locations. Some of these relations are affordance-based (e.g., *hammer* and *nail*), and some are more conventional (e.g., *chopsticks* and *sushi*).

There is an ever-increasing number of studies showing that in sentence understanding, event knowledge of this type affects comprehension from the very first stages: there is no temporal separation between lexical or event-based information. These studies are thus directly aimed against the dual-stage theory. We understand sentences incrementally: each incoming word activates rich world knowledge, which is integrated with the rest. A rich source of information comes from priming studies, which so far have shown that:

- Specific verbs prime the typical nouns appearing in their different slots. For example, verbs prime their protypical semantic roles:

  (1) Agent. The verb *arrest* primes *cop*; the verb *serve* primes *waiter*
  (2) Patients. The verb *arrest* primes *robber*; the verb *serve* primes *customer*
  (3) Instruments. The verb *stir* primes *spoon*; the verb *cut* primes *chainsaw*

- Specific nouns prime the verbs with which they appear in thematic scenes:

  (1) the noun *waiter* primes *serving* (Agent)
  (2) the noun *guitar* primes *strumming* (Patient)
  (3) the noun *chainsaw* primes *cutting* (Instrument)
  (4) the noun *cafeteria* primes *eating* (Location)

- Specific nouns can also prime other nouns which participate in the same scene:

  (1) some event nouns prime people (*sale–shopper*) and objects (*trip–luggage*) commonly found at those events
  (2) some location nouns prime people/animals (*hospital–doctor*) and objects (*barn–hay*) commonly found at those locations
  (3) some instrument nouns prime things on which those instruments are commonly used (*key–door*), though not the types of people who tend to use them (*hose–gardener*).

These links are sensitive to grammatical choices: for example, verbs related to events carried out in a typical location (e.g., *cook–kitchen*) do not prime these location nouns in just any verbal form: perfective forms do not prime them (e.g., *had cooked*), but imperfective forms do (e.g., *was cooking* does prime *kitchen*). These results are consistent with other research that has shown that imperfective aspect prompts the simulation of the internal structure of an event (while perfective aspect makes us simulate the event as a finished whole; Madden and Zwaan, 2003). Other studies have shown how these choices are modulated by context; typically, the word *saved* would prime *money*, but that depends on the agent that is found before; if the agent of the verb has been *the lifeguard*, then *money* is not primed (since it would activate a different scene with a different sense of the polysemous verb *save*: saving money vs. saving a person).

All these examples show how quite specific and detailed world knowledge is active in sentence meaning construction since the first moments, always modulated, of course, by the discursive context. For example, when talking about food, different thematic instruments will be associated with different types of restaurants (compare the restaurant you might think about when you hear *chopsticks* vs. *silverware*, for example); different types of foods will be associated with the specific places where you eat the food (*cotton-floss* is associated with fairs and circuses, *popcorn* with cinemas, and *hamburgers* with cafeterias and fast-food restaurants), and some foods are even associated with specific times of the year (e.g., *turkey* is a typical Christmas food in many countries of the world).

Figure 8.4 Some Thematic Associations within the Domain of Food

There are studies that have shown the exclusively thematic origin of these associations. For example, the conjunction of two words like *piano* and *move* has been shown to prime a third one, *backache*. These words are not categorically related, nor have a direct associative link and thus can only be related by relying on our world knowledge in some common scene (somebody moving a heavy piano with the end result of backache). The same has been shown to happen with other groups of words such as *director, bribe* and *dismissal*.

In summary, we have a great deal of very specific knowledge about events in the world; this knowledge is activated by the lexemes found in a given discourse context, in such a way that each word creates expectations of what you are about to hear next. If you hear about a hammer, this creates expectations about what is coming next (the probability of the word *nail* is high), because you know what hammers are used for. This type of real-world, thematic, frame-based knowledge has shown to play a very important role in many areas of cognition; in language, it has been proved to influence areas like the ones we have covered (e.g., sentence parsing and understanding or word sense disambiguation); in other areas of cognition, it has been shown to influence categorization, similarity rating, memory, inference and analogy.

In the next section, we review how all the different types of information covered so far in the chapter can be seen to interact with grammar, by reviewing one specific example: the Commercial Transaction Frame.

8.7.1 The Commercial Transaction Frame

In this frame, we find a scene with at least four elements; Person A (the SELLER) has some object (that we call the GOODS) that Person B (the BUYER) wants. Person B gives Person A something (usually MONEY) in exchange for the object. This is basically what goes on in a commercial transaction scene (see Figure 8.5):

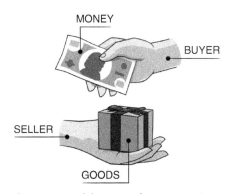

Figure 8.5 The Commercial Transaction Frame: Frame Elements

There are many different verbs that can be used to activate this frame, each of them showing a slightly different perspective or point of view. The way in which this works is by changes in the linking of frame-specific roles. For example, if you link the SELLER with the grammatical function 'subject', you get the verb *sell*. On the other hand, if 'subject' is linked to the BUYER, then the verb resulting is *buy*. Every time you make a change in linking you are shifting the prominence or salience of the different elements. Normally, the element that gets the grammatical function of 'subject' is the element that is given more emphasis. Each verb tells you how to express grammatically the frame-specific role. Some possibilities are listed in Table 8.7:

Table 8.7 *The Commercial Transaction Frame: Verbs and their Linkings*

	Buyer	Goods	Seller	Money
Buy	subject	object	from	for
Sell	to	object	subject	for
Cost	oblique	subject	⊘	object
Spend	subject	on	⊘	object

This is why all the sentences in example (10) make reference to the same scene, though each of them chooses a different perspective:

(10) a. *Natasha bought a car from Boris for €200*
      b. *Boris sold a car to Natasha for €200*
      c. *The car cost €200 to Natasha*
      d. *Natasha spent €200 on the car*

Note that each verb gives you a list of elements that must be obligatorily expressed (subject and object, for example), and also the elements that cannot be expressed with that verb. For example, you cannot mention the SELLER with the verb *cost: The car cost Natasha €200 from Boris.*

Also, if we change the requirements that the different frame elements must meet, or add further constraints on other frame elements, we get a great deal of additional verbs, much more specific. This is what is found in the list in (11):

(11) *bribe   present trade   auction import*
      export   haggle   refund   award   swindle
      shoplift raffle   peddle   inherit   finance

All these verbs make reference to this frame, but they include some variations, by adding more specific information to the details of the event, like some special characteristics of the SELLER, the BUYER, the GOODS or the MONEY, or adding some other element like the PLACE (the only thing that distinguishes importing and exporting is the place of BUYER and SELLER). In this way, very rich scenes can be activated; just think about the verb *auction* and the characteristic way in which auctioneers quickly chant the prices offered by bidders and their stereotyped closing formula: *Going, going, gone! Sold to the lady in the second row!* (and then the SELLER will signal the completion of the transaction with a gavel bang).

Quite frequently, mentioning one element can activate a whole frame. This is what we find in (12):

(12) a. 'Specific' sellers
    pusher/dealer landlord   sponsor
    vendor   salesman merchant

  b. 'Specific' money
    rent   bill/check fare/toll fee
    salary wages   capital

Whenever the frame element *rent* is mentioned, a special configuration of the whole commercial transaction frame is recovered, in which the BUYER is called the *tenant*, the SELLER is the *landlord*, the MONEY that is paid is called the *rent* and the GOODS that you buy are the right to inhabit a house (that belongs to the landlord). In the same way, mentioning a *dealer* will activate some specific GOODS: what a *dealer* sells is drugs. In this way, we see how frames/schemas are the way to encode very detailed world knowledge.

8.8 Concluding Remarks

Semantic roles are theoretical entities that play an essential role in most linguistic theories. They are crucial in the structuring of complex scenes, in which several elements are involved in complex relationships, and they help relate semantic content with syntactic behaviour. The use of one semantic role over another can have a great influence on how we conceptualize a situation (as we saw in the study introduced in Chapter 6, Section 6.9, about the effect that using an agentive or a non-agentive role had for the perception of blame; Fausey and Boroditsky, 2010). Nonetheless, their use is riddled with knotty problems.

To start with, the debate about the right level of generalization of semantic roles, as generic labels such as AGENT, PATIENT, INSTRUMENT, etc. on the one hand, or as more specific ones, as in frame-specific roles, on the other, is probably not one that can be solved. As we have mentioned, neither of both options is the 'correct' one; it all depends on the part we want them to play in our explanatory schemes. For very general and ample generalizations about the syntactic behaviour of most arguments (like the general linking of agents to subjects, for example), the generic level can be enough; for more specific and content-bound generalizations, a finer-grain is needed.

With all probability, these wider categories of AGENT, PATIENT, etc., arise from abstracting away of more specific frame-roles. If this is the case, we would expect semantic roles to show prototype effects, since we can have 'better' and 'worse' examples of AGENT (cf. Figure 8.6).

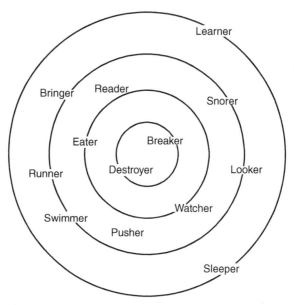

Figure 8.6 Prototypical Structure of the Category AGENT

As we have explained in Chapter 4, categories that are structured proto-typically cannot be described with a single set of 'necessary and sufficient conditions' which apply to all the exemplars in the category. What we expect instead is 'family-resemblances' among the exemplars; local similarities of groups of items that can be described only by their own set of generalizations. This is quite probably what we should expect in the case of semantic roles: not all agents are going to behave in the same way. This is then another reason why finding a universal set of semantic roles is so hard. And also why, instead of looking for generalizations that apply across the board to all verbs, many authors of different persuasions have opted for looking at smaller areas of the category. For example, Pinker (1989) resorts to **narrow semantic classes** in order to explain the correct argument structure generalizations that children engage in. Narrow semantic classes have also been applied to the linking of semantic roles with grammatical functions, which greatly facilitates the task (e.g., Davis and Koenig, 2000; Jackendoff, 1990).

There are other unanswered questions in the study of semantic roles; for example, their mixed status, as linguistic and conceptual entities, still needs to be clarified; we do not know whether to regard notions like AGENT or PATIENT as semantic primitives or we can decompose them; the ascription of noun phrases to a semantic role is still a thorny issue, and it is still quite easy to come up with sentences that are difficult to categorize using semantic roles. However, as we have mentioned at the beginning of this section, despite all these problems, disregarding them in linguistic analysis is a luxury no theory can afford, since they are truly the portals that connect the realms of syntax and semantics.

8.9 Chapter Summary

In this chapter, we have looked at how we arrive at the meaning of sentences. We have examined the information that is supplied by a crucial element in sentences: the verb. Verbs are 'predicates', relational elements that have to be combined with arguments; the combination of a verb and its arguments is the key element in the meaning of a sentence. Verbs specify how many arguments they need to complete their meaning, the roles that those arguments will play in the event or scene they describe and also how those elements will be expressed linguistically. The semantic relations between an argument and a predicate can be classified in a number of different 'semantic roles', like agent, patient or instrument. Semantic roles are linked with grammatical functions to construct the whole meaning of a sentence. We have also looked at propositions, the union between a predicate and its arguments that some authors have described as 'units of meaning', the most adequate level to capture the meaning of sentences. We have presented both empirical evidence in favour of their existence and some of the main criticisms aimed at them. We have also examined some of the problems faced by semantic roles, such as the difficulty of agreeing on their number and exact coverage, and the two extremes for their definition, the more abstract, syntactically based option and the more specific, semantic-based one.

The rest of the chapter has been devoted to the exploration of one of these two possibilities: highly specific semantic roles, which capture information at the level of specific events. We have reviewed empirical evidence that shows that thematic event-based knowledge is activated incrementally in the understanding of sentences. Finally, we have seen how all these different sources of information can be put together by examining the function of a concrete frame, that of commercial transactions. The chapter has closed with a summary of the main challenges of semantic roles and a re-appraisal of their importance in the field of semantics.

Exercises

Exercise 8.1 Explain the relation between participants and grammatical elements in the following sentences. How many event participants and how many grammatical elements are there in each sentence? Is there a one-to-one-relationship?

- *I wash myself everyday*
- *I sent Mary a couple of books last week*
- *It surprises me that you think I'm crazy*
- *The prices go up*
- *The Beatles conquered America*
- *John and Paul wrote many songs together*
- *It has been raining cats and dogs for the last three hours*
- *Nasty things were said in the divorce court-room*

Exercise 8.2 Identify the predicates and the arguments in the following list of sentences. Try to organize them in lists of propositions.

- *The cow jumped over the moon*
- *Jane has hired a very efficient secretary*
- *The frightened hobbit fought the hideous orc*
- *The dinner Mary is cooking smells great*
- *Your sister is sleeping on the couch*
- *We got the idea from a magazine*
- *The truth is out there*
- *He hammered the nail into the wall*
- *He hammered the nail into the floor*

Exercise 8.3 Identify the semantic roles in the following examples:

- *The dragon burned the city with its fiery breath*
- *The sun melted the ice*
- *I heard a strange noise in the attic*
- *Her silly stories amused the children*
- *She crutched her brother the ball*
- *I saw the girl from my window*
- *Your sister is sleeping in the couch*
- *I thought I knew what I was doing*
- *Please, tell your mother that I want an answer soon*

- *We got the idea from a decoration magazine*
- *I want you to sing me a birthday song*
- *He gave the door a hand of paint*
- *The police searched the house from noon till midnight*
- *Cry me a river*
- *Jesus changed water into wine*
- *The falling tree destroyed my bicycle*
- *Her stories bored the children to death*
- *This suitcase weighs twenty kilos*
- *Our team lost the game*
- *We were playing tic-tac-toe*

Exercise 8.4   Try to find out the organization of the frame underlying these groups of words. Which would be the frame-roles needed and how would you define them? Can you think of additional words to each one?

- *patient, doctor, medicine, illness, treatment, prescription, nurse*
- *attack, retreat, defend, parley, counter-attack*
- *come, go, advance, arrive, ascend, escape, exit, fall, leave, enter*

Exercise 8.5   Here you have again the list of verbs mentioned in example (11). Can you specify what type of additional information they bring to the COMMERCIAL TRANSACTION FRAME?

bribe	*present*	*trade*	*auction*	*import*
export	*haggle*	*refund*	*award*	*swindle*
shoplift	*raffle*	*peddle*	*inherit*	*finance*

Can you do the same with the specific frame elements in example (12)?

pusher/dealer	*landlord*	*sponsor*
vendor	*salesman*	*merchant*
rent	*bill/check*	*fare/toll*
fee	*salary*	*wages*

Key Terms Introduced in this Chapter

predicate
argument
adjunct
semantic role

predication
adicity
agent
instrument
stimulus
patient
experiencer
content
beneficiary
theme
source
goal
path
location
participant role
non-participant role
double-tier
proposition
linking theory
subject hierarchy
argument-structure constructions
thematic/frame-semantic/encyclopaedic knowledge
frame-specific roles
commercial transaction frame

Further Reading

One of the first proposals for semantic roles came from Fillmore (1968), who was inspired by the work of Tesnière (1959). Frawley (1992) includes a good discussion of semantic roles. The main reference in propositions as representation of sentences and texts is Kintsch (1998; 2001). There are many papers making reference to the new trend of specific event-knowledge in the processing of sentences; names such as Ken McRae, Mary Hare or Jeff Elman are strongly associated with this area (see for example, Ferretti *et al.*, 2001 or McRae *et al.*, 1998). Section 8.7.1 draws from Fillmore's Frame Semantics (Fillmore, 1982); the FrameNet project, which can be accessed at https://framenet.icsi.berkeley.edu, contains many more examples like this one.

CHAPTER 9

Discourse Meaning and Pragmatics

In this chapter ...

We examine how people interpret linguistic material in the wider realm of discourse comprehension. In order to recover the communicative intention of the speaker, we normally have to go beyond the words uttered and enrich them with inferences derived from the context at hand. This thorny issue becomes more tractable if we consider language as a collaborative activity: meaning is constructed from the speaker's linguistic cues and the hearer's understanding of the contextual situation. Both participants in the communicative setting derive expectations about the intentions of their interlocutor from the context and the goals of the social situation they are engaged in. In this chapter, the complex notion of context will be divided into: (1) information that comes from the physical place and time where the communication takes place; (2) the context provided by what has been said so far (called the co-text); and (3) context provided by the shared knowledge between speaker and hearer. For this last type of context, we will resort to the notion of 'common ground' (the knowledge that both speaker and hearer are aware that they share with each other) as well as to our knowledge of scenes and frames. We will see how knowing the way in which we are supposed to interact with the other person provides a great wealth of information that facilitates the recovery of inferences. We will also examine two classic notions in pragmatics, Grice's Conversational Maxims and Searle's Speech Acts, in connection with the general framework described in the chapter.

9.1 Discourse, Context and Use

> What words mean is a matter of what people mean by them (Grice, 1975: 340)

In this last chapter, like in all good stories, it is time to try to tie up all the loose ends, always a challenging task in the field of semantics. So far, we have been looking at how we construct meaning by examining the types of meaning evoked by the different linguistic levels, mainly the lexical one. We have spent some time looking at the meanings associated with words (Chapter 4), how words can refer to different meanings (i.e., polysemy; Chapter 5), and how word meanings are related to each other (Chapter 5); we have also seen how the meanings activated by verbs and other predicates organize the meaning of sentences (along with constructional meanings) in Chapter 8.

In our discussion, we have tried to avoid the trap of the **decoding** view. According to that view, when speakers want to convey a message, they encode it using a linguistic code and then produce the appropriate vocal signals; the addressee hears these signals, and, using the same linguistic code, 'decodes' them back into the original message. Unfortunately, this is not the way language works. Think of a dialogue like the one in (1):

(1)   Speaker A: *The phone!*
       Speaker B: *I'm in the shower!*

According to the decoding view, this dialogue is rather strange. The meaning of *phone* corresponds to the electrical device we use to transmit speech, so that is what should be evoked in the mind of the addressee. If that is the case, and the hearer recalls the image of a telephone, the answer seems odd: it merely informs Speaker A of the activity being carried out at that moment (taking a shower) in a way that may seem unrelated to the first utterance (think of a dialogue like '*The wall!*' '*I'm eating a sandwich!*', which has a similar form, but is even more difficult to understand). However, what is actually activated by this dialogue is something rather different. If you are in your house and somebody yells *The phone!!*, what you would normally understand is something like 'The phone is ringing; somebody go get it!'. In that case, the answer in (1) would in all probability be understood as something like 'I'm in the shower and therefore, I cannot pick up the phone'. Clearly, in order to understand one another, speakers need to go *beyond* what their words say literally; there is no way that we can analyse the individual meaning of the words in (1) to make them mean what we have described as an ordinary interpretation of the dialogue (Figure 9.1).

Figure 9.1 A Dialogue Interpreted in Context

In the **inferential** view of language, on the other hand, linguistic material plays only a partial (though basic) role in the whole process of meaning construction. Language is just a cue, a rough sketch, so to speak, of the complete meaning to be recovered. It is the hearer, who using his/her knowledge of the situation (i.e., context), must make an educated guess about what the other person really wants to communicate. The hearer will thus add whichever inferences are needed in order to cross the gap between what is said and what is meant.

Quite probably, these two related notions, context and inferences, are the main conundrums in semantic theory nowadays. **Context** permeates all semantic phenomena, to the extent that there is no agreement on what type of semantic information is 'context-free'. In fact, many authors support the extreme view that there is no such thing as context-independent information (Elman, 2009; Evans, 2009; Kintsch, 2001; Prinz, 2002; Spivey, 2007; Wittgenstein, 1957, *inter alia*). As we saw in our *coffee* example in Chapter 1, a word is typically associated with a great number of facts, many of them coming from our encyclopaedic knowledge. Parts of this information may be activated more frequently (or more automatically) than others, but there is no fail-safe way of telling beforehand what will be needed in a communicative exchange. Drawing a clear line between 'core' and 'peripheral' knowledge turns out to be an exceedingly complex issue; the distinction is bound to be a completely graded, statistical issue. In the inferential view, word meanings are always dynamic, context-dependent and ad hoc: in the same way as no man ever steps in the same river twice (for it's not the same river and he's not the same man, as Heraclitus said), the meaning of a word can be said to be never exactly the same on two different occasions. This means that we still have a lot of work to do. As Lebois *et al.* (2015: 31) state:

> Much remains to be understood and established about the dynamic activation of conceptual information. Future research needs to specify how situational context and task demands control the context-dependent construction of semantic representations.

For our current purposes, though, the main role of context is guiding the inferences that are needed in order to achieve the main goal in a communicative event: the recognition of the **communicative intention of the speaker.** In order to do this, two things are necessary. To start with, speaker and addressee must have a certain degree of shared knowledge. Then, they have to use this knowledge to 'guess' what the other person might be thinking. On the one hand, the speaker must try to formulate the message in a way that will allow the hearer to recover correctly his/her communicative intention and, on the other, the hearer must analyse the situation and try to guess correctly the communicative intention of the speaker. That is, both speaker and hearer must possess 'theory of mind' abilities.

A unifying approach is to conceptualize **language as a cooperative activity.** In this view, speaking a language is like dancing a waltz or playing tennis: something you do with another person. So, it makes little sense to try to describe language just from the point of view of the speaker: there is a hearer at the other end, and only by taking into account both ends can language and meaning be appropriately described. Comprehension thus results from coordinating the efforts of two agents; it is a meeting of the speaker's meaning and the hearer's understanding. In other words, meanings are not to be found in the speaker's words, but in the interaction between speaker and hearer. One very important advantage of this view is that it allows us to consider language from both a psychological and social perspective: the study of language can be claimed to belong both to cognitive and to social science.

From an evolutionary perspective, cooperation has been described as one of the hallmarks of human nature: we are where we are now because we learned to cooperate in a new and more efficient way; other advanced primates cannot do it in the same way that we do. Such a desire to cooperate is innate; if you drop a clothespin in front of a 2-year-old, she will probably pick it up for you. Babies as young as 12 months will point at something that an adult pretends to have lost. The evolutionary advantages of coordinated action are self-evident (improved hunting or warfare, pooling of techniques for tool making or shelter construction, strengthening of social bonds, etc.).

Scholars such as Michael Tomasello argue that at a point in their evolution, humans learned to interpret the actions of others from an intentional point of view: we learned to infer what the other person wanted by projecting from what we would want in their position. Linguistic communicative cooperation (i.e. language) is thus part of a wider adaptation for collaborative actions. Linguistic labels can be seen not only as organizational tools for our minds (as we saw in Chapter 4), but also as ways of aligning the conceptual representations of a community of speakers, allowing us to share our thoughts. In this view, what is innate is not our capacity for language, but our capacity for **engaging in collaborative activities** and **inferring the intentions of others**. We have dedicated mechanisms for this purpose, such as joint attention, shared intentions within common social goals and theory of mind capabilities (already introduced in Chapter 6, when talking about the acquisition of word meanings). This general cooperative character underlying our linguistic behaviour has already been noted within language studies: philosopher of language Paul Grice established his **Cooperative Principle** (in the form of several 'maxims' that we all seem to follow when we are speaking), which can be integrated into this more general view. We will examine Grice's ideas in more detail in section 9.6 below.

This chapter focuses, then, on these two complex but nevertheless key concepts: context and communicative intentions. The first three sections 9.2, 9.3 and 9.4, will be devoted to examining in some detail the notion of context. Follwing Saeed (2009), we will distinguish three types of context. Section 9.2 will be devoted to examining the contextual information coming from the physical environment where the communicative event takes place; Section 9.3 will examine the context provided by what has already been said in the communicative exchange (sometimes called **co-text**). Section 9.4 will examine the most complex of all sources of context, that is, the one formed by the knowledge shared by speaker and hearer. The second half of the chapter, formed by Sections 9.5, 9.6 and 9.7, will be devoted to examining the recovery of communicative intentions. More specifically, in Section 9.5 we will see how knowledge of social routines can guide the recovery of inferences related to communicative goals; Section 9.6 will examine Grice's Cooperative Principle, as well as his conversational maxims. Finally, Section 9.7 will look at speech acts, which are directly related to the communicative intentions of speakers.

9.2 Spatio-Temporal Context: Deixis

A basic communicative event typically takes place in some place and at some given time (or at least, synchronous, face-to-face communication is the original and most basic communicative situation; in modern times, digital communication has incorporated many variants of this initial setting). There are certain linguistic elements that make reference to this immediate context: these elements are known as **deictic** (the noun is **deixis**, which comes from a Greek word that means 'to point out, to show'). These expressions normally take as a reference point the act of speaking, and derive considerations of space and time from this focal point. The main deictic categories involve information about three elements of this spatio-temporal scene: the physical space where the communication is being held, the time at which it is taking place and the persons involved in it.

9.2.1 Space Deixis

The speaker is the most important element in deixis (followed closely by the hearer), and is normally called the **deictic centre**. Thus, we take into account the place where the speaker is, the time at which the speaker speaks and who the speaker is (and to whom s/he is speaking). In English, there are two notions related to **space** that we can point out: distance from the speaker (near or far) and, taking into account motion, direction (towards or away from the speaker). Spatial deixis shows up in different types of words:

(A) *Adverbs: here, there, left, right ...*

The meaning of the adverbs *here* and *there* has to be interpreted in relation to proximity or non-proximity to the speaker: *here* could be paraphrased approximately as 'close to the speaker' and *there* as 'away from the speaker'. They do not indicate fixed points, since the location they make reference to changes all the time, 'moving along' as the speaker changes place: the location that *here* designates depends on the position of the speaker. Additional words in English would be *yonder* (indicating a greater distance from the speaker and hearer), *hither* ('to this place'), *thither* ('to that place') or *thence* ('from that place'). Many other languages use a three-way distinction; for example, Spanish has *aquí, ahí* and *allí* (more or less, meaning 'close to the Speaker', 'close to the Hearer' and 'away from both'), in few languages have even more.

(B) *Demonstratives: this/these, that/those*

Again, these elements serve to point out locations which are either close to the Speaker (*this/these*) or away from the Speaker (*that/those*). And again other distinctions are possible; there are languages with three, four, five or even more demarcations of distance.

(C) *Verbs: come, go*

Verbs can indicate spatial deixis by encoding whether a given movement is produced towards or away from the speaker. For example, in English, there are verbs such as *come* and *go*, which can only be understood with respect to the position of the Speaker: *come* means roughly, 'movement towards the place where the speaker is', and *go* means 'movement away from the speaker'. Thus, we can often estimate the position of the speaker from the use of these verbs. For example, in (2):

(2) a. *Please come to my house*
    b. *Please go to my house*

we would interpret that the speaker is in the house in (2a) but away from the house in (2b). That is why an expression like *?come away* would be difficult to interpret (compare with *go away* or *come closer*).

This description can be elaborated a bit, because sometimes the reference point can be moved away from the place where the utterance takes place. For example, the expression *Will you come to my party?* takes as a focal point the future location of the party, even if the speaker is not yet there; Yule (1996) calls this phenomenon **deictic projection**. Displacement towards the past is also possible; we can say something like *Yesterday, while I was in my office, Jane came to say hello*, and we would use the verb *come* even if we are not in the office at the moment of speaking. Sometimes, the verb *come* involves not just the place where the speaker is, but also the place where the hearer is. Consider example (3):

(3) *Jane came to the office yesterday morning.*

This sentence can be felicitously uttered if the speaker is at the office in the moment of speaking, if the hearer is at the office in the moment of speaking (in a telephone conversation, for example), or if either the speaker or the hearer were in the office the day before. Another very common example would be the phrase that is often uttered when one hurries up to open the door: *I'm coming!* We would be using as a reference point the location where we will be in a very short time (or where our interlocutor is). This deictic projection is also done in story-telling: we can easily switch the deictic centre and locate ourselves in the place where the story is being told (*So I met Harry in this bar, and he says 'Hey, Sally, what are you doing here?'*). A further example of displacement is the sentence *I'm not here now, but you can leave me a message after the beep*, to be recorded in a telephone answering machine.

Systems of spatial deixis can be projected to other domains; this is what happens in **discourse** or **textual deixis.** This is what we see in the examples in (4):

(4)   a. *Here we find again the example seen in Chapter 1*
       b. *There, we presented an explanation that we will expand now*

In both cases, we are using deictic spatial terms to locate textual material. Another device for expressing textual deixis related to space is the verticality of the English words *above* and *below*. Both are used to refer to elements that have already been mentioned in discourse, or that will be mentioned presently.

9.2.2 Time Deixis

There are many ways of expressing **time deixis** in English, that is, locating some event with respect to the deictic centre created by the moment of speaking. There are words or expressions that are used only in a temporal context: *now, later, then, tomorrow, yesterday, soon, recently, currently,* etc. Other expressions involve measurements of time used with demonstratives (or a similar functioning element): *this month, next year, two centuries ago.* Note that some terms do not make a distinction between past or future, and just indicate a 'point in time'; the rest of the information is picked out from the verb or some other element, as we see in (5):

(5)   a. *John was here then*
       b. *John will be here then*
       c. *When I was 18 … oh, life was easy then*
       d. *The movie starts at 8:30; I'll see you then*

Grammatical tense itself is deictic, since notions such as present, past or future depend on the moment of speaking. Other expressions of time function in the same way: if you found a note in my office saying *I'll be back in 40 minutes*, you would have no way of knowing when exactly I'm coming back, unless I had mentioned the exact time at which I wrote the note. As we hinted in Chapter 1, we can do pretty sophisticated temporal operations, such as opening temporal periods in the past or the future which serve as 'background' for the precise allocation of a temporal point (e.g., *While I was studying my degree, I suddenly discovered I loved semantics* or *I hope to have a steady job by the time I have my first child*).

Space expressions can also be used with a temporal sense; for example, when watching a movie you can say *Watch out! Here is the part when the Alien comes out of his belly!* We also find the same deictic projection as in space deixis; in story telling, we can move the **deictic centre** and reinterpret the real meaning of the adverb:

(6)   *I met Sally two days ago and she told me, 'Hey I didn't know you were in London now'.*

In this case, we would interpret the time that *now* makes reference to as two days prior to the time of the utterance.

Finally, we can also use temporal deixis to indicate distance from reality, not just from the moment of speaking. Thus, to indicate that something is impossible or unreal, we use the subjunctive mood, which coincides with the past tense (as if it had happened in a remote past): *If I were a rich man . . .*

9.2.3 Person Deixis

All languages have ways to mark the roles of the participants in the linguistic exchange: mainly, who is the current speaker and who is the addressee(s), and additionally, other participants mentioned in the conversation. The linguistic elements that indicate this are personal pronouns. It may take some time for children to discover the meaning of these elements, since, for example *I* and *you* are completely deictic and thus their reference is constantly changing in a conversation. That is why at first, they may get *you* and *me* wrong: since they are addressed as *you* all the time, they sometimes think that their own name is *you*, so, they will say *you want* to mean 'I want', or *pick you* for 'pick me'. This mistake is seen even in deaf children, whose personal pronouns may seem iconic, since they consist of pointing to the speaker or the hearer.

Almost all languages establish then a distinction between speaker (first person), hearer (second person) and neither-speaker-nor-hearer (third person), normally enriched with some other type of information, typically number and the gender of the person(s) alluded to. In the case of English, there are seven personal pronouns: *I, you, he, she, it, we* and *they*. They display variations along the three parameters mentioned: the central and basic distinction of *person* (first, second or third), *number* variations (singular or plural) and in some cases, *gender*. Not all the combinations of these variants are exploited in English. For example, gender distinctions are only used in the case of third person singular (*he/she/it*). In Romance languages, the gender distinction tends to be exploited more fully, since it tends to be applied to all the plural forms as well; Arabic extends the gender distinction further, to the second person singular, distinguishing between *anta* ('you' masculine, singular) and *anti* ('you' feminine, singular). In Japanese, there is even a gender variation for the first person singular. The logical possibilities, of course, include variation of gender for all pronouns.

The distinction in *number* can also be different in different languages: English lacks a plural version of the second person: *you* is used both for addressing a single person or a group of them. There is some evidence that English speakers miss this possibility, since they have created different versions of a second person plural for its use in informal speech. This is the case of the expression *you guys* (which is valid for both masculine and feminine use); other regional variants of this would be *y'all* in Southern American English, and *you lot* in British English. Another option that is not exploited by English regards the possibilities of the first person plural. The

241

fact is that this form is ambiguous in English, since it can include or exclude the hearer. For example:

(7)   a. *We are going to the party; are you coming or not?*
      b. *We are going to the party; get ready and let's go*

In (7a), the pronoun *we* does not include the hearer, while in (7b) it does. According to Yule (1996: 12), this distinction can sometimes be expressed in English by the contrast between *let's go*, and *let us go*; the latter would correspond to the exclusive one. Many languages of the world have different pronouns for this distinction (which receives the technical term of 'clusivity').

We could consider **social deixis** a variant or specialization of person deixis. In addition to the information about who is speaking to or about whom, we can include additional information that indicates the social relationships among the participants in the linguistic act. This is usually done by marking in a special way the higher status of some participant (that is why these expressions are sometimes called **honorifics**). In English there used to exist a distinction between *thou* and *you* (and their accusative counterparts, *thee* and *you*) that is now archaic and only survives in some religious formulas (as in the commandments: *Thou shalt not commit adultery*). In many Indo-European languages, however, respect or deference pronouns are still pretty much in use: Spanish *tú/usted*, French *tu/vous*, German *du/Sie*, Italian *tu/Lei*, etc. These variations normally make use of the iconic relation between distance/proximity. So, the use of the 'high-respect' pronoun is combined with a third person verb, instead of the second person. In this way, we talk to someone who is in front of us, involved in the current exchange, but using a verbal form reserved for somebody who is away (neither speaker nor hearer). There is thus a projection from physical distance to the social distance between speaker and hearer.

Again, other languages have many more distinctions; Japanese is the most cited example. In this language, the social position of first, second and third persons must be considered, affecting not only the choice of personal pronoun but also other linguistic elements, such as verbal endings. As a matter of fact, verbs in Japanese are marked for the social status of the subject, of the direct object and of the indirect object. Japanese has six levels of formality for the pronoun *I* and five for the pronoun *you*. To speak correct Japanese, thus, you have to be aware of the many subtleties of social relations.

9.3 Discourse/Text Context

Besides the circumstances of the physical context (time, place and person), we can also use as context whatever has already been said in a communicative event (i.e., the previous discourse). This receives sometimes a different and specific name, **cotext**. All languages can make use of this information, and there are a number of linguistic phenomena that depend heavily on it: we can indicate whether something has already been mentioned or not (as in the use of the definite article vs. the indefinite article), we can refer back to things already mentioned (as in anaphor); we can use previous discourse to 'leave out' certain parts of language (as in ellipsis), etc. In this section we review some phenomena that depend on discourse context.

9.3.1 Anaphor and Cataphor

Anaphor is a way of making reference to something already mentioned without having to repeat the same word(s); personal pronouns are usually used for this. We find this in example (8):

(8)   *Mary Poppins₁ was a big hit in the '60s. She₁ won everybody's heart with her umbrella.*

There are very complicated linguistic analyses (especially in generative and post-generative syntactic theories) that try to show how syntax constrains the range of possible co-reference between anaphor and the entity it refers to, which is called its **antecedent**. Other theories include a wider number of possible strategies to link an anaphor with its antecedent; a partial list of such strategies could be the one presented in Table 9.1 (adapted from Barsalou, 2014):

Table 9.1 *Strategies for Linking an Anaphor with its Antecedent*

- *Recency.* When you encounter a possible anaphor, choose the most recent referent in focus: *Irene ate apple pie; Claire₁ ate cake. Later she₁ had coffee.*
- *Salience.* When you encounter a possible anaphor, choose the referent in focus that is most salient grammatically: *It was Paula₁ who called Iraide; she₁ wanted to discuss her new book*
- *Gender.* When you encounter a possible anaphor, choose the referent that keeps the same gender: *Ian₁ and Anna left when he₁ got tired*
- *Number.* When you encounter a possible anaphor, choose the referent in focus that agrees in number: *When the cup₁ and the glasses fell, it₁ broke*
- *Grammatical role.* When you encounter a possible anaphor, choose the referent in focus that keeps the same grammatical role: *Bert₁ saw Barnie, and then he₁ hid behind a tree*
- *World knowledge.* When you encounter a possible anaphor, choose the referent in focus that seems plausible based on general knowledge: *Pope Francis and Barack Obama₁ met for lunch; he₁ was accompanied by his wife.* This individual factor is one of the main reasons why the automatic recovery of antecedents by computers is so difficult.

Some intriguing research has shown the usefulness of some anaphors, such as personal pronouns. According to an fMRI study by Almor *et al.* (2007), pronouns aid brain function. The reason is that every time we mention a proper name, our brain creates a representation of the person; thus, if in discourse, we repeat the same proper noun several times, a new complex representation will be created each time. This excessive activity can be reduced by using a pronoun, which does not create a new representation and thus does not force our memory to hold yet another element active.

Cataphor is a related phenomenon, much less frequent than anaphor: it refers to the case in which we have to look for the reference of a linguistic item in the forthcoming discourse:

(9)   a. *When I saw <u>him</u>₁ in the metro I could not believe my eyes: <u>George Clooney</u>₁ in person!*
    b. *<u>It</u>₁ bugs me <u>that you don't want to go to the cinema tonight</u>₁*

9.3.2 Ellipsis

There are a number of constructions in which the linguistic material needed for their semantic interpretation is absent, but is easily recoverable from the immediate linguistic context. This is what we call **ellipsis**. For example, consider the examples in (10):

(10)   a. *I'm really bored*
    b. *I'd like to go to the beach next summer*
    c. *I'm going to have my ear pierced*
    d. *Me too*

The meaning of (10d) depends completely on whatever has been said before. So, depending on whether the previous sentence had been (10a), (10b) or (10c), the interpretation would change to *I'm really bored, too, I'd also like to go to the beach next* and *I'm also going to have my ear pierced*, respectively. We have to take into account what has been said to supply only the parts of the sentences that are strictly necessary. In all the examples in (11–13), we are able to supplement the answers with parts of the questions being asked:

(11)   a. *Who did she give the present to?*
    b. *To John (i.e., she gave the present to John)*

(12)   a. *Why did she kill him?*
    b. *She was bored (i.e., she killed him because she was bored)*

(13)   a. *Was the door locked or unlocked when we left?*
    b. *Locked (i.e., the door was locked when we left)*

Ellipsis can also be considered as yet another example of metonymic thought; you name one part, and the rest is automatically activated; that is, ellipsis can be thought of as an example of a 'part-for-whole' metonymy.

9.4 Shared/Common Knowledge as Context

This last category is probably the main one and the most difficult to deal with. Actually, the sources of contextual information we have just reviewed in the previous sections could be said to be part of it. This type of knowledge is formed by the **common ground** shared by a speaker and a hearer (Clark, 1996; Stalnaker, 2002): what they both know, and they know that they both know. This can then include the information coming from the physical environment of the communicative event of the sort that we just reviewed in Section 9.2, but also from additional perceptual details, such as a noise that is heard during the conversation, or the fact that it is (or it is not) raining. Everything that is happening during the conversation and noticed by both participants can thus be included in their common ground. This also applies to all the things that have been said (the co-text that we covered in Section 9.3); the common ground thus is increasingly expanded as the conversation unfolds and information is shared. As a matter of fact, this is the etymological origin of the verb *communicate*: it means 'to make common'.

But besides the information gleaned from the physical context and the discourse context, we also make guesses about the (shared) knowledge that our interlocutor brings to the communicative exchange, and we use that information to shape our message accordingly. In Clark's words:

> The speaker designs his utterance in such a way that he has good reason to believe that the addressee can readily and uniquely compute what he meant on the basis of the utterance along with the rest of their **common ground** (Clark *et al.*, 1983, p. 246).

Consider the examples in (14), taken from Saeed (1997), who adapted them from Clark (1978):

(14)   a. *Two bottles of Heineken, please!*
       b. *Two Heinekens, please!*
       c. *Two bottles, please!*
       d. *Two, please!*

If you are in a bar where all brands of beers are sold, both in draught and in bottles, you will need to express your wishes using a similar expression to (14a). However, if you are in another type of place, say, the bar at a theatre, where only bottles are sold and draught beer is not available, then you can use sentence (14b) since no mistake is possible. In a context where only Heineken beer is sold, both in bottle and in draught, you would only have to specify (14c). Finally, in a context where the only thing being sold is Heineken bottles, you can utter sentence (14d) without the possibility of misunderstanding.

There are in fact many experiments showing that we do adapt our message to the knowledge we assume our interlocutor to have. For example, in Krauss and Fussell (1991), a person asked for directions to passersby in the city of Boston. In some cases, he pretended to be from another city (informing explicitly the people he asked); in some others, he asked the same questions but with a Boston accent. The answers he got were markedly different: when people assumed he was not from Boston, the directions supplied were longer and much more detailed.

Generally speaking, the bigger the overlap in our common ground is, the less explicit the linguistic message has to be: old friends and couples can communicate almost with no words. A great part of the knowledge we share with our interlocutors comes from the different communities that we belong to (what we could call 'cultural knowledge'). Roughly, a **community** can be defined as a group of people with whom you have something in common. In this sense, we are all members of many different communities: the community of citizens of a given city, a given neighbourhood, a country or a continent; of co-workers at a job, or university students, residents in a building, members of a political group, a religion, a hobby, a job, fans of a TV series or a musical group, the community of your close group of friends, and a very long etcetera. It can go down to quite small or private communities, things that you share only with one person (e.g., your partner, your sibling or your best friend). Each community possesses some knowledge that is more or less shared by all its members; when we communicate, we make use of this shared knowledge to guess what our hearer brings to the task when trying to make sense of our message. Of course, there are also facts that are shared by all humans: embodied, biological, physical knowledge from being in the world, like the universal laws of cause and effect, knowing that if you do not breathe, drink or eat, you die, or the fact that you can pull a rope but you cannot push it. We can more or less easily assign our interlocutors to the different communities they might belong to by indirect evidence (their external appearance, their clothes, their accent, the role in a situation, specific information that may come up in their speech), or sometimes by direct evidence (they may tell us, for example).

Another substantial part of our shared knowledge comes from our knowledge of scenes, frames or scripts. We have already discussed scenes and frames several times throughout the book. **Scripts** are knowledge structures that include a more or less fixed and stereotypical sequence of events, with specific information about the different stages of the activity; each stage can be considered a scene with its own sub-goals. We actually introduced scripts in Chapter 6, when we saw how babies use the knowledge of frequent sequences of events (the bath routine, the eating routine, going out to the park) as an aid to guess the meaning of new words used in these interactive scenes.

Adults derive inferences from their knowledge of these scripts all the time. An example that is typically invoked in this case is the famous RESTAURANT script, made up of different stages such as going to the restaurant, finding a seat, waiting for the waiter to bring you the menu, reading the menu, ordering your meal, getting the meal delivered by the waiter, eating the food, paying the bill and leaving (Schank & Abelson, 1977). We know this is the typical sequence of events in a restaurant, and this is why in a text like the one in (15), we can supply missing information, making inferences from all the things we know normally happen at a restaurant:

(15) John went to a restaurant; he sat down and the waiter gave him a menu. John ordered pizza and was served quickly and efficiently; he left a large tip.

After reading this, we would automatically infer (though it is not mentioned in the text) that John was sitting at a table during the meal, that he read the menu, that the pizza was prepared by a chef, that John ate the pizza, that John asked the waiter for the bill, that John was satisfied by the whole thing (since he left a large tip), etc. It is also our knowledge of frames and scripts that explains certain grammatical uses, from reference to anaphor: you say *the key of my car*, and people understand it because we know that cars only have one key; the same with *the menu* in a restaurant (not *a menu*), and a myriad of other examples.

Many other expressions make use of our knowledge of scripts; quite frequently, naming just one of the stages of the whole process is enough to activate, in a part-for-whole metonymy, the whole event. We already commented on some of these cases: expressions such as *Saying 'I do'*, or *Walking down the aisle* will activate the whole marriage script just by naming one of the stages. This is what we find in the expressions in (16):

(16)   a. *I need to go to the bathroom*
       b. *I can't believe they went to bed on their first date*
       c. *-How did you get to the hotel?*
          -I waved down a taxi
       d. *I took my computer to the repair shop*
       e. *I'll write you a cheque*

Examples (16a) and (16b) are especially frequent and useful as euphemisms. It is clear that once you get to the bathroom in (16a) or to the bed in (16b), there are further stages in those scripts, but naming just the first one is enough to activate the whole event. The sentence *Where can I wash my hands?* can also be a euphemism for going to the toilet, but in that case, we make reference to the final stage in the script. The answer to the question in (16c) is meaningful because it activates a complex scene in which we know that taxis are vehicles that take people to places for money, that you can call the attention of a taxi driver by waving (a culturally sanctioned way of requesting the taxi services), that the driver will then stop to pick you up, take you to your point of destination and then charge you a fee, which will roughly depend on the distance travelled (see Figure 9.2). In (16d) you understand that taking the computer to a repair shop is only the first stage of the script; the technicians will fix the problem and call you back when it's ready. In (16e), writing a cheque is only one action, but the ensuing stages of the script allow the inference that the receiver of the cheque will get some money. This script-based, part-for-whole-metonymy is a very frequent and efficient method of deriving inferences.

Figure 9.2 Different Stages in the Taxi-Script

Finally, jokes are often based on a clash of background frames: when the joke starts, you activate the (seemingly) relevant background frame and derive a number of inferences. When the closing punchline makes you quickly change to a different frame, a new set of inferences is suddenly created and a humorous effect arises from the clash. Something like this (hopefully) happens in (17):

(17)   My boyfriend just told me that he needs more space.
       So I bought him a 10-terabyte hard drive

9.5 Communicative Intentions

We get to the final stage, in which we recover the communicative intention of the speaker applying our theory-of-mind capabilities. Theory of Mind (ToM), as we already know, can be defined as 'the capacity to interpret others' actions in terms of intentions, beliefs, knowledge, and other mental states' (Lin *et al.* 2010: 551). Of course, we do not do this in the vacuum, but within a certain interpersonal setting; as we have seen, we are helped by our knowledge of cultural practices and expectations. The thematic knowledge we have been discussing (such as the commercial transaction frame we saw in Chapter 8, or the scripts we just mentioned in the previous section) quite often involves not only very detailed information about the roles of the participants in the event, but also the different actions these participants are supposed to engage in during the different stages of the event. This includes the expected local and global goals of the activity, that is, the expected intentions of the participants at each point in the event. This knowledge provides speakers with expectations about the direction and purpose of the actions taken, which supplies a highly structured setting for the extraction of inferences. Think about the commercial transaction frame again: you know the sequence of actions (from both the point of view of the buyer and of the seller), you know how to behave and you know what the response to your behaviour will probably be. The following is a typical exchange at a buying event, adapted from Clark (1996). A careful analysis of the conversation in (18) will show us how the intentions of each participant in each moment of the exchange can be easily guessed from our expectations of the way the event should unfold:

(18)   a. Buyer: (catches the eye of the attendant)
   b. Seller: *I'll be right there*
   c. Buyer: *Ok*
   d. Seller: *This magazine ... and a pack of chewing gum*
   e. Buyer: *That's 2 euros ten*
   f. Seller: *Ok; let me see; this a five-euro note and ... here, this is ten cents*
   g. Buyer: *Ten cents. Ok. Your change is three euros*
   h. Seller: *Right, thank you.*

The interaction starts with (18a), when the buyer establishes eye contact with the seller; in this specific context, this is enough to convey the message that he or she wishes to start the commercial transaction event. The answer in (18b), *I'll be right there*, can thus be interpreted approximately as 'I recognize your desire of starting the commercial event; let me finish what I'm doing right now, and we will start quite soon'. The *ok* in (18c) just acknowledges the understanding and acceptance of the previous message. The phrase in (18d) only makes sense within this particular stage of the exchange; it would be difficult to understand if it were the seller who uttered it (your typical reaction would probably be 'uh?'). Said by the buyer at this moment, though, it can be understood as 'please, tell me how much I have to pay for this magazine', which the seller interprets correctly, since (18e) is the price which the buyer must pay. (18f) is another expression that can only be correctly understood at this point of the exchange (it would make little sense at the beginning, for example), and the same would apply to the rest of the dialogue.

A similar procedure would be found in many other well-structured situations such as asking for directions, trying to chat someone up at a party, participating in an academic conference or performing a visit to someone at the hospital. This knowledge of the expected goals and intentions of participants in a given scene also explains why sometimes we can communicate our intentions merely with gestures. If you are at a bar, and you are the customer, you can look at the waiter and just point at your empty beer glass, and quite probably he will be able to infer your intention from his understanding of the current situation (Figure 9.3): as a waiter, he is supposed to provide drinks for you, the customer, and if you direct his attention to the fact that your glass is empty, he will guess that you are asking him to fill it up again. Thus, we see how cooperative actions go beyond mere language, but provide a rich background against which we can effectively communicate.

Figure 9.3 Communicating Intentions with a Single Gesture in a Highly Structured Situation

9.6 Grice's Cooperative Principle

As I have just mentioned, this general social cooperative attitude can help us explain a great portion of our linguistic activity, filling that often mysterious gap between what is actually said and what is understood. The first person to speak about the rules that govern linguistic interactions from the point of view of cooperation was philosopher Paul Grice, who noticed that whenever two people hold a conversation, they follow a given 'code of behaviour' that makes a conversation possible. He identified a general **Cooperative Principle**: the assumption, held by the participants in a communicative exchange, that both are trying to be cooperative in their utterances. Grice spelled out this cooperative behaviour in the four maxims included in Table 9.2:

Table 9.2 *Grice's Conversational Maxims*

(A) The Maxim of Quality: Be Truthful
    a. Do not say what you believe is false.
    b. Do not say that for which you lack adequate evidence.

(B) The Maxim of Quantity: Be Informative   a. Make your contribution as informative as is required for the current purposes of the exchange (i.e., not more or less informative).
(C) The Maxim of Relation: Be Relevant   a. Make your contributions relevant to the topic of the exchange.

(D) The Maxim of Manner: Be clear
    a. Avoid ambiguity and obscurity.
    b. Be brief and orderly.

The fact that we follow these cooperative rules explains many of the inferences that we draw. For example, how would you interpret the hearer's answer in (19)?

(19) Speaker: *Would you like a coffee?*
      Hearer: *Thanks, coffee will keep me awake*

The answer depends on the type of activity both speakers are engaged in. If the speaker knows that the hearer wants to avoid sleep (because they are both preparing an exam for the next morning), the answer has to be understood as 'yes, thanks, I would like a coffee'. However, if the speaker knows that the hearer wants to go to bed early (because the next day he has an early appointment or whichever reason), then the answer is understood as 'no, thanks, I don't want a coffee'. We are thus guided by expectations of the behaviour, purposes and desires of the others (what we have described as 'theory of mind abilities'). And we also expect them to collaborate with us: this explains many of the linguistic strategies for courtesy. For example, if we inform our interlocutor about our desire for something, we expect him/her not only to recognize that desire, but also to act collaboratively and do something to help us reach our goal. This is why a sentence like *I would like a beer* (under the appropriate circumstances) would normally be interpreted as a request to the hearer: 'Please, get me a beer'.

It should not be assumed that we *always* follow these 'ideal' rules when we speak. However, we use them to build special inferences on the utterances produced: these inferences are called **conversational implicatures** (or just **implicatures,** for short). Austin showed how even the breaking of these rules (which receives the name of **flouting**) can be used to derive special communicative effects (i.e., can be used to generate implicatures). When one maxim is violated, speakers notice that there is something special about the utterance ('marked', we could say, using the same terminology we have applied throughout the book), and this automatically triggers off an implicature. For example, in example (20), the maxim of quantity is broken (flouted):

(20) Teacher: *I hope you have completed Exercises 1 and 2*
      Student: *Ah, I've completed Exercise 1*

The student's reply seems to be incomplete, since there is no mention of Exercise 2, which was explicitly mentioned in the teacher's question. However, since we notice that the maxim of quantity has been flouted, we extract an implicature that informs us that the student has not completed Exercise 2. Another example of how these maxims work would be the exchange in (21):

(21) Boy: *Would you like to come to the party tonight?*
      Girl: *Oh, I have a paper due tomorrow*

At first, it could seem that the girl's reply is breaking the maxim of relation, since she is not answering directly the question by saying yes or no. However, if we assume that she is trying to be relevant, we just take this reply as a point on which to build our inferences, so that the communicative event can be understood as relevant and meaningful (and we know that the answer is 'no').

The maxim of relation holds a special status, because it has been the basis for one of the most prominent pragmatic theories for the analysis of meaning, **Relevance Theory.** Though it is difficult to summarize such a complex theory in a few lines (it is actually more a theory of cognition than a theory of language), it basically claims that humans start from the assumption that all utterances are relevant in a given conversation, and will accordingly generate the inferences needed until the utterance is found relevant for the communicative exchange (Sperber and Wilson, 1995).

Sometimes, single words convey implicatures; such is the case of words like *even* or *yet*; Grice called these cases **conventional implicatures** (because they are conventionalized and do not depend on context). Consider these examples:

(22)　a. *Even John danced last night*
　　　b. *He's not here yet*
　　　c. *I used to smoke a lot*

From example (22a), we would infer that John normally does not dance (and also that everybody else was dancing); in example (22b), we would understand that the person who is not there will arrive shortly; in (22c) the implicature is that I do not smoke a lot right now.

9.7 Speech Acts

Guided by our knowledge of social situations and using our theory of mind abilities, we can derive expectations of the goals and desires of the participants in a communicative exchange in a way that will allow us to recover communicative intentions. Now, these intentions can be classified into different types or categories, and this is where **speech act theory** comes in. Recognizing the type of speech act that an utterance is related to is a basic first step in recognizing the communicative intention of the speaker. Is the speaker asking something, promising something, or does he want me to do something? This is what the theory of speech acts examines.

Speech act theory started in the fifties with philosopher John Austin. He was interested in the cases in which language is not just representational, that is, it is not just used to describe the world, but it is used to change it somehow. As he said, sometimes we use language not *to say* things but *to do* things. He gave a number of examples of what he called **performatives**. Think of the expressions in (23):

(23)　a. *You're fired!*
　　　b. *I promise I'll be there tomorrow*
　　　c. *I bet you 10 euros he'll make it to the top*

In each of these cases, something 'happens' when we utter these words. If you are in a job situation and your boss utters (23a), you would regard this expression as more than a mere statement. The moment those words are uttered, something changes in the world: you are suddenly out of a job. Something similar happens in (23b), we commit ourselves to a future action by promising something and the promise comes into existence the moment you say the words; the same happens with the bet in (23c). The difference with other expressions is then clear: if you say *I paint the door*, nothing happens: the door is still not painted. But if you say *I promise to paint the door*, a public commitment to painting the door is now in place. Austin called these cases in which utterances create some change of state in the world **performative utterances** and they were the beginning of **speech act theory**. He gave some of them more specific labels, such as apology, complaint, compliment, invitation, promise, request, threat, etc.

The appropriate circumstances that have to be present for a given speech act to be properly performed and recognized are known as **felicity conditions**. Thus, there are certain felicity conditions for the example (23a): the Speaker has to be the boss of the Hearer, and must have the power to order the cessation of the contract at will. In the same way, *I declare you husband and wife* is a formula that will produce the intended effect only if the given felicity conditions are met: the Speaker must be a priest (or someone with the legal power to carry out the task), the setting must be a special ceremony, etc. Note that this is completely different from **truth conditions**, which we covered in Chapter 3. Felicity conditions say nothing about whether something is true or not, but only about the conditions that must be met in order for a sentence such as the one in 23a to have any real effect; exactly the opposite holds for truth conditions.

In speech act theory, three different but related acts can be recognized in the production of any utterance:

(1) **Locutionary act**, or the basic act of an utterance. Whenever we produce a meaningful linguistic expression, we are producing a locutionary act.

(2) **Illocutionary act.** This is a second dimension that is added to the first one, and refers to the communicative force (the speaker's intention) when producing an utterance. As we mentioned in some other part of the course, the same sentence can be uttered with different communicative intentions:

(24)   a. *'I'll be back,'* promised MacArthur
       b. *'I'll be back,'* threatened Terminator
       c. *'I'll be back,'* reassured her Casanova
       d. *'I'll be back,'* lamented Sysyphus

The same sentence can be uttered to make a statement, an offer, an explanation, or with other communicative purposes; this is what is known as the *illocutionary force* of an utterance (Figure 9.4).

(3) **Perlocutionary act.** This refers to the effect that we create with an utterance. For example, in order to use the verb *to convince* properly, somebody's words have to have an effect on the hearer. To convince somebody, not only do you have to utter a number of words, but also

Figure 9.4 Same Sentence, Different Illocutionary Forces

your hearer has to believe you and must change his/her mental state accordingly: only then can the act of 'convincing' be said to be in place. Other examples like this one would be *inspiring, persuading, impressing, deceiving, embarrassing, misleading, intimidating* or *irritating*.

As we have hinted before, we could say that the different speech acts form a 'typology of communicative intentions'. There are many ways of classifying speech acts; a classic typology is Searle and Venderveken (1985) who distinguish five different broad types:

(A) DECLARATIVES

These speech acts bring about a change in the world via their utterance. As we have mentioned before, the given felicity conditions must be met, especially the special institutional role of the speaker, a specific context, etc.

(25)   a. Priest: *I now pronounce you husband and wife*
       b. Referee: *You're out!*
       c. Jury Foreman: *We find the defendant guilty*

Uttering (25a) with the correct felicity conditions will change the civil status of the couple, who go from 'single' to 'married' in that very moment. When the referee utters (25b), the player is no longer active in the game; once the utterance in (25c) is produced, the status of a person changes, going from accused to convicted.

(B) ASSERTIVES

These speech acts state what the speaker believes to be the case or not. Statements of some fact, assertions, descriptions and conclusions are all examples of speakers' beliefs about the state of the world.

(26) a. *There are seven days in a week*
      b. *Laughter is the best medicine*
      c. *The Earth is not flat*

(C) EXPRESSIVES

The speech acts that state what the speaker feels. They express psychological states and can be statements of pleasure, pain, likes, dislikes, etc.

(27) a. *I'm really glad you could come*
      b. *I feel so lonely*
      c. *I can't get no satisfaction*

(D) DIRECTIVES

The speech acts that speakers use to make someone else do something; they are commands, orders, requests, suggestions, which can be positive or negative.

(28) a. *Take me to your leader*
      b. *Buy our new book with a 10 per cent discount*
      c. *Don't lose my number*

(E) COMMISSIVES

The speech acts that speakers use to commit themselves to some future action. They express what the speaker intends. They are promises, threats, refusals, etc.

(29) a. *I'll be back*
      b. *I'm gonna love you like nobody's loved you*
      c. *We will rock you*

Of course, this list does not exhaust all the possibilities; more categories would be needed for cases like compliments (*Nice job!*), greetings (*Good morning!*) and farewells. Clark (1996) complains that some speech acts are not codified but can nevertheless be recognized on the fly (again another example of ad hoc categories in language).

In any case, speech acts are important for a number of reasons; not only do they provide a typology of communicative intentions, but they are also key elements in bringing together language and action, much in line with embodied approaches. In this sense, for example, a directive is a request for the hearer to perform some action; the answer to the question *Can you pass the salt?* could perfectly be wordless: just passing the salt would show that you have recovered correctly the meaning of sentence. Cooking recipes are another good example of a language-action connection.

Yet another important aspect of speech acts is that they can only be understood in a social setting. Take the class of declaratives, for example, the utterances that bring about a change in the world via their utterance. They only make sense within a strongly conventionalized social setting, and would actually be meaningless outside of those situations. The same could be said about the rest of them. A directive describes the desire of an agent to evoke a response in another agent; this is possible only in some settings. We know when and how it is socially acceptable to use a directive with our interlocutor, and we shape our messages accordingly (only the person with higher social status can use a direct order, for example). In fact, none of these speech acts would make sense without including them in a collaborative setting.

9.7.1 Direct and Indirect Speech Acts

In general terms, there is a very clear relationship between the three basic forms of a sentence (declarative, interrogative and imperative) and the three more general communicative intentions (statement, question and command). In this way, we normally use declaratives to make statements (as in 30a), interrogatives to ask questions (30b), and imperatives to make commands (30c):

(30)   a. *You wear a seat belt*
       b. *Are you wearing a seat belt?*
       c. *Wear a seat belt!*

These cases, in which there is a direct relationship between the sentence form and its function, are called **direct speech acts**. However, as philosopher John Searle noted, this perfect fit between structures and functions is not universal, and we find cases where we use:

- a declarative to make a request (e.g., *It's a bit cold here*, a request to close the window)
- a declarative to make a command (e.g., *Officers will wear evening dress*)
- an interrogative to make a command (e.g., *Can you shut up?*)
- an interrogative to make an assertion (e.g., *Do you think I'm stupid?*)

Clark (1996) finds eleven different illocutions connected to the imperative, as can be seen in Table 9.3:

Table 9.3 *Different Illocutions Linked to the Imperative*

Commands	*To the rear, march*
Requests	*Please, pass the horseradish*
Promises	*Mow the lawn and I'll pay you a dollar*
Threats	*Stop or I'll shoot*
Warnings	*Watch out*
Offers	*Have some cake*
Well-wishings	*Have a nice trip*
Advice	*For a nice martini, mix six parts of gin with one part vermouth*
Curses	*Go to hell*
Exclamations	*Well, look at you*
Exhortations	*Fly American Airlines*

Recognizing the type of speech act from an utterance is not always that easy, since the information can sometimes be implicit and recoverable only from the context. At other times, there are highly conventional phrases to convey a communicative intention (think about the phrase *If you don't like it, you know where the door is*) and even conventionalized strategies. For example, there is a politeness strategy in English connected with directives: expressing a command with a direct speech act form (i.e., an imperative) is often considered too harsh, so it is more common to use strategies such as asking about the hearer's ability to perform an action (*Can you close the door?*) or his/her will or desire (*Will you close the door?*). Politeness strategies have been thoroughly studied; some classic references are Brown and Yule (1983), Levinson (1983) and Brown and Levinson (1987).

9.8 Chapter Summary

In this chapter we have presented language from an inferential point of view. In this view, language just gives us a 'blueprint' and we have to use context information and knowledge of the world to cross the gap between what we say and what we mean. We have seen how, when speaking, we calculate what (and how much) our addressee knows and we take it into account in the formulation of our message, hoping that our addressee will perform the right inferences and recover the meaning that is *implicit* in our words. This takes place within a social context involving the pragmatics of embodied interaction of persons.

We have just outlined a rough (but, hopefully, illuminating) sketch of how we derive inferences from specific social situations, as well as expectations about the behaviour of our interlocutors in those situations. We have covered how we can use (1) information coming from the physical context in which the communicative event takes place (when we say something – temporal deixis, where we say something – spatial deixis and who is involved in the exchange – personal deixis); (2) information coming from what has already been said (i.e., the co-text), which is the basis of grammatical phenomena such as anaphor, cataphor and ellipsis; and (3) information extracted from what speaker and hearer know that they both know (their common ground). In this sense, we have seen how knowledge of the structure of our social interactions as well as our theory of mind capabilities both help us derive the intentions of the interlocutor in communicative exchanges. Everything has been interpreted under the general perspective of language as a collaborative activity; in this sense, Grice's cooperative principle (spelled out in his four conversational maxims) is an effort of showing in which ways we interact with other people collaboratively in communicative exchanges. Finally, Searle's speech act theory has been examined as a typology of the communicative intentions that we recognize in speakers.

Exercises

Exercise 9.1   Think of how context can change the following utterances; what would the intended meanings be in each case? If an answer is needed, what would be a relevant answer in each case?

- *What would you like for dinner?* Situation A: asked while sitting at a restaurant. Situation B: asked while shopping at a supermarket.
- *I'm hot!* Situation A: in an African country. Situation B: in a casino. Situation C: describing yourself to a member of the opposite sex.
- *My battery is dead.* Situation A: your car is stopped on a forbidden zone, and a policeman comes to issue a ticket. Situation B: you walk into a repair shop and inform the man there about your situation.
- *It's getting late.* Situation A: you are at home, getting ready for a party, and you say this to your partner, who is still not ready. Situation B: you have spent some time at a party, and you say this to your partner, who is talking to some friends.
- *It's been a long time.* Situation A: you meet a friend in the street. Situation B: you present your latest book to your audience.
- *The door.* Situation A: somebody's knocking at the door, and your housemate, who is in the kitchen, says this. Situation B: You arrive home,

enter the house and hang your coat; your housemate, who enters after you, leaves the door open; you say this to him/her. Situation C: You are a painter, and you are painting different parts of a house; you say this to your co-worker.

Exercise 9.2   Read this famous dialogue from Lewis Carroll's *Through the looking-glass*:

– *'I don't know what you mean by 'glory,' ' Alice said.*
– *Humpty Dumpty smiled contemptuously. 'Of course you don't – till I tell you. I meant 'there's a nice knock-down argument for you!' '*
– *'But 'glory' doesn't mean 'a nice knock-down argument',' Alice objected.*
– *'When I use a word,' Humpty Dumpty said, in rather a scornful tone, 'it means just what I choose it to mean – neither more nor less.'*
– *'The question is,' said Alice, 'whether you can make words mean so many different things.'*

What do you think about Alice's answer? How far do you think can we take the influence of context? Can we make words mean whatever we want with the right amount of context?

Exercise 9.3   What is the inference required to make the answers to these questions relevant?

(a) – *Why don't we go the cinema tomorrow night?*
       – *Oh, my parents are coming for dinner*
(b) – *Sit down and eat something with us*
       – *Thanks, I've already eaten*
(c) – *How did you get here so fast?*
       – *Joe has a BMW*
(d) – *I'm pregnant*
       – *And what are you going to do?*
(e) – *Do you want to come up for a drink?*
       – *Thanks, but I don't think your girlfriend would like the idea*

Exercise 9.4   Identify the deictics in these sentences; are they place, time, or person deictics?

– *Could you please come over here this afternoon?*
– *Well, I have to go to Edinburgh today*
– *Hmm. How about this Thursday?*
– *I must go to the United States by the end of this week; perhaps you would like to come with me?*

Exercise 9.5   Identify the type of speech act that is used (declarative, representative, expressive, directive or commissives):

a) *Passengers are requested to wear their seat-belt fastened until the lights are turned off*
b) *I can't stand losing you*
c) *(watching TV) Do you have to keep on changing channels all the time?*
d) *The Harry Potter book series has been incredibly successful*
e) *Take your stinking paws off me, you damned dirty ape!*
f) *You make me feel (like a natural woman)*
g) *I'm gonna wait till the midnight hour*
h) *After looking at all the resumés, we've reached a decision: you are hired.*
i) *As God is my witness, I'll never be hungry again*
j) *Frankly, my dear, I don't give a damn*
k) *I have seen things you people wouldn't believe*
l) *Have you tried using H&S for your dandruff?*
m) *I hereby resign the office of President of the United States*

Exercise 9.6   Which is the cooperative principle which is broken here?

A: *Does your dog bite?*
B: *No*
    (A reaches down to pet the dog. The dog bites the man's hand)
A: *Ouch! Hey! You said that your dog doesn't bite*
B: *He doesn't. But that's not my dog.*
A: *Call me a taxi*
B: *Ok, you are a taxi*

Exercise 9.7   The following hedges are used by speakers to warn the hearer that some cooperative principle could be compromised. Can you tell to which cooperative principle are these hedges related?

• *As far as I know; to the best of my knowledge; I may be mistaken but . . .; I'm not sure but . . .; I think that . . .; I guess*
• *As you probably know; to cut a long story short; I won't bore you with all the details*
• *By the way; and also; well; anyway*
• *I'm not sure if this makes sense*

Exercise 9.8   Look at the following clip; describe to another person what is going on. Are you attributing mental states and intentions to the participants? (Taken from Heider and Simmel, 1944). Clip: http://vimeo.com/36847727.

Key Terms Introduced in this Chapter

discourse
pragmatics
decoding view of language
inferential view of language
context
inference
communicative intention
theory of mind
language as a cooperative activity
spatial/temporal/personal/social deixis
discourse/textual deixis
honorifics
deictic centre
deictic projection
co-text
anaphor, cataphor and ellipsis
common ground
scripts
cooperative principle
conversational maxims
conversational implicatures
conventional implicatures
flouting
relevance theory
felicity conditions
speech act
performatives
locutionary, illocutionary and perlocutionary act
declarative/representative/expressive/directive/commissive speech act
direct and indirect speech act

Further reading

There are a number of very good introductions to pragmatics; one of the best places to start is Yule (1996); a classic reference is Levinson (1983). The idea of language as a joint activity and the notion of common ground are explained at length in Clark (1996). Michael Tomasello has written a number of very readable and interesting books about the cultural origins of cognition (Tomasello, 1999) or the origins of human communication (Tomasello, 2008); his ideas on cooperation are explained in Tomasello (2009). Relevance theory is considered as a 'post-Gricean' theory, since it bases its premises on just one of Grice's maxims (the maxim of relation); the classic reference is Sperber and Wilson (1995); there are other current theories based on Grice (called 'neo-Gricean'), which think that reducing every to just one maxim is not possible; a comparison of both approaches can be found in the introduction of Levinson (2000). The typology of speech acts is taken from Searle and Venderveken (1985); Searle (1990) is a classic reference for speech act theory.

Glossary

ad hoc category   Category that is formed on the spot, without being stored in long-term memory. It tends to contain elements that bear little resemblance among themselves.

adicity   The number of arguments that a given predicate takes.

affordances   The possibilities for physical interaction that an object offers a biological entity; they are normally perceived in an automatic way and are species-dependent.

amodal symbolic systems   Systems of rules that try to capture the computations we perform with amodal (i.e., abstract) symbols (that is, their combinations) in order to carry out cognitive tasks.

antonymy   The relation existing between two words that are opposed in meaning in a binary fashion.

classical view of categories   Theory of categorization based on the 'necessary' and 'sufficient' conditions that an element needs to comply with in order to be included in a category.

cognitive/embodied semantics   Branch of semantics that deals with issues of meaning, relating them to its psychological, neurological and cultural bases.

common ground   All the knowledge that is shared by speaker and hearer; it influences how the speaker shapes the message to be communicated and it helps the hearer recover the speaker's communicative intention.

computational theory of mind; computationalism   Theory that tries to explain the behaviour of cognitive agents by exploiting the parallels between the human brain and digital computers. According to this theory, cognition amounts to the algorhythmic combination of symbols (i.e., rules), which defines what cognition is and how it should be explained.

constructional meaning   Meaning assigned to a grammatical construction, even devoid of lexical content (i.e., just the grammatical configuration).

cue validity; cue strength   An attribute or characteristic of an element has 'high cue validity' if it is by itself (or in combination with a few other attributes) enough to classify an element as belonging to a category; this is also called its 'cue strength'. On the contrary, when an attribute is not very decisive in establishing the categorization, and its influence is lower, we say it has 'low cue validity' (or weak cue strength).

deictic centre   Point with respect to which time and space are calculated in deictic expressions, typically the point where the speaker is located (e.g., 'here') and the moment at which the utterance is produced (e.g., 'now').

deictic projection/displacement   There are linguistic resources which 'move' the deictic centre from the 'here and now' to some other alternative point in space/time, which then becomes the deictic centre (e.g., *When I met John at his house, he said: 'this is your first visit* **here***, right?'*).

deictics   Elements that make reference to aspects of the context and are thus inherently variable and dependent on contextual details; they can be related to spatial context (e.g., 'here'), temporal context (e.g., 'now'), personal context (e.g., 'you'), etc.

denotational theories of meaning   Theories of meaning that are based on the study of the correspondences between linguistic expressions and elements in the world (or in any possible world).

embodiment; embodied cognition thesis   A thesis about the functioning of cognition that proposes that thoughts and higher-level processes involve the activation of the modality areas of the brain, including sensorimotor, emotional and introspective areas.

exemplar theories   Theories of categorization that argue that we do not abstract away from the different details of the different exemplars of a category in order to build an abstract 'prototypical' exemplar, but instead keep in memory all the different instances of the members of the category.

felicity conditions   Conditions that must be met for a given speech act to be effective; for example, the utterance *I declare you husband and wife* only has a real effect under certain 'felicity conditions': the speaker must be legally allowed to say it, the interlocutors must be in agreement with the act, the context must be a special ceremony, and so on.

flouting   Technical name received by the breaking of a conversational maxim.

formal semantics   Branch of semantics that deals with issues of meaning by using the tools of formal logic (see also **amodal symbolic systems**).

frames   Frames are groups of facts about the world that are lumped together and capture co-occurrences of elements in the world. These structures, which can contain highly cultural knowledge, are the background against which the meanings of words are extracted.

high-dimensional models of semantics   Computational technique that allows us to extract the meaning of words just from their co-occurrence with other words in large corpora.

hyperonymy   When two words are related by a 'specificity' link (that is, one of them is more specific than the other), the more general one is a hyperonym of the other. E.g., *animal* is a hyperonym of *dog*.

hyponymy   When two words are related by a 'specificity' link (that is, one of them is more specific than the other), the more specific one is a hyponym of the other. E.g., *dog* is a hyponym of *animal*.

joint-attentional frames   A 'joint-attentional frame' is the set of objects and events that are within the focus of attention by both speaker and hearer in a communicative event.

Language of Thought Hypothesis; mentalese   Both these labels refer to the format in which our thought is coached; it is quite similar to a linguistic code in its characteristics, though it does not correspond to any specific human language.

lexical contrast   Strategy followed by children in language acquisition in which, when a given meaning for a word is shared by speaker and hearer in a given communicative exchange, speakers will preferentially use that meaning and will tend not to resort to possible additional meanings for that word.

Linguistic Relativity Hypothesis   Hypothesis that affirms that languages have an influence on how people organize their conceptual structure.

marked and unmarked   An unmarked element is the default, neutral, element; a marked element is the less typical one, associated with more specific information.

meronymy/partonymy   Relationship between two words in which one of them is considered a part of the other (e.g., *eye* is a meronym of *face*).

metaphorical expression   Each of the different linguistic expressions that can be linked to one conceptual metaphor.

necessary and sufficient conditions   According to the classical theory of categorization, the conditions that an object must unavoidably comply with in order to be included in a category are 'necessary conditions'; the list of conditions which are enough to classify an object within the category, with no other requirements, are called 'sufficient conditions'.

opposites   The relation existing between two or more words that are opposed in meaning.

phonosemantics   Discipline that deals with sound symbolic effects (see **Sound symbolism**)

possible world   Any world that can be imagined, containing any element we can think of, including those non-existing in the real world, such as unicorns or united Europeans.

priming   Facilitation effect that one word exerts on the next one (read or heard), thus proving their connection at a mental level.

proposition   Minimal unit of meaning, formed by the combination of a predicate with its arguments.

prototype effects   These are cognitive effects that are created by the prototypical organization of categories: thus, prototypical exemplars of the category are recognized faster, show up first (and more frequently) in listing tasks, are learned earlier by children and receive higher 'goodness-of-exemplar' ratings.

prototype structure; prototype   Structure of conceptual categories, in which one member of the category acts as the 'prototype', that is, the most typical example of the category; elements are compared with this prototype in order to establish whether they belong to the category or not. Prototypical categories admit degrees, that is, there can be more 'central' or more 'peripheral' members (see also **'prototype effects'**).

regular and irregular polysemy   In regular polysemy, there is a 'rule' that relates a group of words with their polysemous extensions, in a more or less predictable way. In irregular polysemy, the relationship among the different senses is less predictable and more context dependent.

Sapir-Whorf Hypothesis   See **Linguistic Relativity Hypothesis**.

schemas   Another name for 'frames'.

scripts   A sequence of actions that is stored as a unit and describes a given complex event.

Semantic Differential Technique   Technique created by Charles Osgood and his collaborators that used (at least) three dimensions of meaning as rating scales in order to characterize the connotative structure of a given word; typically, those three categories were valency (good–bad), potency (strong–weak) and activation (high–low).

semiotics   Discipline that deals with the study of signs, that is, how one entity can stand for another.

sentiment analysis   Computational technique that tries to predict whether texts are expressing favourable or unfavourable views about a given subject. More broadly, it tries to detect the emotional communicative intention (or emotional state of the author), using complex computational analyses that start (among other things) from the connotations of the words contained in the text.

simulation   Re-enactment of the brain areas activated during the real-world experience with an object or action when that object/action is used in high-level cognitive tasks such as memory or language.

sound symbolism   Cases in which the sounds in a language are related to the meaning they convey in some motivated, non-arbitrary way.

source–path–goal image schema   Image schema in which the motion of objects is distilled onto a 'schematic' structure consisting of the object moving, the point where motion starts (source), the trajectory it follows (path) and the point of destination (goal).

statistical learning abilities   Capacities of children to find the statistical structure of the elements occurring in their environment.

syntactic bootstrapping   Theory that proposes that the syntactic form of an unknown word helps to restrict its possible meanings, a process that greatly helps children's acquisition of language.

theory of mind   Capacity of humans to infer the mental state of others.

truth conditions   The truth conditions of a word or a linguistic expression are the conditions which should be met in the world (or a possible world) for that word or expression to be used truthfully.

truth-conditional semantics   Branch of semantics that is based on finding out the conditions that should be met in a possible world in order to use a linguistic expression truthfully.

weak compositionality   In weak compositionality, the meaning of the whole is derived from the combination of the meaning of the parts, but in a non-deterministic fashion, allowing for 'emergent' meanings to arise (that is, meanings which are not activated by any of the individual components of the whole).

whole object bias   Tendency shown by children to ascribe new words to whole objects rather than to parts of objects.

word association strength   The probability that one word is mentioned after another one in a word association test; the higher the probability, the stronger the association.

References

Aitchison, J. (2012). *Words in the Mind: An Introduction to the Mental Lexicon.* Oxford and New York: Basil Blackwell.

Allan, K. (1986). *Linguistic Meaning.* 2 volumes, London: Routledge and Kegan Paul.

Almor, A., Smith, D. V., Bonilha, L., Fridriksson, J. and Rorden, C. (2007). What is in a name? Spatial brain circuits are used to track discourse references. *Neuroreport* 18(12), 1215–1219.

Altmann, G. T. M. (1997). *The Ascent of Babel.* Oxford University Press.

Apresjan, J. (1974). Regular polysemy. *Linguistics* 142, 5–32.

Arbib, M. A., Gasser, B. and Barrés, V. (2014). Language is handy but is it embodied? *Neuropsychologia* 55, 57–70.

Arias-Trejo, N. and Plunkett, K. (2009). Lexical priming effects during infancy. *Philosophical Transaction of the Royal Society B* 364, 3633–3647.

Bach, E. (1989). *Informal Lectures on Formal Semantics.* Albany, NY: SUNY Press.

Baldwin, D. A. (1991). Infants' contribution to the achievement of joint reference. *Child Development* 62, 875–890.

Barcelona Sanchez, A. (ed.) (2000). *Metaphor and Metonymy at the Crossroads. A Cognitive Perspective.* Berlin/New York: Mouton de Gruyter.

Barsalou, L. W. (1983). Ad hoc categories. *Memory and Cognition* 11, 211–27.

(1987). The instability of graded structure: Implications for the nature of concepts. In Neisser, U. (ed.), *Concepts and Conceptual Development: Ecological and Intellectual Factors in Categorization.* Cambridge University Press, pp. 101–140.

(1999). Perceptual symbol systems. *Behavioral and Brain Sciences* 22(4), 577–660.

(2008). Grounded cognition. *Annual Review of Psychology* 59(1), 617–645.

(2010). Grounded cognition: past, present, and future. *Topics in Cognitive Science* 2, 716–724.

(2014). *Cognitive Pyschology: an overview for cognitive scientists.* New York: Psychology Press.

Barsalou, L. W. and Wiemer-Hastings, K. (2005). Situating abstract concepts. In Pecher, D. and Zwaan, R. A. (eds.), *Grounding Cognition: The Role of Perception and Action in Memory, Language, and Thinking.* Cambridge University Press, pp. 129–163.

Bergen, B. (2012). *Louder than Words: the New Science of How the Mind Makes Meaning.* New York: Basic Books.

Bierwisch, M. (1971). On classifying semantic features. In Steinberg, D. and Jakobovitz, L. A. (eds.), *Semantics: An Interdisciplinary Reader in Philosophy, Linguistics and Psychology.* Cambridge University Press, 410–435.

Bloom, P. (2000). *How Children Learn the Meanings of Words*. Cambridge, MA: MIT Press.

Boot, I. and Pecher, D. (2010). Similarity is closeness: Metaphorical mapping in a perceptual task. *Quarterly Journal of Experimental Psychology* 63, 942–954.

Borghi, A. M., Glenberg, A. M. and Kaschak, M. P. (2004). Putting words in perspective. *Memory and Cognition*, 32(6), 863–873.

Boroditsky, L. (2000). Metaphoric structuring: Understanding time through spatial metaphors. *Cognition* 75(1), 1–28.

(2011). How language shapes thought. *Scientific American* 304(2), 63–65.

Boroditsky, L. and Gaby, A. (2010). Remembrances of times East: Absolute spatial representations of time in an Australian Aboriginal community. *Psychological Science* 21, 1635–1639.

Boroditsky, L. and Prinz, J. (2008). What thoughts are made of. In Semin, G. and Smith, E. (eds.), *Embodied Grounding: Social, Cognitive, Affective, and Neuroscientific Approaches*. New York: Cambridge University Press.

Boroditsky, L., Ham, W. and Ramscar, M. (2002). What is universal about event perception? Comparing English and Indonesian speakers. In Gray, W. D. and Schunn, C. D. (eds.), *Proceedings of the 24th Annual Meeting of the Cognitive Science Society*. Mahwah, NJ: Erlbaum, pp. 136–141.

Boroditsky, L., Schmidt, L. and Phillips, W. (2003). Sex, syntax and semantics. In Gentner, D. and Goldin-Meadow, S. (eds.), *Language in Mind: Advances in the Study of Language and Thought*. Cambridge, MA: MIT Press.

Boutonnet, B. and Lupyan, G. (2015). Words jump-start vision: a label advantage in object recognition. *Journal of Neuroscience* 32(25), 9329–9335.

Bowdle, B. F. and Gentner, D. (2005). The career of metaphor. *Psychological Review*, 112, 193–216.

Bowers, J. S. and Pleydell-Pearce, C. W. (2011). Swearing, euphemisms, and linguistic relativity. *PloS one* 6(7), e22341.

Bréal, M. (1924/1897). *Essai de sémantique: science des significations*. Paris: Gérard Monfort.

Bresnan, J. and Kanerva, J. (1989). Locative inversion in Chichewa. *Linguistic Inquiry* 20, 1–50.

Brown, G. and Yule, G. (1983). *Discourse Analysis*. Cambridge University Press.

Brown, P. and Levinson, S. C. (1987). *Politeness: Some Universals in Language Usage*. Cambridge University Press.

Brown, R. (1957). Linguistic determinism and the part of speech. *Journal of Abnormal and Social Psychology* 55, 1–5.

Brugman, C. (1981). *The Story of 'Over'*. MA Thesis. Berkeley, CA: University of California. (Also: Duisburg/Essen: LAUD, 1983.)

Bylund, E. and Athanasopoulos, P. (2014). Language and thought in a multilingual context: The case of Xhosa. *Bilingualism: Language and Cognition* 17 (2014), 431–441.

Cacciari, C. and Glucksberg, S. (1994). Understanding figurative language. In Gernsbacher, M. A. (ed.), *Handbook of Psycholinguistics*. New York: Academic Press, pp. 447–477.

Cangelosi, A., Greco, A. and Harnad, S. (2002). Symbol grounding and the symbolic theft hypothesis. In Cangelosi, A., Greco, A. and Harnad, S. (eds.), *Simulating the Evolution of Language*. Berlin: Springer Verlag, pp. 191–210.

Capitani, E., Laiacona, M., Mahon, B. and Caramazza, A. (2003). What are the facts of category-specific deficits? A critical review of the clinical evidence. *Cognitive Neuropsychology* 20, 213–262.

Carroll, J. B. (1956). *Language, Thought, and Reality: Selected Writings of Benjamin Lee Whorf*. Boston: MIT Press.

Carston, R. (2002). *Thoughts and Utterances. The Pragmatics of Explicit Communication*. Oxford: Blackwell.

Casasanto, D. (2008). Similarity and proximity: When does close in space mean close in mind? *Memory and Cognition* 36(6), 1047–1056.

Casasanto, D. and Boroditsky, L. (2008). Time in the mind: Using space to think about time. *Cognition* 106, 579–593.

Casasanto, D. and Dijkstra, K. (2010). Motor action and emotional memory. *Cognition*, 115(1), 179–185.

Chen, K. (2013). The effect of language on economic behavior: Evidence from savings rates, health behaviors, and retirement assets. *American Economic Review* 103(2), 690–731.

Chen, M. L. and Waxman, S. R. (2013). 'Shall we blick?': Novel words highlight actors' underlying intentions for 14-month-old infants. *Developmental Psychology* 49(3), 426–431.

Chierchia, G. and McConnell-Ginet, S. (2000). *Meaning and Grammar: an Introduction to Semantics*. Cambridge, MA: MIT Press.

Chomsky, N. (1981). Lectures on Government and Binding: The Pisa Lectures. Holland: Foris Publications. (Reprint. 7th Edition. Berlin and New York: Mouton de Gruyter, 1993).

Clark, H. H. (1978). Inferring what is meant. In Levelt, W. J. M. and Flores d'Arcais, G. B. (eds.), *Studies in the Perception of Language*. London: Wiley, pp. 295–321.

(1996). *Using Language*. Cambridge University Press.

Clark, H. H., Schreuder, R. and Buttrick, S. (1983). Common ground and the understanding of demonstrative reference. *Journal of Verbal Learning and Verbal Behavior* 22, 245–258.

Connell, L. and Lynott, D. (2009). Is a bear white in the woods? Parallel representation of implied object color during language comprehension. *Psychonomic Bulletin and Review* 16, 573–577.

Copestake, A. and Briscoe, E. J. (1995). Semi-productive polysemy and sense extension. *Journal of Semantics*, 12, 15–67.

Costa, A., Foucart, A., Hayakawa, S., Aparici, M. and Apesteguia J. *et al.* (2014). Your morals depend on language. *PLoS ONE* 9(4): e94842.

Croft, W. (1991). *Syntactic Categories and Grammatical Relations: The Cognitive Organization of Information*. University of Chicago Press.

Cruse, D. A. (1986). *Lexical Semantics*. Cambridge University Press.

(2000). *Meaning in Language: an Introduction to Semantics and Pragmatics*. Cambridge University Press.

Damasio, A. R. (1989). Time-locked multiregional retroactivation: A systems level proposal for the neural substrates of recall and recognition. *Cognition* 33 (1–2): 25–62.

Davis, A. and Koenig, J. P. (2000). Linking as constraints on word classes in a hierarchical lexicon. *Language* 76, 56–91.

De Vega, M., Glenberg, A. and Graesser, A. C. (2008). *Symbols and Embodiment: Debates on Meaning and Cognition.* Oxford University Press.

Deerwester, S., Dumais, S. T., Furnas, G. W., Landauer, T. K. and Harshman, R. (1990). Indexing by latent semantic analysis. *Journal of the American Society for Information Science* 41 (6), 391–407.

Diesendruck, G., Markson, L. and Bloom, P. (2003). Children's reliance on creator's intent in extending names for artifacts. *Psychological Science* 14, 164–168.

Dik, S. C. (1978). *Functional Grammar.* Amsterdam: North-Holland.

Dirven, R. and Pörings, R. (2002). *Metaphor and Metonymy in Comparison and Contrast.* Berlin: Walter de Gruyter.

Dodds, P. S., Clark, E. M., Desu, S., Frank, M. R., Reagan, A. J., Williams, J. R. *et al.* (2015). Human language reveals a universal positivity bias. *Proceedings of the National Academy of Sciences* 112(8), 2389–2394.

Dove, G. (2011). On the need for embodied and dis-embodied cognition. *Frontiers in Psychology* 1, 242.

Dowty, D. (1991). Thematic proto-roles, argument selection, and lexical semantic defaults. *Language* 67(3), 547–619.

Drivonikou, G. V., Kay, P., Regier, T., Ivry, R. B., Gilbert, A. L. *et al.* (2007). Further evidence that Whorfian effects are stronger in the right visual field than the left. *Proceedings of the National Academy of Sciences (PNAS)* 104, 1097–1102.

Elman, J. L. (2009). On the meaning of words and dinosaur bones: Lexical knowledge without a lexicon. *Cognitive Science* 33, 547–582.

Estes, Z., Golonka, S. and Jones, L. L. (2011). Thematic thinking: The apprehension and consequences of thematic relations. *Psychology of Learning and Motivation* 54: 249–294.

Evans, V. (2009). *How Words Mean: Lexical Concepts, Cognitive Models and Meaning Construction.* Oxford University Press.

Fauconnier, G. and Turner, M. (2002). *The Way We Think: Conceptual Blending and the Mind's Hidden Complexities.* New York: Basic Books.

Fausey, C. and Boroditsky, L. (2010). Subtle linguistic cues influence perceived blame and financial liability. *Psychonomic Bulletin and Review* 17(5), 644–650.

Fausey, C. and Boroditsky, L. (2011). Who dunnit? Cross-linguistic differences in eye-witness memory. *Psychonomic Bulletin and Review* 18(1), 150–157.

Fausey, C., Long, B., Inamori, A. and Boroditsky, L. (2010). Constructing agency: the role of language. *Frontiers in Psychology* 1, 162.

Ferretti, T. R., McRae, K. and Hatherell, A. (2001). Integrating verbs, situation schemas, and thematic role concepts. *Journal of Memory and Language* 44: 516–547.

Filipović, L. (2013). Constructing causation in language and memory: Implications for access to justice in multilingual interactions. *International Journal of Speech, Language and the Law* 20, 1–19.

Filipović, L. and Ibarretxe-Antuñano, I. (2015). Motion. In Dąbrowska, E. and Divjak, D. (eds.), *Handbook of Cognitive Linguistics*. Berlin: Mouton de Gruyter, pp. 526–545.

Fillmore, C. J. (1968). The case for case. In Bach, E. and Harms, R. (eds.), *Universals in Linguistic Theory*. New York: Holt, Rinehart and Winston, pp. 1–88.

(1982). Frame semantics. In Linguistic Society of Korea (ed.), *Linguistics in the Morning Calm*. Seoul: Hanshin, pp. 1–88.

(1984). Lexical semantics and text semantics. In Copeland, J. E. (ed.), *New Directions in Linguistics and Semiotics*. Houston: Rice University, pp. 123–147.

(1985). Frames and the semantics of understanding. *Quaderni di Semantica* 6(2), 222–254.

Fillmore, C. J. and Atkins, B. T. S. (2000). Describing polysemy: The case of 'crawl'. In Ravin, Y. and Leacock, C. (eds.), *Polysemy: Theoretical and Computational Approaches*. Oxford University Press, pp. 91–110.

Firth, J. R. (1957). *Papers in Linguistics 1934–1951*. London: Oxford University Press.

Fodor, J. (1983). *The Modularity Of Mind*. Cambridge, MA: MIT Press.

Frawley, W. (1992). *Linguistic Semantics*. Hillsdale: Lawrence Erlbaum Associates.

Frege, G. (1884/1980). The Foundations of Arithmetic. Trans. J. L. Austin. Second Revised Edition. Evanston, IL: Northwestern University Press.

Gardner, H. (1985). *The Mind's New Science*. New York: Basic Books.

Garrett, M. F. (1992). Disorders of lexical selection. *Cognition*, 42, 143–180.

Geeraerts, D. (1993). Vagueness's puzzles, polysemy's vagaries. *Cognitive Linguistics* 4, 223–272.

Gentner, D. (1978). A study of early word meaning using artificial objects: What looks like a jiggy but acts like a zimbo? *Papers and Reports on Child Language Development* 15, August.

(2001). Spatial metaphors in temporal reasoning. In Gattis, M. (ed.), *Spatial Schemas in Abstract Thought*. Cambridge, MA: MIT Press, pp. 203–222.

Gentner, D., Bowdle, B., Wolff, P. and Boronat, C. (2001). Metaphor is like analogy. In Gentner, D., Holyoak, K. J. and Kokinov, B. N. (eds.), *The Analogical Mind: Perspectives from Cognitive Science*. Cambridge MA: MIT Press, pp. 199–253.

Gibbs, R. (1994). *The Poetics of Mind: Figurative Thought, Language and Understanding*. Cambridge University Press.

(ed.) (2008). *The Cambridge Handbook of Metaphor and Thought*. New York: Cambridge University Press.

Gibson, J. J. (1979). *The Ecological Approach to Visual Perception*. Boston: Houghton Mifflin.

Gil, D. (2013). Riau Indonesian: a language without nouns and verbs. In Rijkhoff, J. and van Lier, E. (eds.), *Flexible Word Classes: Typological Studies of Underspecified parts of speech*. Oxford University Press, pp. 89–130.

Givón, T. (1984). *Syntax: A Functional-Typological Introduction*. Amsterdam: John Benjamins.

(1990). *Syntax: A Functional-Typological Introduction*, vol. 2. Amsterdam: John Benjamins.

(1998). Toward a neurology of grammar. *Behavioral and Brain Sciences* 21(1), 154–155.

(2002). *Bio-linguistics*. Amsterdam: John Benjamins.

(2005). *Context as Other Minds: The Pragmatics of Sociality, Cognition and Communication*. Amsterdam: John Benjamins.

Glenberg, A. M. and Kaschak, M. P. (2002). Grounding language in action. *Psychonomic Bulletin and Review*, 9, 558–565.

Glenberg, A. M. and Robertson, D. A. (1999). Indexical understanding of instructions. *Discourse Processes*, Vol 28(1), pp. 1–26.

(2000). Symbol grounding and meaning: A comparison of high-dimensional and embodied theories of meaning. *Journal of Memory and Language* 43(3), 379–401.

Glucksberg, S. (1998). Understanding metaphors. *Current Directions in Psychological Science*, 7, 39–43.

(2003). The psycholinguistics of metaphor. *Trends in Cognitive Sciences* 7(2), 92–96.

Goddard, C. and Wierzbicka, A. (eds.) (1994). *Semantic and Lexical Universals: Theory and Empirical Findings*. Amsterdam: John Benjamins.

(eds.) (2002). *Meaning and Universal Grammar: Theory and Empirical Findings* (2 volumes). Amsterdam/Philadelphia: John Benjamins.

Goldberg, A. (1995). *Constructions*. University of Chicago Press.

(2006). *Constructions at Work: The Nature of Generalization in Language*. Oxford/New York: Oxford University Press.

González J., Barrós-Loscertales, A., Pulvermüller, F., Meseguer, V., Sanjuán, A. *et al.* (2006). Reading cinnamon activates olfactory brain regions. *Neuroimage* (15), 906–912.

González-Marquez, M., Mittelberg, I., Coulson, S. and Spivey, M. (2007). *Methods in Cognitive Linguistics*. Berlin: John Benjamins.

Grady, J. (1997). *Foundations of Meaning: Primary Metaphors and Primary Scenes*. PhD Dissertation. Berkeley, CA: University of California.

Grice, P. (1975). Logic and conversation. In Cole, P. (ed.), *Syntax and Semantics. Volume 9: Pragmatics*. New York: Academic Press, pp. 113–128.

Griffiths, T., Steyvers, M. and Tenenbaum, J. (2007). Topics in Semantic Representation. *Psychological Review* 114, 211–244.

Grimshaw, J. (1990). *Argument Structure*. Cambridge, MA: MIT Press.

Gruber, J. (1976). *Lexical Structure in Syntax and Semantics*. New York: North Holland.

Harnad, S. (1990). The symbol grounding problem. *Physica D* 42: 335–346.

Harris, C. L., Aycicegi, A. and Berko Gleason, J. (2003). Taboo words and reprimands elicit greater autonomic reactivity in a first than in a second language. *Applied Psycholinguistics* 24, 561–578.

Hauk, O. and Tschentscher, N. (2013). The Body of Evidence: What Can Neuroscience Tell Us about Embodied Semantics? *Frontiers in Psychology* 4, 13 February.

Heider, F. and Simmel, M. (1944). An experimental study in apparent behavior. *The American Journal of Psychology* 57, 243–259.

Hirsh-Pasek, K., Golinkoff, R. M. and Naigles, L. (1996). Young children's use of syntactic frames to derive meaning. In Hirsh-Pasek, K. and Golinkoff, R. M. (eds.), *The Origins of Grammar: Evidence from Early Language Comprehension*. Cambridge, MA: MIT Press, pp. 123–158.

Hirst, G. (1987). *Semantic Interpretation and the Resolution of Ambiguity*. Cambridge University Press.

Hsu, N. S., Kraemer, D. J. M., Oliver, R. T., Schlichting, M. L. and Thompson-Schill, S. L. (2011). Color, context, and cognitive style: Variations in color knowledge retrieval as a function of task and subject variables. *Journal of Cognitive Neuroscience* 23(9), 2544–2557.

Hunston, S. and Francis, G. (2000). *Pattern Grammar: A Corpus-Driven Approach to the Lexical Grammar of English*. Amsterdam: John Benjamins.

Hurford, J. R. (2003). The neural basis of predicate-argument structure. *Behavioral and Brain Sciences* 26(3), 261–283.

Hurford J. and Heasley, B. (1983). *Semantics: a Coursebook*. Cambridge University Press.

Ibarretxe-Antuñano, I. (1999). Polysemy and Metaphor in Perception Verbs: A Cross-Linguistic Study. PhD Thesis. University of Edinburgh.

(2008). Vision metaphors for the intellect: Are they really cross-linguistic? *Atlantis* 30(1), 15–33.

Ibbotson, P. (2013). The Scope of Usage-Based Theory. *Frontiers in Psychology* 4, 255, 1 May.

Ibbotson, P., Lieven, E. and Tomasello, M. (2013). The attention-grammar interface: eye-gaze cues structural choice in children and adults. *Cognitive Linguistics* 24(3), 457–448.

Jackendoff, R. (1972). *Semantic Interpretation in Generative Grammar*. Cambridge, MA: MIT Press.

(1976). Toward an explanatory semantic representation. *Linguistic Inquiry* 7(1), 89–150.

(1990). *Semantic Structures*. Cambridge, MA: MIT Press.

Johnson, M. (1987). *The Body in the Mind: The Bodily Basis of Meaning, Imagination and Reason*. University of Chicago Press.

Jones, S. (2002). *Antonymy: A Corpus-Based Perspective* (Routledge Advances in Corpus Linguistics). London: Routledge.

Jostmann, N. B., Lakens, D. and Schubert, T. W. (2009). Weight as an embodiment of importance. *Psychological Science* 20, 1169–1174.

Kamide, Y., Altmann, G. T. M. and Haywood, S. L. (2004). The time-course of prediction in incremental sentence processing: Evidence from anticipatory eye movements. *Journal of Memory and language* 49(1), 133–156.

Kaschak, M. P. and Glenberg, A. M. (2000). Constructing meaning: The role of affordances and grammatical constructions in sentence comprehension. *Journal of Memory and Language* 43(3), 508–529.

Keil, F. (1994). Explanation, association, and the acquisition of word meaning. *Lingua* 92, 169–190.

Kersten, A. W., Meissner, C. A., Lechuga, J., Schwartz, B. L., Albrechtsen, J. S. and Iglesias, A. (2010). English speakers attend more strongly than Spanish speakers to manner of motion when classifying novel objects and events. *Journal of Experimental Psychology: General* 139, 638–653.

Kiefer, M., Sim, E. J., Herrnberger, B., Grothe, J. and Hoenig, K. (2008). The sound of concepts: Four markers for a link between auditory and conceptual brain systems. *Journal of Neuroscience* 28:12224–12230.

Kintsch, W. (1988). The role of knowledge in discourse comprehension construction-integration model. *Psychological Review* 95, 163–182.

(1998). *Comprehension: A Paradigm for Cognition.* Cambridge University Press.

(2001). Predication. *Cognitive Science* 25: 173–202.

Kittay, E. (1987). *Metaphor: Its Cognitive Force and Linguistic Structure.* Oxford/ New York: Clarendon Press/Oxford University Press.

Koenig, J. P., Mauner, G. and Bienvenue, B. (2003). Arguments for adjuncts. *Cognition* 89, 67–103.

Köhler, W. (1947). *Gestalt Psychology*, 2nd edition. New York: Liveright.

Koster, C. H. A. (2004). Transducing Text to Multiword Units. *Workshop on MultiWord Units MEMURA at the Fourth International Conference on Language Resources and Evaluation, LREC-2004.* Lisbon, Portugal.

Kövecses, Z. and Radden, G. (1998). Metonymy: Developing a cognitive linguistic view. *Cognitive Linguistics* 9(1), 37–77.

Krauss, R. M. and Fussell, S. R. (1991). Perspective-taking in communication: Representations of others' knowledge in reference. *Social Cognition* 9, 2–24.

Kreidler, C. (1998). *Introducing English Semantics.* London: Routledge.

Krupnik, I. and Müller-Wille, L. (2010). Franz Boas and Inuktitut Terminology for Ice and Snow: From the emergence of the field to the 'Great Eskimo Vocabulary Hoax', in SIKU, *Knowing Our Ice; Documenting Inuit Sea Ice Knowledge and Use.* Springer Verlag.

Kutas, M. and Federmeier, K. D. (2000). Electrophysiology reveals semantic memory use in language comprehension. *Trends in Cognitive Science* 4(12), 463–470.

Kutas, M. and Hillyard, S. A. (1980). Reading senseless sentences: Brain potentials reflect semantic incongruity. *Science* 207: 203–208.

Labov, W. (1973). The boundaries of words and their meanings. In Bailey, C.-J. N. and Shuy, R. W. (eds.), *New Ways of Analysing Variation in English.* Washington: Georgetown University Press.

Lakoff, G. (1992). Metaphor and war: The metaphor system used to justify war in the Gulf. In Pütz, M. (ed.), *Thirty Years of Linguistic Evolution: Studies in Honor of Renè Dirven on the Occasion of his Sixtieth Birthday.* Amsterdam: John Benjamins, pp. 463–481.

Lakoff, G. and Johnson, M. (1980). *Metaphors We Live By.* University of Chicago Press.

(1999). *Philosophy in the Flesh: The Embodied Mind and its Challenge to Western Thought.* New York: Basic Books.

Landau, B. and Jackendoff, R. (1993). 'What' and 'where' in spatial language and spatial cognition. *Behavioral and Brain Sciences* 16, 217–238.

Landau, M. J., Meier, B. P. and Keefer, L. (2010). A metaphor-enriched social cognition. *Psychonomic Bulletin and Review*, 136(6), 1045–1067.

Landauer, T. K. and Dumais, S. T. (1997). A solution to Plato's problem: The Latent Semantic Analysis theory of the acquisition, induction, and representation of knowledge. *Psychological Review* 104, 211–240.

Landauer, T. K., Foltz, P. W. and Laham, D. (1998). Introduction to Latent Semantic Analysis. *Discourse Processes* 25, 259–284.

Langacker, R. W. (1987). *Foundations of Cognitive Grammar*. Stanford University Press.

(1991). *Foundations of Cognitive Grammar. Vol II: Descriptive Application*. Stanford University Press.

Lany, J. and Saffran, J. R. (2013). Statistical learning mechanisms in infancy. In Rubenstein, J. L. R. and Rakic, P. (eds.) *Comprehensive Developmental Neuroscience: Neural Circuit Development and Function in the Brain*, volume III. Amsterdam: Elsevier, pp. 231–248.

Lebois, L. A. M., Wilson-Mendenhall, C. D. and Barsalou, L. W. (2015). Are automatic conceptual cores the gold standard of semantic processing? The context-dependence of spatial meaning in grounded congruency effects. *Cognitive Science* 39, 1764–1801.

Lehrer, A. (1974). *Semantics Fields and Lexical Structure*. Amsterdam: North Holland.

Levinson, S. C. (1983). *Pragmatics*. Cambridge University Press.

(1996). Frames of reference and Molyneux's question: Cross-linguistic evidence. In Bloom, P., Peterson, M., Nadel, L. and Garrett, M. (eds.), *Language and Space*. Cambridge, MA: MIT press, pp. 231–248.

(2000). *Presumptive Meanings: The Theory of Generalized Conversational Implicature*. Cambridge: MIT press.

Lin, S., Keysar, B. and Epley, N. (2010). Reflexively mindblind: Using theory of mind to interpret behavior requires effortful attention. *Journal of Experimental Social Psychology* 46, 551–556.

Löbner, S. (2013). *Understanding Semantics*. London: Blackwell.

Louw, W. E. (1993). Irony in the text or insincerity in the writer? The diagnostic potential of semantic prosodies. *Text and Technology: In Honour of John Sinclair*. Amsterdam: John Benjamins, pp. 157–176.

Louwerse, M. (2011). Symbol interdependency in symbolic and embodied cognition. *Topics in Cognitive Science* 3, 273–302.

Louwerse, M. and Jeuniaux, P. (2008). Language comprehension is both embodied and symbolic. In De Vega, M., Glenberg, A. M. and Graesser, A. C. (eds.), *Symbols, Embodiment, and Meaning*. Oxford University Press, pp. 309–326.

(2010). The linguistic and embodied nature of conceptual processing. *Cognition* 114, 96–104.

Lund, K. and Burgess, C. (1996). Producing high-dimensional semantic spaces from lexical co-occurrence. *Behavior Research Methods, Instruments, and Computers*, 28(2), 203–208.

Lupyan, G. (2008a). The conceptual grouping effect: Categories matter (and named categories matter more). *Cognition* 108, 566–577.

Lupyan, G. (2008b). From chair to 'chair': A representational shift account of object labeling effects on memory. *Journal of Experimental Psychology: General* 137(2), 348–369.

Lyons, J. (1977). *Semantics 1 and 2*. Cambridge University Press.

MacDonald, M. C., Pearlmutter, N. J. and Seidenberg, M. S. (1994). Lexical nature of syntactic ambiguity resolution. *Psychological Review* 101, 676–703.

Madden, C. J. and Zwaan, R. A. (2003). How does verb aspect constrain event representations? *Memory and Cognition* 31, 663–672.

Malt, B. C. and Wolff, P. (eds.) (2010). *Words and the Mind: How Words Encode Human Experience*. Oxford University Press.

Mandelbaum, D. (ed.) (1958). *Selected Writings of Edward Sapir in Language, Culture and Personality*. University of California Press.

Manning, C. D. (2003). Statistical approaches to natural language processing. In Nadel, L. (ed.), *Encyclopedia of Cognitive Science*. London: Nature Publishing Group.

Markman, E. M. (1991). The whole-object, taxonomic, and mutual exclusivity assumptions as initial constraints on word meanings. In Gelman, S. A. and Byrnes, J. P. (eds.), *Perspectives on Language and Thought: Interrelations in Development*. New York: Cambridge University Press, pp. 72–106.

Markson, L. and Bloom, P. (1997). Evidence against a dedicated system for word learning in children. *Nature*; 385(6619, 27 February): 813–815.

Marmor, G. S. (1978). Age at onset of blindness and the development of the semantics of color names. *Journal of Experimental Child Psychology* 25(2), 267–278.

Maurer, D., Pathman, T. and Mondloch, C. J. (2006). The shape of boubas: Sound–shape correspondences in toddlers and adults. *Developmental Science* 9(3), 316–322.

McCloskey, P. (2013). DOE rolls semantic search for science research. Blog archive, retrieved from https://gcn.com/Blogs/Pulse/2013/04/DOE-rolls-out-semantic-search-for-science-research.aspx?p=1.

McRae, K., Spivey-Knowlton, M. J. and Tanenhaus, M. K. (1998). Modeling the influence of thematic fit (and other constraints) in on-line sentence comprehension. *Journal of Memory and Language* 38, 283–312.

Meier, B. P. and Robinson, M. D. (2004). Why the sunny side is up. *Psychological Science* 15, 243–247.

Meier, B. P., Schnall, S., Schwarz, N. and Bargh, J. A. (2012). Embodiment in social psychology. *Topics in Cognitive Science* 4, 705–716.

Meier, B. P., Sellbom, M. and Wygant, D. B. (2007). Failing to take the moral high ground: psychopathy and the vertical representation of morality. *Personality and Individual Differences* 43(Sep), 757–767.

Mervis, C. B. (1987). Child-basic object categories and early lexical development. In U. Neisser (ed.), *Concepts and Conceptual Development: Ecological and Intellectual Factors in Categorization*. Cambridge University Press, pp. 201–203.

Meteyard, L., Cuadrado, S. R., Bahrami, B. and Vigliocco, G. (2012). Coming of age: a review of embodiment and the neuroscience of semantics. *Cortex* 48, 788–804.

Murphy, G. (1996). On metaphoric representation. *Cognition* 60, 173–204.
  (1997). Reasons to doubt the present evidence for metaphoric representation. *Cognition* 62, 99–108.
  (2002). *The Big Book of Concepts*. Cambridge, MA: MIT Press.

Murphy, G. L. and Andrew, J. M. (1993). The conceptual basis of antonymy and synonymy in adjectives. *Journal of Memory and Language* 32, 301–319.

Murphy, M. L. (2003). *Semantic Relations and the Lexicon*. Cambridge University Press.

Murphy, S. T. and Zajonc, R. B. (1993). Affect, cognition, and awareness: Affective priming with optimal and suboptimal stimulus exposures. *Journal of Personality and Social Psychology* 64, 723–739.

Murray, L. and Trevarthen, C. (1985). Emotional regulations of interactions between two-month-olds and their mothers. In Field, T. M. and Fox, N. A. (eds.), *Social Perception in Infants*. Norwood, NJ: Ablex, pp. 177–197.

Myers, E. B. and Blumstein, S. E. (2005). Selectional restriction and semantic priming effects in normals and Broca's aphasics. *Journal of Neurolinguistics* 18(3), 277–296.

Nelson D. L., McEvoy, C. L. and Schreiber, T. A. (1998). *The University of South Florida Word Association, Rhyme, and Word Fragment Norms*. Available at www.usf.edu/FreeAssociation.

Oztürk, O., Krehm, M. and Vouloumanos, A. (2013). Sound symbolism in infancy: Evidence for sound–shape cross-modal correspondences in 4-month-olds. *Journal of Experimental Child Psychology* 114, 173–186.

Paivio, A. (1971). *Imagery and Verbal Processes*. New York: Holt, Rinehart, and Winston.

Panther, K. and Radden, G. (eds.) (1999). *Metonymy in Language and Thought*. Amsterdam/Philadelphia: John Benjamins Publishing Company.

Panther, K.-U. and Thornburg, L. L. (eds.) (2003). *Metonymy and Pragmatic Inferencing*. Pragmatics and Beyond New Series 113. Amsterdam/Philadelphia: John Benjamins Publishing Company.

Paradis, C. and Willners, S. (2007). Antonyms in dictionary entries: Methodological aspects. *Studia Linguistica* 61(3), 261–277.

Paradis, C., Willners, S. and Jones, S. (2009). Good and bad opposites using textual and experimental techniques to measure antonym canonicity. *The Mental Lexicon* 4(3), 380–429.

Partington, A. (1998). *Patterns and Meanings – Using Corpora for English Language Research and Teaching*. Amsterdam/Philadelphia: John Benjamins.

Pavlenko, A. (2002). Conceptual change in bilingual memory: A neo-Whorfian approach. In Fabbro, F. (ed.), *Advances in the Neurolinguistics of Bilingualism*. Udine, Italy: Forum, pp. 69–94.

(2005). Bilingualism and thought. In De Groot, A. and Kroll, J. (eds.), *Handbook of Bilingualism: Psycholinguistic Approaches*. Oxford University Press, pp. 433–453.

(2011). Thinking and speaking in two languages: Overview of the field. In Pavlenko, A. (ed.), *Thinking and Speaking in Two Languages*. Bristol, UK: Multilingual Matters, pp. 237–257.

Pecher, D., Zeelenberg, R. and Barsalou, L. W. (2003). Verifying different-modality properties for concepts produces switching costs. *Psychological Science*, 14(2), 119–124.

Peirsman, Y. and Geeraerts, D. (2006). Metonymy as a Prototypical category. *Cognitive Linguistics* 17(3), 269–316.

Pinker, S. (1989). *Learnability and Cognition: the Acquisition of Argument Structure*. Cambridge: MIT Press.

(1994). *The Language Instinct*. New York: Harper Perennial Modern Classics.

(2007). *The Stuff of Thought: Language as a Window Into Human Nature*. New York: Viking.

Prinz, J. (2002). *Furnishing the Mind: Concepts and Their Perceptual Basis*. Cambridge, MA: MIT Press.

Pulvermüller, F. (2002). A brain perspective on language mechanisms: From discrete neuronal ensembles to serial order. *Progress in Neurobiology 67*, 85–11.

Pulvermüller, F., Hauk, O., Nikulin, V. V. and Ilmonlemi, R. J. (2005). Functional links between motor and language systems. *European Journal of Neuroscience 21*, 793–797.

Pustejovsky, J. (1995). *The Generative Lexicon*. Cambridge: MIT Press.

Pylyshyn, Z. W. (1981). The imagery debate: Analogue media versus tacit knowledge. *Psychological Review 88*, 16–45.

(1984). *Computation and Cognition: Towards a Foundation for Cognitive Science*. Cambridge, MA: MIT Press.

Rakison, D. H. and Krogh, L. (2012). Does causal action facilitate causal perception in infants younger than 6 months of age? *Developmental Science 15*, 43–54.

Ramachandran, V. S. and Hubbard, E. M. (2001). Psychophysical investigations into the neural basis of synaesthesia. *Proceedings of the Royal Society of London, B 268*, 979–983.

Regier, T. and Kay, P. (2009). Language, thought and color: Whorf was half right. *Trends in Cognitive Sciences 13*, 439–446.

Riemer, N. (2010). *Introducing Semantics*. Cambridge University Press.

Rosch, E. (1973). On the internal structure of perceptual and semantic categories. In Moore, T. E. (ed.), *Cognitive Development and the Acquisition of Language*. New York: Academic Press, 111–144.

(1975). Cognitive representations of semantic categories. *Journal of Experimental Psychology: General 104*: 192–233.

(1978). Principles of categorization. In Rosch, E. and Lloyd, B. B. (eds.), *Cognition and Categorization*. Hillsdale: Lawrence Erlbaum, 27–48.

Rosch, E. and Mervis, C. B. (1975). Family resemblances: Studies in the internal structure of categories. *Cognitive Psychology 7*, 573–605.

Rosch, E., Mervis, C. B., Gray, W. D., Johnson, D. M. and Boyes-Braem, P. (1976). Basic objects in natural categories. *Cognitive Psychology 8*, 382–439.

Rouder, J. N. and Ratcliff, R. (2006). Comparing exemplar- and rule-based theories of categorization. *Current Directions in Psychological Science 15*, 9–13.

Rumelhart, D. E., McClelland, J. L. and the PDP Research Group (1986). *Parallel Distributed Processing: Explorations in the Microstructure of Cognition, Vol. 1: Foundations*. Cambridge, MA: MIT Press.

Saeed, J. (1997/2009). *Semantics*. London: Blackwell.

Sapir, E. (1929). The Status of Linguistics as a Science. *Language 5*(4), 207–214.

Saussure, F. (1916). *Cours de Linguistique Général*. Bally, C. and Sechehaye, A. (eds.) with the collaboration of A. Riedlinger. Paris/Lausanne: Payot.

Schubert, T. W. (2005). Your highness: Vertical positions as perceptual symbols of power. *Journal of Personality and Social Psychology 89*, 1–21.

Schwartz, M. F., Kimberg, D. Y., Walker, G. M., Brecher, A., Faseyitan, O. *et al.* (2011). A neuroanatomical dissociation for taxonomic and thematic knowledge in the human brain. *Proceedings of the National Academy of Sciences* 108, 8520–8524.

Searle, J. (1980). Minds, brains and programs. *Behavioral and Brain Sciences* 3(3), 417–457.

(1990). Epilogue to the Taxonomy of Illocutionary Acts. In Carbaugh, D. (ed.), *Cultural Communication and Intercultural Contact*. Hillsdale, NJ: Lawrence Erlbaum Associates.

Searle, J. R. and Vanderveken, D. (1985). *Foundations of Illocutionary Logic*. Cambridge University Press.

Sebeok, T. A. (1994). *An Introduction to Semiotics*. London: Pinter.

Shank, R. C. and Abelson, R. P. (1977). *Scripts, Plans and Understanding: an Inquiry into Human Knowledge Structures*. Hillsdale, NJ: Erlbaum.

Sherman, G. D. and Clore, G. L. (2009). The color of sin: White and black are perceptual symbols of moral purity and pollution. *Psychological Science* 20, 1019–1025.

Shepard, R. N. and Cooper, L. A. (1992). Representation of colors in the blind, color-blind, and normally sighted. *Psychological Science* 3(2), 97–104.

Simmons, W. K., Martin, A. and Barsalou, L. W. (2005). Pictures of appetizing foods activate gustatory cortices for taste and reward. *Cerebral Cortex* 15(10), 1602–1608.

Simmons, W., Ramjee, V., Beauchamp, M., McRae, K., Martin, A. and Barsalou, L. (2007). A common neural substrate for perceiving and knowing about color. *Neuropsychologia* 45(12), 2802–2810.

Sinclair J. (1996). The search for units of meaning. *Textus IX*, 75–106.

Snider, J. G. and Osgood, C. E. (1969). *Semantic Differential Technique: A Sourcebook*. Chicago: Aldine.

Solomon, K. O. and Barsalou, L. W. (2004). Perceptual simulation in property verification. *Memory and Cognition*, 32(2), 244–259.

Spelke, E. S. and Kinzler, K. D. (2007). Core knowledge. *Developmental Science* 10, 89–96.

Sperber, D. and Wilson, D. (1995). *Relevance: Communication and Cognition, Second Edition*. Oxford/Cambridge: Blackwell Publishers.

Spivey, M. (2007). *The Continuity of Mind*. Oxford University Press.

Spivey, M. J. and Geng, J. J. (2001). Oculomotor mechanisms activated by imagery and memory: Eye movements to absent objects. *Psychological Research* 65, 235–241.

Sproat, R. (1992). *Morphology and Computation*. Cambridge, MA, MIT Press.

Srinivasan, M. and Rabagliati, H. (2015). How concepts and conventions structure the lexicon: Cross-linguistic evidence from polysemy. *Lingua* 157, 124–152.

Stalnaker, R. C. (2002). Common ground. *Linguistics and Philosophy* 25: 701–721.

Stanfield, R. A. and Zwaan, R. A. (2001). The effect of implied orientation derived from verbal context on picture recognition. *Psychological Science* 12, 153–156.

Steels, L. (2001). Grounding symbols through evolutionary language games. In Cangelosi, A. and Parisi, D. (eds.), *Simulating the Evolution of Language*. London: Springer Verlag, pp. 211–226.

(2003). Evolving grounded communication for robots. *Trends in Cognitive Science* 7, 308–312.

(2010). Modeling the Formation of Language: Embodied Experiments. In Nolfi, S. and Mirolli, M. (eds.), *Evolution of Communication and Language in Embodied Agents*. Berlin: Springer, pp. 235–262.

Stephens, R. and Umland, C. (2011). Swearing as a response to pain: Effect of daily swearing frequency. *Journal of Pain* 12(12), 1274–1281.

Strack, F., Martin, L. and Stepper, S. (1988). Inhibiting and Facilitating Conditions of the Human Smile: A Nonobtrusive Test of the Facial Feedback Hypothesis. *Journal of Personality and Social Psychology* 54(5): 768–777.

Stubbs, M. (1995). Collocations and semantic profiles: On the cause of the trouble with quantitative methods. *Functions of Language* (2)1, 1–33.

(2001). *Words and Phrases: Corpus Studies of Lexical Semantics*. London: Blackwell.

Sweetser, E. (1990). *From Etymology to Pragmatics: Metaphorical and Cultural Aspects of Semantic Structure*. Cambridge University Press.

Swinney, D. (1979). Lexical access during sentence comprehension: (Re) consideration of context effects. *Journal of Verbal Learning and Verbal Behavior* 18, 645–659.

Tan, L. H., Chan, A. H. D., Kay, P., Khong, P.-L., Yip, L. K. C. and Luke, K.-K. (2008). Language affects patterns of brain activation associated with perceptual decision. *Proceedings of the National Academy of Sciences* 105, 4004–4009.

Taylor, J. R. (1995/2004). *Linguistic Categorization*. Oxford University Press.

Tesnière, L. (1959). *Éléments de syntaxe structural*. Paris: Klincksieck.

Thibodeau, P. H. and Boroditsky, L. (2011). Metaphors we think with: The role of metaphor in reasoning. *PLoS ONE* 6(2): e16782.

Tomasello, M. (1999). *The cultural origins of human cognition*. Cambridge, MA: Harvard University Press.

(2000). A usage-based approach to child language acquisition. *Annual Meeting of the Berkeley Linguistics Society* 26(1), 305–319.

(2003). *Constructing a Language: A Usage-Based Theory of Language Acquisition*. Cambridge, MA: Harvard University Press.

(2008). *Origins of Human Communication*. Cambridge, MA: MIT Press.

(2009). *Why We Cooperate*. Cambridge, MA: MIT Press.

Trier, J. (1931). *Der Deutsche Wortschatz im Sinnbezirk des Verstandes*. Heidelberg: *Winter*.

Tuggy, D. (1993). Ambiguity, polysemy, and vagueness. *Cognitive Linguistics* 4–3, 273–290.

Tyler, L. and Moss, H. (1997). Functional properties of concepts: Studies of normal and brain damaged patients. *Cognitive Neuropsychology* 14, 511–545.

Ungerer, F. and Schmid, H. (2006). *An Introduction to Cognitive Linguistics*. Harlow, UK: Pearson Education Limited.

Valenzuela, J. (2010). Cognitive linguistics and computational modeling. *Textus XIII: Special Issue, Cognition and the Brain in Language and Linguistics*, 763–794.

Valenzuela, J. and Soriano, C. (2009). Are conceptual metaphors accessible on-line? Is control really up? A psycholinguistic exploration of the CONTROL IS UP metaphor. In Valenzuela, J., Rojo, A. and Soriano, C. (eds.), *Trends in*

Cognitive Linguistics: Theoretical and Applied models. Frankfurt: Peter Lang, pp. 31–50.

Van Valin, R. D. (2004). Semantic macroroles in role and reference grammar. In Kailuweit, R. and Hummel, M. (eds.), *Semantische Rollen*. Tubingen: Gunter Narr Verlag, pp. 62–82.

Verfaillie, K. and Daems, A. (1996). The priority of the agent in visual event perception: On the cognitive basis of grammatical agent–patient asymmetries. *Cognitive Linguistics* 7, 131–147.

Vigliocco, G. and Vinson, D. P. (2007). Semantic Representation. In G. Gaskell (ed.), *Handbook of Psycholinguistics*. Oxford University Press.

Waddington, C. H. (1960). Evolutionary adaptation. In Tax, S. (ed.), *Evolution After Darwin*, Vol. I. University of Chicago Press, pp. 385–386.

Waxman, S. R. (2004). Everything had a name, and each name gave birth to a new thought: Links between early word-learning and conceptual organization. In Hall, D. G. and Waxman, S. R. (eds.), *From Many strands: Weaving a Lexicon*. Cambridge: MIT Press.

Waxman, S. R. and Markow, D. R. (1995). Words as invitations to form categories: Evidence from 12- to 13-month-old infants. *Cognitive Psychology* 29, 257–302.

Whorf, B. L. (1940). Science and Linguistics. *Technology Review* 42(6): 229–231, 247–248. Also in Carroll J. B. (ed.), *Language, Thought and Reality* (1956). Cambridge, MA: MIT Press.

Wierzbicka, A. (1988). *The Semantics of Grammar*. Amsterdam: John Benjamins.

Wilensky, R. (1989). Primal content and literal content: An antidote to literal meaning. *Journal of Pragmatics* 13, 163–186.

Williams, L. E. and Bargh, J. A. (2008). Experiencing physical warmth promotes interpersonal warmth. *Science* 322(5901), 606–607.

Wilson M. (2002). Six views of embodied cognition. *Psychonomic Bulletin Review* 9, 625–636.

Winawer, J., Witthoft, N., Frank, M. C., Wu, L., Wade, A. R. and Boroditsky, L. (2007). Russian blues reveal effects of language on color discrimination. *Proceedings of the National Academy of Sciences* 104, 7780–7785.

Winter, B. and Matlock, T. (2013). Making judgments based on similarity and proximity. *Metaphor and Symbol*, 28, 1–14.

Wittgenstein, L. (1957). *Philosophical Investigations*. Translated by G. E. M. Anscombe. Oxford: Basil Blackwell.

Wu, L. and Barsalou, L. W. (2009). Perceptual simulation in conceptual combination: Evidence from property generation. *Acta Psychologica* 132(2), 173–189.

Yule, G. (1996). *Pragmatics*. Oxford University Press.

Zhong, C. B. and Liljenquist, K. (2006). Washing away your sins: Threatened morality and physical cleansing. *Science*, 313, 1451–1452.

Zwaan, R. A. (2000). The role of linguistic cues in situation-model construction. *International Journal of Psychology* 35(3–4), 392.

(2009). Mental simulation in language comprehension and social cognition. *European Journal of Social Psychology* 37, 1142–1150.

(2014). Embodiment and language comprehension: Reframing the discussion. *Trends in Cognitive Sciences* 18(5), 229–234.

Zwaan, R. A., Madden, C. J., Yaxley, R. H. and Aveyard, M. E. (2004). Moving words: Dynamic representations in language comprehension. *Cognitive Science* 28, 611–619.

Zwaan, R. A., Stanfield, R. A. and Yaxley, R. H. (2002). Language comprehenders mentally represent the shapes of objects. *Psychological Science* 13, 168–171.

Index